Canon EOS R5 Mark II

Photography Handbook

The Complete Guide to Mastering Digital Photography and Videography with Expert Tips & Insights

Divine Favour

Copyright © 2024 **Divine Favour**

This book or parts thereof may not be reproduced in any form, stored in any retrieval system, or transmitted in any form by any means—electronic, mechanical, photocopy, recording, or otherwise—without prior written permission of the publisher, except as provided by United States of America copyright law and fair use.

Disclaimer and Terms of Use

The author and publisher of this book and the accompanying materials have used their best efforts in preparing this book. The author and publisher make no representation or warranties with respect to the accuracy, applicability, fitness, or completeness of the contents of this book. The information contained in this book is strictly for informational purposes. Therefore, if you wish to apply the ideas contained in this book, you are taking full responsibility for your actions.

Printed in the United States of America

TABLE OF CONTENTS

TABLE OF CONTENTS III

CHAPTER 1 1

INTRODUCTION 1

   OVERVIEW OF CANON EOS R5 MARK II AND ITS ACCESSORIES 1
   HANDLING 2

THE CANON EOS R5 MARK II'S AUTOFOCUS 4

   EYE CONTROL 5
   FRAME RATE 6
      Pre-Continuous Shooting 6
      Dual Shooting (stills and videos) 7
      High ISO 7
      Processing in the Camera 9
      Image Stabilization 10
   ACCESSORIES 10
      Best All-in-one Lens for Canon EOS R5 Mark II 10
      Why does this Lens Stand Out? Why does it Work Well with the Canon EOS R5 Mark II? 11
   WHAT ARE THE BEST PRIME TELEPHOTO LENSES FOR THE CANON EOS R5 MARK II? 13
   BEST TELEPHOTO ZOOM LENSES FOR CANON EOS R5 MARK II 18
   THE BEST STANDARD PRIME LENSES FOR THE CANON EOS R5 MARK II 23
   COMPARISON: CANON RF 50MM F/1.2 L USM VS CANON RF 50MM F/1.8 STM 27
   BEST STANDARD ZOOM LENSES FOR CANON EOS R5 MARK II 27
   COMPARISON: CANON RF 24-70MM F/2.8 L IS USM VS CANON RF 28-70MM F/2 L USM 31
   BEST WIDE-ANGLE ZOOM LENSES FOR CANON EOS R5 MARK II 32
   BEST WIDE-ANGLE PRIME LENSES FOR CANON EOS R5 MARK II 37
   BEST PORTRAIT LENSES FOR CANON EOS R5 MARK II 41
   BEST MACRO LENSES FOR CANON EOS R5 MARK II 44

CHAPTER 2 47

INITIAL SETUP: CHARGING THE BATTERY AND ATTACHING THE LENS 47

   CHARGING THE BATTERY 47
   CHARGE TIME AND CONDITIONS 49
   PRE-CHARGING REQUIREMENTS 50
   SAFETY AND BATTERY MAINTENANCE TIPS 50
   PUTTING IN THE BATTERY 50
   REMOVING THE BATTERY 51

CHAPTER 3 52

CAMERA SETUP 52

The Set-up Menu	55
Set-up Menu Options	55
Record Functions+Card/Folder Sel.	55
File Numbering	62
Movie Clip Numbering	63
File Name	65
Format Card	68
Auto Rotate	69
Add Movie Rotate Information	70
Date/Time/Zone	70
Language	71
System Frequency	72
Help Text Size	73
Beep	73
Volume	74
Screen Brightness/Viewfinder Brightness	75
Screen/Viewfinder Color Tone	75
Fine-Tune Viewfinder Color Tone	76
Screen and Viewfinder Display	76
UI Magnification	77
HDMI Resolution	78
Cooling Fan Settings	78
Shutter at Shutdown	79
Sensor Cleaning	79
Power Saving	80
Reset Camera	81
Custom Shooting Mode (C1–C3)	81
Save/Load Camera Settings On Card (R5 II only)	83
Battery Information	83
Registering Your Battery Packs	85
Copyright Information	86
Manual/Software URL	86
Certification Logo Display	86
Firmware	87
CHAPTER 4	**88**
WORKING WITH THE AF SYSTEM	**88**
AF Operation	88
One-Shot AF	88
Servo AF	89
Manual Focus	90
AF Method	90
Face+Tracking AF	91

Spot AF	93
1-Point AF	94
Expand AF Area	94
Expand AF Area: Around	95
Zone AF	95
Large Zone AF (Vertical)/(Horizontal)	96
Magnified View	97
Fine-Tuning Your Autofocus	98

CHAPTER 5 101

AUTOFOCUS MENU 101

AF Menu Options	101
AF Operation	*101*
Subject to Detect	*101*
Eye Detection	*103*
Action Priority	*103*
MF Peaking Settings	*103*
Focus Guide	*104*
AF-Assisted Beam Firing	*104*
Lens Electronic MF	*105*

CHAPTER 6 107

EXPLORING CANON EOS R5 MARK II'S VIDEO CAPABILITIES 107

Introduction to the R5 Mark II's 8K Video Recording	107
The Movie Shooting Menu	109
Movie Recording Size	*109*
High frame rate	110
Main Recording Format:	*111*
RAW Movies	*111*
Recording Proxy Movies	111
Movie Cropping	112
Dual Shooting (Still Photos and Movies)	113
Sound Recording	113
Audio Format:	114
Audio Settings:	*114*
Recording Level	115
Wind Filter	115
Attenuator	116
Microphone Directionality	116
Audio Status	116
HDR Movie Mode	116
Shadow Compensation	117
Saturation	117

LIMITING THE MAXIMUM BRIGHTNESS. 117
TIME-LAPSE MOVIE 118
SELECT [MAIN REC.]. FORMAT]. 120
MOVIE SELF-TIMER 121
TALLY LAMP 122
PRE-RECORDING SETTINGS 123
SELECT [RECORDING TIME]. 123
RECORD THE MOVIE. 123
IS (IMAGE STABILIZER MODE) 123
FALSE COLOR SETTINGS 125
FALSE COLOR DISPLAY 125
ZEBRA SETTINGS 126
SHOOTING INFORMATION DISPLAY 127
STANDBY: LOW RESOLUTION 127
CANON LOG HDMI OUTPUT RANGE 127
TIME CODE 128
OTHER MENU FUNCTIONS 129
    HDMI Display *129*
    HDMI RAW Output *130*
MANUAL EXPOSURE SETTINGS FOR VIDEO 131
MOVIE PLAYBACK AND EDITING 133

CHAPTER 7 135

THE PHOTO SHOOTING MENU 135

IMAGE QUALITY 135
PICTURE SIZE 135
PICTURE STYLE 135
WHITE BALANCE 135
AUTO LIGHTING OPTIMIZER 136
HIGH ISO NR 136
LENS ABERRATION CORRECTION 136
LONG EXPOSURE NOISE REDUCTION 136
HIGH ISO SPEED NOISE REDUCTION 136
MULTIPLE EXPOSURE 137
HDR MODE 137
INTERVAL TIMER 137
TIME-LAPSE MOVIE 137
IMAGE QUALITY 137
CROPPING/ASPECT RATIO 139
EXPO.COMP./AEB: 0 – 140
ISO SPEED SETTINGS 140
ANTI-FLICKER SHOOTING 141
ANTI-FLICKER SHOOT: DISABLE 141

HIGH-FREQUENCY ANTI-FLICKER SHOOTING	142
RECOMMENDED TV SETTING	143
FOR MANUAL SETTING:	143
FLASH FUNCTION SETTINGS	145
Flash Firing	*145*
E-TTL Balance	*145*
E-TTL II Metering	*146*
Continuous Flash Control	*147*
Sync Speed Priority	*147*
SLOW SYNCHRO	149
FLASH FUNCTION SETTINGS	150
SHUTTER SYNC	152
FLASH EXPOSURE COMPENSATION	153
FLASH EXPOSURE BRACKETING	154
FLASH CUSTOM FUNCTION SETTINGS	154
CLEAR SETTINGS	154
METERING MODE	155
EVALUATIVE METERING	155
PARTIAL METERING	156
SPOT METERING	156
CENTER-WEIGHTED AVERAGE METERING	157
PRACTICAL TIPS FOR USING METERING MODES:	157
AE FOR PRIORITY SUBJECTS DURING AF	157
PICTURE STYLE	158
SYMBOLS	162
SETTINGS AND EFFECTS	163
MONOCHROME ADJUSTMENT	164
SELECTING PICTURE STYLES	164
DEFINING PICTURE STYLES	165
ADJUSTING STYLES WITH THE PICTURE STYLE EDITOR	166
UPLOADING A PICTURE STYLE TO THE CAMERA	167
COLOR SPACE	168
CLARITY	171
HIGHLIGHT TONE PRIORITY	172
WHITE BALANCE	172
WHITE BALANCE SHIFT/BRACKETING	174
LENS ABERRATION CORRECTION	176
LONG EXPOSURE NOISE REDUCTION	178
HIGH ISO SPEED NOISE REDUCTION	181
DUST DELETE DATA	182
DUST DELETE DATA APPENDING	184
MULTIPLE EXPOSURE	185
MULTIPLE EXPOSURE CONTROL	187

Number of Exposures 188
Save Source Images 188
Continue Multiple Exposure 189
Focus Bracketing 190
Set [Depth composite] 191
Set [Crop depth comp.] 191
Set [Flash interval] 192
Take the picture 192
Interval Timer 193
Silent Shutter Function 193
Shutter Mode 194
Release Shutter Without Card 195
Touch Shutter 196
High-Speed Display 196
Metering Timer 196
Display Simulation 197
Optical Viewfinder Simulated View Assist 198
Blackout-Free Display 198
Shooting Information Display 199
Reverse Display 200
Viewfinder Display Format 200
Display Performance 201

CHAPTER 8 202

EOS R5 MARK II CUSTOM SETTINGS 202

Tab Menus: Custom Functions 202

Restrict Shooting Modes 202
Exposure Level Increments 203
ISO Speed Setting Increments 203
Speed from Metering/ISO Auto 203
Bracketing Auto Cancel 203
Bracketing Sequence 204
Number of Bracketed Shots 204
Safety Shift 205
Same Expo. for New Aperture 205
AE Lock Meter. Mode after Focus 206
Set Shutter Speed Range 206
Mech Shutter/Elec 1st-curtain 206
Electronic 207
Set Aperture Range 207
AE Microadjustment 207
FE Micro Adjustment 208
Limit Continuous Shot Count 208

Add Cropping Information 208
Av Setting Without Lens 209
Default Erase Option 209
Release Shutter w/o Lens 210
Retract Lens On Power Off. 210
Add IPTC Information 210
Custom Function C. Fn 5 210

CHAPTER 9 211

IMAGE REVIEW AND PLAYBACK 211

PLAYBACK MENU 211
PROTECT IMAGES 212
ERASE IMAGES 213
ROTATE STILLS 214
CHANGE MOVIE ROTATE INFO 215
RATING 216
IMAGE COPY 218
PRINT ORDER 220
RAW PROCESSING 222
IN-CAMERA UPSCALING 224
RESIZE 225
CROPPING 226
SLIDE SHOW 227
VR PREVIEW 228
SETTING IMAGE SEARCH CONDITIONS 228
RESUMING FROM PREVIOUS PLAYBACK 229
VIEW FROM LAST SEEN 229
MAGNIFICATION (APPROXIMATE) 229
BLUR/OUT-OF-FOCUS IMAGE DETECTION 230
DISPLAYING THE HIGHLIGHT ALERT 231
PLAYBACK INFORMATION DISPLAY 231
AF POINT DISP. 232
PLAYBACK GRID 232
MOVIE PLAY COUNT 232

CONCLUSION 233

INDEX 234

Chapter 1

Introduction

Overview of Canon EOS R5 Mark II and its Accessories

The R5 Mark II is a significant improvement over the R5 that came before it, in addition to the standard upgrades one would anticipate from a Mark II edition of an outstanding camera. It has some cool new features. Creative photographers now have a lot more options thanks to these new features. I'm sure that both professional and amateur photographers will love them because it's a beautiful camera to use, and the pictures it takes are just as good as we expect from Canon.

There's a lot more I can say about these new features, but here's a quick rundown of what's new on the Canon EOS R5 Mark II:

- A brand-new pre-capture shooting tool that will change the game for me and make sure I don't miss the important moment. There's a new Canon camera called the EOS R1 and the R5 Mark II that both have this feature. I'm excited about it!
- Eye Control AF lets you look at people or things in the camera to choose what to focus on. This is one of the best things about the R1 and R3, so it's great that the R5 Mark II has it too.
- Other new autofocus features, such as People Priority AF, Action Priority AF, Register People Priority AF, and much better focus tracking, let us arrange in creative ways, knowing that the camera will handle the rest.
- A brand-new stacked CMOS sensor that lets you get faster frame rates, better autofocus, a wider dynamic range, and more accurate white balance and metering.
- Better electronic shutters that allow you get frame rates of up to 30fps. Now you can choose an electronic shutter monitor that doesn't black out, and shutter speeds go up to 1/32,000. This means you can use your lenses wide open in the sunniest conditions without needing an ND filter. It is now possible to use flash with the electronic shutter, and the rolling shutter blur has been cut down.
- The video tools on the R5 Mark II are also much better. Unfortunately, I only take still pictures, so I haven't tried out the video features. However, Canon has added

some great new features that allow you shoot stills and record video at the same time. Features like these make the EOS R5 Mark II the best camera for hybrid photographers. They'll get me to start taking videos as well as stills on my trips.

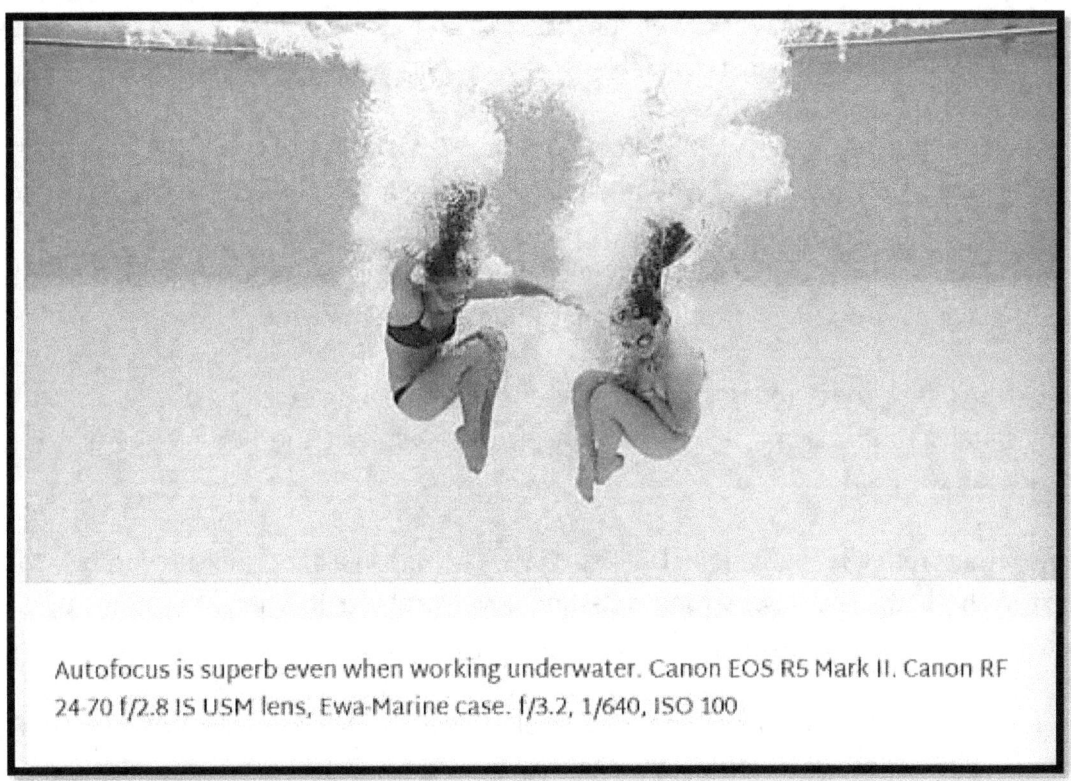

Autofocus is superb even when working underwater. Canon EOS R5 Mark II. Canon RF 24-70 f/2.8 IS USM lens, Ewa-Marine case. f/3.2, 1/640, ISO 100

Handling

Photographers who have used the Canon EOS R5 will find the R5 Mark II easy to use. The R5 Mark II weighs 746g with the card and battery, while the R5 weighs 738g. Most of the buttons are also in the same places. The top left of the camera has changed a lot. Instead of the on/off switch, there is now a switch that goes from stills to video. This is a great feature for hybrid photographers because it lets you switch between modes quickly.

As a portrait photographer, I love that the largest file size remains at 45MP. You can print this picture very large for wall art or crop it to make the arrangement better without losing too much quality. Canon has also added a very useful function called in-camera upscaling.

With the press of a button, you can make a JPEG image four times its original size. We'll talk more about this later.

Canon kept the R5's two card spots for the R5 Mark II. One is for CF Express cards and the other is for SD cards. This works well for me. I back up my RAW files to a fast CF Express card and my JPEG files to an SD card.

The LP-E6P is the new battery that comes with the R5 Mark II. The LP-E6-NH, which many of us have been using with our R5 cameras, can be used with the R5 Mark II, but only in certain situations. For example, some of the new features, like pre-continuous shooting or dual shooting, need a new battery. You should have the old batteries on hand in case something goes wrong, but if you can, you should use the new ones.

The battery life is good, and one charge was enough for a long morning of taking pictures of my family. There hasn't been a full side-by-side test, but the battery seems to last longer than the R5.

It is weatherproof like the Canon EOS R5, so it will be fine in a light rain shower, but don't put it in the bath. The new, strong hot-shoe cover protects it when you're not using a flash.

The R5 Mark II, like all Canon R series cameras, can be changed in a lot of ways. For example, you can assign different settings to the buttons and knobs and make your most-used features easy to find. Customizing the Q menu and assigning drive mode to a button made trying the EOS R5 Mark II a lot easier. This way, I could quickly switch between lower frame rates for quiet times and 30fps for fast action.

With all the choices you have, I think custom modes are the best way to go for different types of shooting. This week before my pool lesson, I added my underwater settings to C3; this made it easy to set up the camera and put it in its underwater housing while the kids changed. There is also a mode I set up just for looking. Custom modes are a great way to save time if you haven't looked into them yet.

You can save all your camera settings to a card once you're happy with them. This makes it easy to copy them to a second camera body and also save a copy of them on your computer for safety.

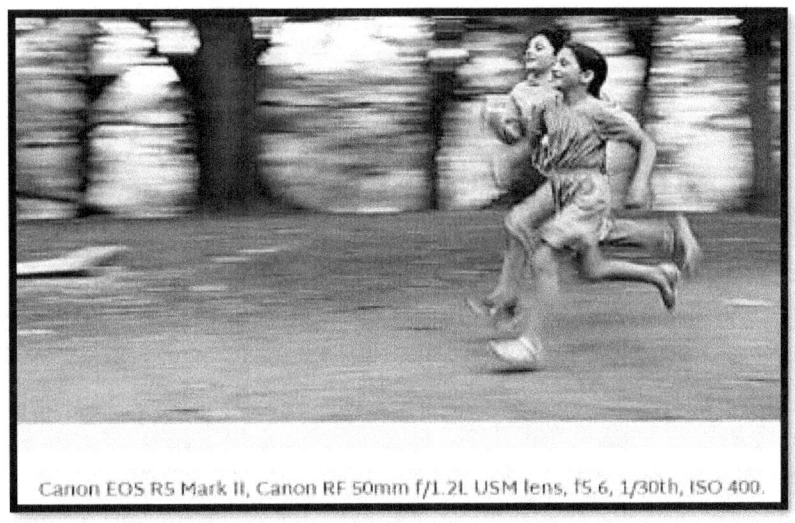
Canon EOS R5 Mark II, Canon RF 50mm f/1.2L USM lens, f5.6, 1/30th, ISO 400.

The Canon EOS R5 Mark II's Autofocus

Because of its new back-illuminated and stacked CMOS sensor and better picture processing system, the EOS R5 Mark II's autofocus has been improved a lot. This means that it takes less time to lock on to something and that tracking is more accurate, even when things are moving quickly. In my tests, the R5 Mark II's focusing felt even better than the R3's, but I haven't had a chance to directly compare the two.

When I use the R5 Mark II, I know that the pictures will always be sharp, so I can focus on framing and let the camera handle the rest. The artistic ideas this will open up are exciting to me.

The constant focus tracking features are what I think are the best new features. The camera is quick and accurate, and it instantly locks on to people's faces and avoids obstacles very well, even when things are tricky, like when kids are running through trees or playing in a cloud of bubbles. That's cool. It was pretty good when I used the R5; this is a big improvement.

If you're used to the R5 and 1-series DSLR cameras, the Servo AF modes were case 1 for general use, case 2 for tennis, case 3 for cycling, and case 4 for football or gymnastics. These have been replaced with an automatic mode or a manual mode where you can set the parameters to make the autofocus tracking more or less sensitive. On my test shoots, I set mine up to look like case 2 from the R5, which worked great.

Great that the R5 Mark II can track focusing, but how do we tell it what to track?

Eye Control

I was very happy to see that the Canon EOS R5 Mark II had eye control focus, which I had seen on the Canon EOS R3.

With eye control, you can choose your subject just by looking at it, and when you press the AF-ON button, tracking starts. It is amazing and lets you quickly switch between subjects.

To use it, point your camera at a small circle in different parts of the picture and look at it while the camera records your eye movements. It's easy to do, and you can have more than one calibration. For example, you could have one for glasses and another for contacts, or have different calibrations for different people if you have a studio with shared cameras and more than one photographer.

Too bad I had to get new glasses because the eye control feature on my old varifocals doesn't work as well with my new Canon EOS R3 that I loved trying. This feature is turned off for now.

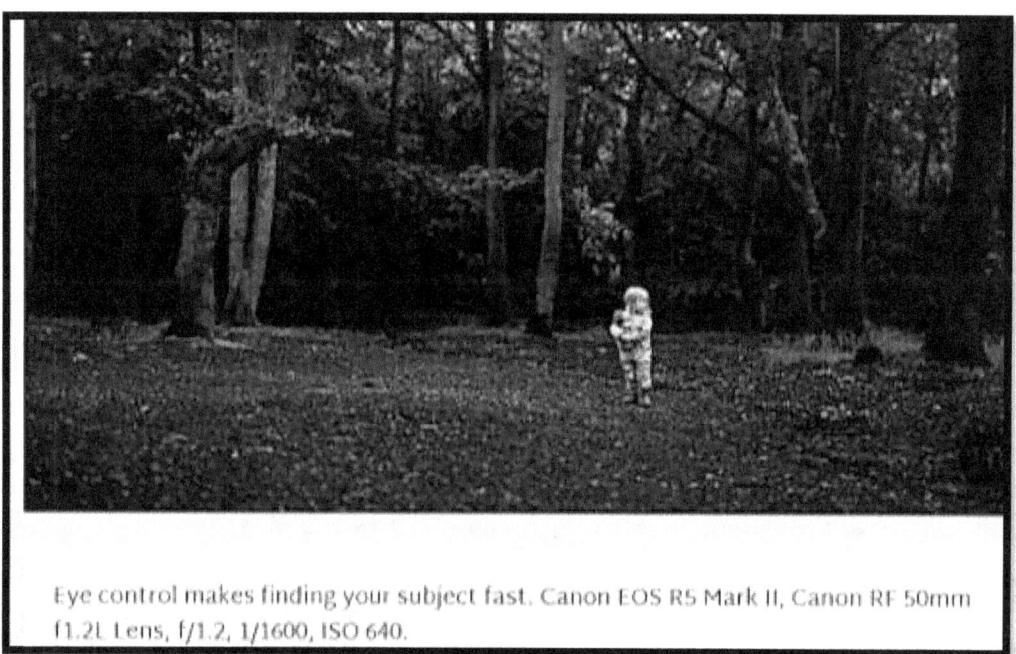

Eye control makes finding your subject fast. Canon EOS R5 Mark II, Canon RF 50mm f1.2L Lens, f/1.2, 1/1600, ISO 640.

Frame Rate

The frame rate of the Canon EOS R5 Mark II has been increased, which will also help us in these fast-paced conditions. The mechanical shutter can shoot about 12 fps, while the electric shutter can shoot up to 30 fps.

You can set different frame rates for each choice. For example, the high speed continuous on the electronic shutter can be 30 or 20 fps, the high speed 20, 15, 12, 10, and 7.5 fps, and the low speed 1, 2, 3, 5, 7.5, 10, 12, and 15. This gives you a lot of freedom to work within the limits you want.

As I take pictures, I like to hear the shutter. It tells me how fast I'm shooting (because you might have also taken a bunch of photos at a high frame rate when you only meant to take one or forgotten to change the shutter speed from 1/15 after some panning shots), and it lets the people in the picture know when the picture has been taken. The electronic shutter on the R5 is very quiet. Sometimes, I like a silent shutter, in an instance like when I want to take a picture of a sleeping baby. But I think most people have trouble telling when a picture is being taken with a silent shutter, so I like that the R5 Mark II lets me set it to play a realistic shutter sound when it's using an electronic shutter.

Pre-Continuous Shooting

One of my favorite things about the new Canon EOS R5 Mark II is pre-continuous shooting, which works well with the fast frame rate and better auto-focus. When you turn on pre-continuous shooting and half-press the shutter button, the camera starts to record pictures, but they stay in its buffer until you fully press the shutter button. You can take up to 15 RAW photos before you press the camera button. This makes it much more likely that you'll catch that magical moment that disappears in an instant.

I wasn't sure how pre-continuous shooting would help me as a family photographer when I first read about it. For example, I could see how very useful it would be in sports to catch the kick that scores the goal or the split second that separates the killer shot and missing the moment. Okay, but what about family photos? I didn't know.

It turns out to be great working with teens who are hard to guess! The shy look of a worried subject, which is often so quick that it's hard to catch, to the moment a child jumps up from the bottom of the pool and makes a waterfall of water. A lot of the time, the action happens so quickly and the buildup is so subtle that you've already missed it. I've already been able to take pictures I wouldn't have been able to before I learned how to set the camera to start shooting before I press the shutter button. I'm sure this will open up many more possibilities in the future.

Of course, I wouldn't want to use this setting all the time because memory cards would fill up very quickly, but this feature is great in the right circumstances. The R5 Mark II, like all Canon R-series cameras, can be customized in a lot of ways. To make it easier to find, I added the pre-shoot setting to my Quick menu.

Dual Shooting (stills and videos)

The Canon EOS R5 Mark II has video features, but I haven't tried them yet because I'm not good at that. However, there was one feature that caught my eye right away: dual shooting, which lets you take both stills and videos at the same time (6 fps 16:9 JPEGs).

I used to not be able to shoot videos because it would take my attention away from my main goal, which was to get great still photos for my clients during my family picture sessions.

With this feature, you can now shoot both video and high-quality JPEG at the same time. This is a very interesting development, and I will look into it more once I get my hands on an R5 Mark II. From the little time I've spent playing around with this feature, I can see that I could get some nice clips for my clients or social media without giving up my main goal of taking still pictures.

I think that social and professional photographers who want to add a few short video clips to their still picture portfolios will love this feature.

High ISO

For family photographers like me who work in people's homes and don't always have control over the lighting, low-light performance is very important. It's more important than some of the flashier new features. I have to work with the light I have most of the time, which isn't much. Flash or LED panels are good sometimes, but not always.

I want to see how far I can push things with each new camera. Most of the time, I shoot with my R5 at ISO 5,000, but sometimes I need to shoot at ISO 10,000. How do I use the R5 Mark II?

It looks like the answer is to go higher than I thought, especially when the new noise reduction tool in the camera is used together.

I tried some ISO 10,000 shots inside during my test shots. The quality is fine for a 24" double-page spread in an album. The camera was set on a kid being thrown in the air at 1/160th, which is a slow shutter speed because the light was low. The kid's eyes are very sharp.

The R5 doesn't look as good at ISO 5,000. Smooth tones and less noise will make it great for taking pictures inside.

I tried going further outside under a dark tree in the woods. When I shot at ISO 51,200, the JPEG was noisy right out of the camera, but the result was surprisingly good after going through the camera's noise reduction. An A2 test print showed that this ISO level could be used for shooting if necessary and that the results could be printed big.

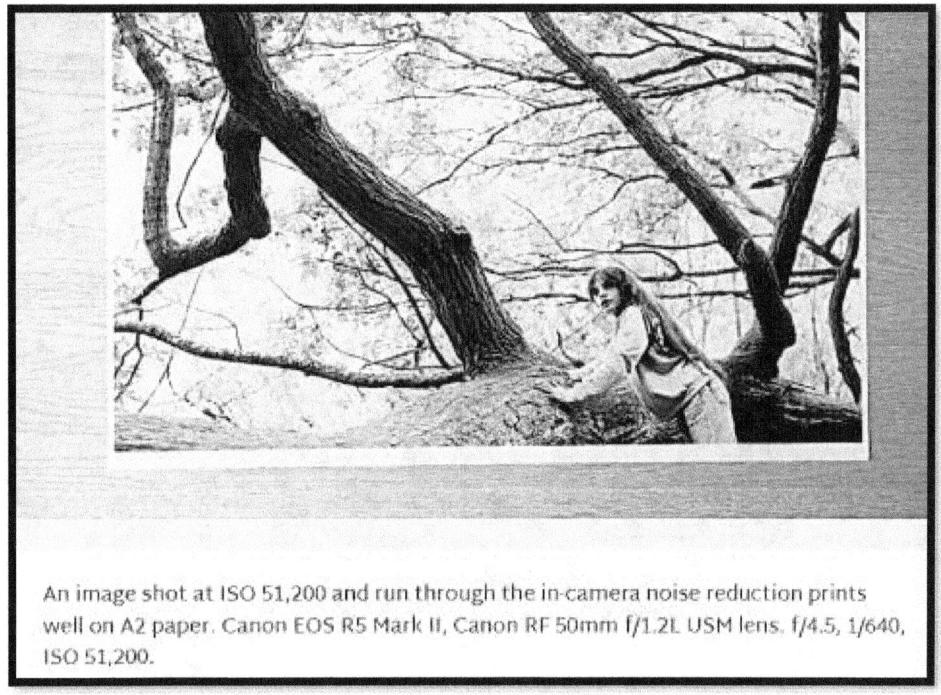

An image shot at ISO 51,200 and run through the in-camera noise reduction prints well on A2 paper. Canon EOS R5 Mark II, Canon RF 50mm f/1.2L USM lens. f/4.5, 1/640, ISO 51,200.

Processing in the Camera

With the touch of a button, the Canon EOS R5 Mark II can take a picture from 8,192 x 5,464 pixels to 16,384 x 10,928 pixels and save it as a JPEG. It can also reduce noise in the image. You can use this with the RAW processing available in the R5 to send pictures to agencies, and it will be very helpful.

The picture can also be shrunk in the camera to make it easier to send (normal JPEG at 24 megapixels, S1 JPEG at 12 megapixels, or S2 JPEG at 3.8 megapixels). The picture can also be cropped and made straight, and the size can be changed to 4:3, 9:16, 3:4, or 16:9.

You can process RAW files in the camera and turn them into JPEG or HEIF files, after which you can then change the picture style, color space, clarity, brightness, noise, white balance, and the lighting optimizer before saving the new file. In case you need to quickly send pictures that have been changed, this feature comes in handy. The R5 Mark II now has a Blur/Out-of-Focus image detection setting that should make it easier to choose images in the camera, but I haven't tested it yet.

I'm sure its main purpose is to help photojournalists quickly edit and send pictures from the field, but I could see myself editing photos and then sending them to my phone through the Canon Connect app to post on social media. It could also be useful for wedding photographers who want to send a few pictures to the couple on the wedding day.

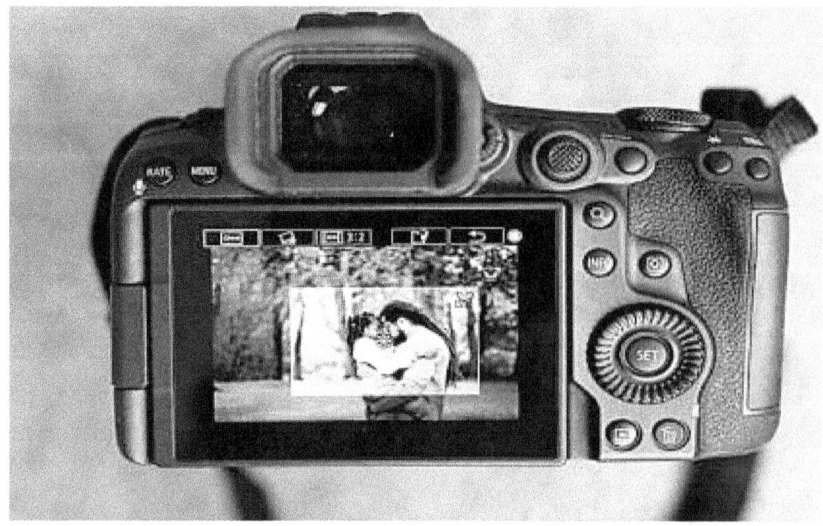

Image Stabilization

In-body image stabilization is better than the R5's already impressive stabilization; when used with in-lens image stabilization, they can give you up to 8.5 stops of total stabilization. In real life, if you take a picture of a little girl standing still while moving an umbrella at 1/15th of a second with the Canon EOS RF 50mm f1.2L lens, she would appear very clear, but the umbrella would not. This will continue to be a very useful feature for people with shaky hands who don't want to carry a tripod. I can see myself using it for creative effects on landscape photography trips, and I will also keep trying out slow shutter speeds on portrait shoots, which is something I like to do sometimes to add a bit of creative blur to an image.

ACCESSORIES
Best All-in-one Lens for Canon EOS R5 Mark II
Canon RF 24-240mm f/4-6.3 IS USM Lens

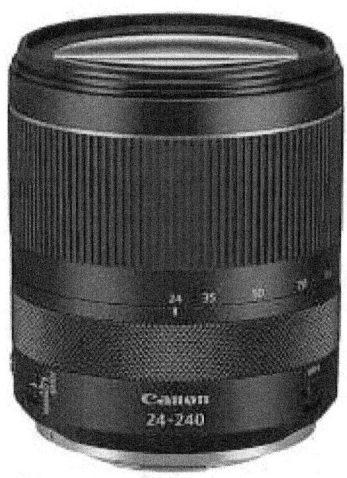

With its wide range of features, the Canon RF 24-240mm f/4-6.3 IS USM lens is one of the best all-in-one lenses for the Canon EOS R5 Mark II. A lot of people think this lens is the best choice for photographers and filmmakers who want to be able to shoot a lot of different things without having to keep switching lenses. It's great for people who are always on the go or don't want to carry around a bag full of lenses because it has all the focal lengths.

Why does this Lens Stand Out? Why does it Work Well with the Canon EOS R5 Mark II?

Versatile Focal Range

One of its best features is the RF 24-240mm focal range. You can take wide-angle pictures starting at 24mm, which are great for scenery, buildings, street photography, and even pictures of big groups of people. When you zoom in 240mm, it will enter telephoto mode, which is great for sports, wildlife, and any other time you need to focus on something far away.

Because it can do so many things, this lens is great for traveling, where you might need to quickly take pictures of both large scenes and small features that are far away. With this lens, you don't have to switch gears to take pictures of a bird in a tree in the afternoon or beautiful scenery in the morning. This all-in-one zoom feature is great for people who don't want to miss a shot.

Image Stabilization

When you use such a wide lens range, especially the longer telephoto range (240mm), the camera shake will be easier to see. Image stabilization (IS) of 5 stops is built into the Canon RF 24-240mm lens. This helps keep your shots straight even if you're holding the camera by hand. This is very important, especially when there isn't much light, or you're zooming in on something far away. The in-body image stabilization (IBIS) of the EOS R5 Mark II will work with the lens's stabilization to give you more room to take clear pictures without a tripod.

This means smoother videos shot with a phone for videographers. If you carry your Canon EOS R5 Mark II around with you and shoot video, you don't have to worry about the shake ruining the shot. This can be very helpful for making trip videos, covering events, or just capturing moments with your family.

Compact and Lightweight Design

When choosing an all-in-one lens, flexibility is one of the most important things to think about. You need something light and strong at the same time. The Canon RF 24-240mm f/4-6.3 IS USM is the right size and has the right features. It's not the smallest lens (about

750g/1.65 lbs), but it's still small enough to be useful on trips because it can be used for so many things. You won't feel too heavy even if you carry the Canon EOS R5 Mark II and lens around with you for a whole day of shooting.

This makes it a great choice if you want to take your camera on holiday, go hiking, or just spend the day exploring. With just one lens in your bag, you won't have to stop and switch lenses, because you can still shoot everything from wide-angle to zoom.

USM Autofocus System

There is a fast and quiet Ultra-Sonic Motor (USM) autofocus system in this lens. This is very important for photographers who need to focus quickly, whether they're shooting moving subjects like athletes or animals, or just catching moments in a busy place like a wedding or street scene.

This autofocus method is even better because it is quiet, so it won't get in the way of recording videos. The buzzing sound of a lens motor is the last thing you want when you're recording something important like an interview or a live event. That won't happen with this lens, so you can focus on getting the best sound and video quality without any interruption getting in the way.

Aperture and Low Light Performance

This lens has an aperture that goes from f/4 to f/6.3. This means that when the lens is fully zoomed out (24mm), it can open up to f/4. This works fine for daily use, especially in well-lit places. But when you zoom in to 240mm, the aperture drops to f/6.3, which means the lens lets in less light.

This aperture range isn't as good for low-light settings as lenses with a constant f/2.8 aperture, but that's what you get for having everything in one package. If you need to take pictures in low light, the EOS R5 Mark II's high ISO performance and in-body stabilization will help. It's still possible to get good pictures when you increase the ISO or slow down the shutter speed, but keep this in mind if you often shoot in low light.

Build Quality

The Canon RF 24-240mm lens is well-made, even though it's not one of their more expensive L-series lenses. Though it's not fully weather-sealed like Canon's expensive lenses, the materials feel strong, and it does hold up against some weather. This is important if you want to use it outside, where dust, light rain, or other weather conditions might happen. Even though you should still be careful in bad weather, this lens can handle normal outdoor use well.

What are the Best Prime Telephoto Lenses for the Canon EOS R5 Mark II?

When it comes to Canon EOS R5 Mark II telephoto prime lenses, picking the right one depends on your needs, like if you want to take pictures of wildlife, sports, birds, or even landscapes from far away. Canon's RF line-up has several powerful cameras that are made to work with mirrorless systems and offer sharpness, image stabilization, and a lot of different shooting choices. Here, we'll look at the **Canon RF 600mm f/11 IS STM**, **Canon RF 800mm f/11 IS STM**, **Canon RF 400mm f/2.8 L IS USM**, and **Canon RF 600mm f/4L IS USM**.

There are different focal lengths and features on these lenses, so each one is good for a different type of shooting. Then you can choose the one that fits your style and needs the best. Let's look at each one in more depth.

1. Canon RF 600mm f/11 IS STM Lens.

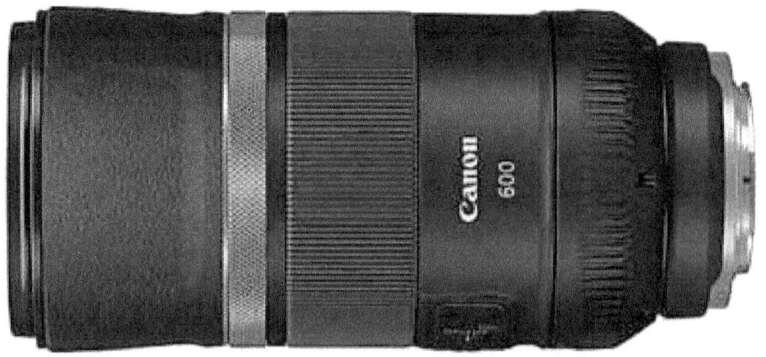

The **Canon RF 600mm f/11 IS STM** is a one-of-a-kind lens because it has a set f/11 aperture and isn't too big for a super-telephoto lens. This makes it a great choice for photographers who want to try telephoto but don't want to spend a lot of money or carry around a heavy lens.

Key Features:

- **Focal Length**: 600mm
- **Aperture**: Fixed f/11
- **Image Stabilization (IS)**: Yes, with up to **5 stops** of compensation
- **Autofocus**: STM (Stepping Motor), which is smooth and quiet, great for both stills and video
- **Weight**: Relatively lightweight at **930g (2.05 lbs)**

What's Great About It?

- **Lightweight and portable:** One of the best things about this long telephoto lens is how portable it is. A lot of 600mm lenses are big, heavy, and hard to move around with. The f/11 aperture, on the other hand, lets Canon keep the size and weight down. Because of this, it's great for photographers who want a super-telephoto lens but don't want to carry around a big lens all day.
- **Affordable**: The price is also a big plus. Other 600mm lenses can cost thousands of dollars, but the RF 600mm f/11 is a lot less expensive. This makes it a great lens for people who are just starting with long telephoto photos.
- **Great for Photographing Wildlife and Birds:** Wildlife and bird photographers will love this lens. With a 600mm lens, you can get close to your subject without scaring them. When used with the EOS R5 Mark II, which has great picture quality and quick focusing, you can get clear pictures of animals in their natural environment.
- **Fixed Aperture Limitations**: The fixed f/11 aperture is bad because it limits the amount of light that can get into the lens. You shouldn't use it when there isn't much light. But because the EOS R5 Mark II has great ISO performance, you can make up for it by raising the ISO or taking in well-lit areas.

2. **Canon RF 800mm f/11 IS STM Lens.**

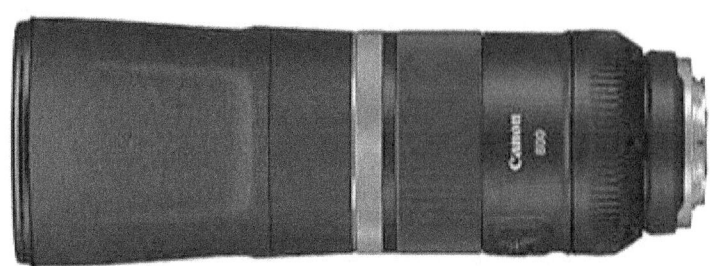

This is another great choice; the **Canon RF 800mm f/11 IS STM**. It has even more reach than the 600mm. In terms of form and features, it's a lot like the 600mm lens. However, it has an 800mm telephoto reach, which makes it an even better tool for shooting at very long distances.

Key Features:

- **Focal Length**: 800mm
- **Aperture**: Fixed f/11
- **Image Stabilization (IS)**: Yes, with up to **4 stops** of stabilization
- **Autofocus**: STM motor for smooth, quiet focusing
- **Weight**: Also lightweight for an 800mm lens at **1260g (2.78 lbs)**

What's Great About It?

- **Extreme Reach**: If you have an 800mm lens, you can take pictures of things that are very far away, and get details with this lens that you wouldn't be able to get with a shorter lens when you're shooting birds in the distance, safari animals, or scenery that are far away.
- **Compact for the Focal Length**: The f/11 aperture keeps the size and weight down, just like the 600mm version. This makes it easier to carry and use than regular 800mm lenses.
- **Affordable Super-Telephoto**: Professional-level 800mm lenses can cost tens of thousands of dollars, but this one is much more affordable, making it a good choice for photographers who want to try out extreme telephoto without spending a lot of money.
- **Fixed Aperture**: Just like the 600mm, the fixed f/11 aperture doesn't work well in low light, so it's best used in well-lit areas or during the day.

3. **Canon RF 400mm f/2.8 L IS USM Lens**

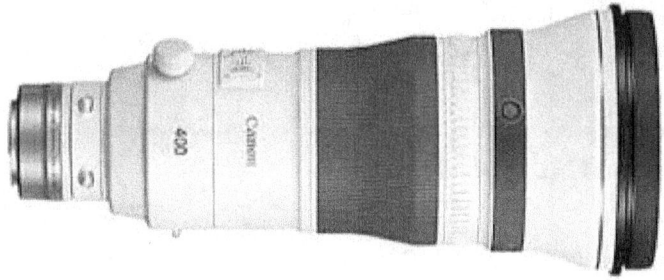

Now let's talk about professional telephoto lenses. The Canon RF 400mm f/2.8 L IS USM is one of them. It's part of Canon's L-series, which means it's made to work and take pictures very well. The f/2.8 aperture makes it great for low-light situations and blurs the background beautifully. This makes it perfect for sports and wildlife photographers who need both reach and speed.

Key Features:

- **Focal Length**: 400mm
- **Aperture**: f/2.8
- **Image Stabilization (IS)**: Yes, with up to **5.5 stops** of stabilization
- **Autofocus**: USM motor for fast and precise autofocus
- **Weight**: Heavier than the 600mm and 800mm at **2840g (6.26 lbs)**

What's Great About It?

- **Professional-Grade Quality**: This lens is made for professionals or serious hobbyists. The f/2.8 aperture is great for low-light situations and makes the depth of field very small, which makes it easy to separate your subject from the background. Wildlife and sports photographers who want to make their subjects stand out will find this very helpful.
- **Versatile Performance**: The 400mm focal length can be used for a lot of different things. Even though it's not as long as 600mm or 800mm, it's still short enough to handle and long enough for most sports and wildlife photos.
- **Superior Build Quality**: The RF 400mm f/2.8 is built like a tank because it is an L-series lens. Because it's weather-sealed, you can use it in any weather without

thinking about damage from dust, water, or rain. It's made to last through the rough conditions of expert use.
- **Price**: Of course, this level of efficiency costs more. This lens costs a lot more than the 600mm and 800mm f/11 options, but pros may find it well worth the extra money.

4. **Canon RF 600mm f/4L IS USM Lens**

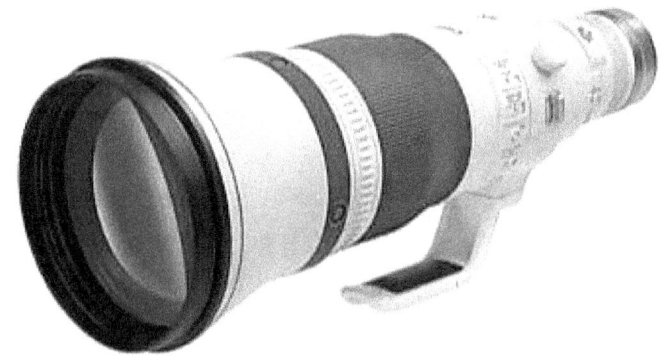

The Canon RF 600mm f/4L IS USM is one of the best telephoto lenses on the market if you need even more reach without giving up your light-gathering ability. It's an L-series lens, like the 400mm f/2.8, so the picture quality and build quality are the best. It's great for wildlife and sports photos, even when there isn't much light because the f/4 aperture lets in a lot of light.

Key Features:

- **Focal Length**: 600mm
- **Aperture**: f/4
- **Image Stabilization (IS)**: Yes, with up to **5 stops** of stabilization
- **Autofocus**: USM motor for fast and accurate autofocus
- **Weight**: Heavier at **3090g (6.81 lbs)**

What's Great About It?

- **Incredible Reach with Fast Aperture**: The 600mm focal length is great for wildlife photographers who need to get close to their subjects without disturbing them.

Also, the f/4 aperture is much faster than the f/11 apertures. This means that you can use this lens in low light and still get sharp, well-exposed pictures.
- **Image Stabilization and Autofocus**: The image stabilization is great, and it can compensate for up to 5 stops. This is very important when taking at such long focal lengths since even a small movement can blur the picture. The **USM autofocus motor** makes sure that you can focus quickly and accurately, which is very important when taking pictures of things that are moving quickly, like birds or activities like sports.
- **Professional Build Quality**: This lens is part of Canon's L-series, so it is made to last. It is weather-sealed and has a tough design that can handle the elements. It's priced right because it's meant to be used by professionals.

Best Telephoto Zoom Lenses for Canon EOS R5 Mark II

1. **Canon RF 100-500mm f/4.5-7.1 L IS USM Lens**

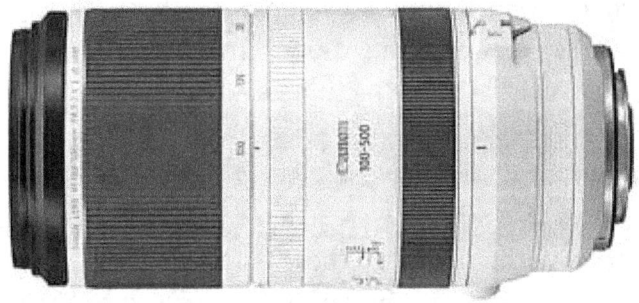

The Canon RF 100-500mm f/4.5-7.1 L IS USM is a high-end telephoto zoom lens in the L series. It is made to produce stunning images at a variety of focal lengths. You can use this lens to take pictures of wildlife, sports, or even landscapes because it has a huge zoom range without losing performance.

Key Features:

- **Focal Length**: 100-500mm
- **Aperture**: Variable f/4.5-7.1
- **Image Stabilization (IS)**: Yes, with up to **5 stops** of compensation
- **Autofocus**: Dual Nano USM motors for fast and silent autofocus
- **Weight**: 1370g (3.02 lbs)

What's Great About It?

- **Versatile Zoom Range**: The 100–500mm focal length gives you a lot of freedom; you can shoot anything from close-up wildlife to faraway views without having to switch lenses. This makes it a great choice for people who need one lens to do a lot of different things. With 100mm, you can see a lot of ground, and with 500mm, you can get very close to things that are far away.
- **Professional-Grade Optics**: The RF 100-500mm has high-end optics because it is an L-series lens. That's because it has Super UD (Ultra-low Dispersion) and UD elements that reduce chromatic distortion and make sure that your pictures are clear and sharp even at the longest focal lengths.
- **Weather Sealing**: This lens is made to last in tough conditions. Because it's fully weather-sealed, you can shoot without thinking about damaging your gear when it's dusty, wet, or humid. It's perfect for photographers who like to be outside and are in tough places like sports fields or safaris.
- **Image Stabilization**: The 5-stop image stabilization that's built-in is great, especially when taking at long focal lengths, where camera shake can be a big problem. It works great with the in-body image stabilization (IBIS) on the EOS R5 Mark II, so you can take sharp pictures even when you hold the lens by hand at 500mm.
- **Aperture Limitations**: The only challenging thing is that the aperture can only be changed between f/4.5 and f/7.1. It doesn't have the fastest aperture, so you might need to raise the ISO when there isn't much light, especially when zoomed to 500mm at f/7.1. However, this lens works well when the lighting is good.

Ideal for:

- People who take pictures of wildlife and birds
- Photographers of sports
- Outdoor and landscape photographers who want a versatile lens
- Travel photographers who want an all-in-one telephoto zoom that works well

2. Canon RF 70-200mm f/2.8 L IS USM Lens

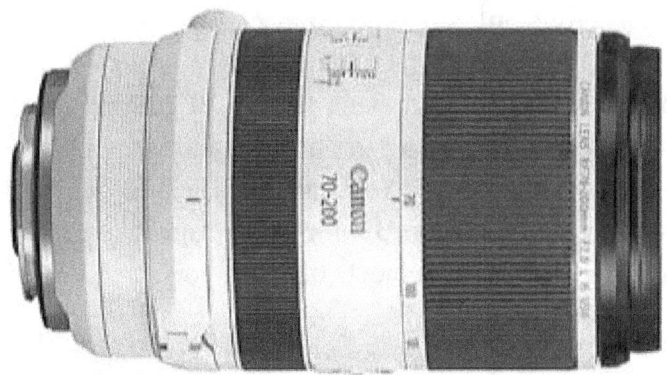

Professional photographers have long loved the Canon RF 70-200mm f/2.8 L IS USM telephoto zoom lens because it is quick and can be used in a lot of different ways. This lens has great image quality, fast autofocus, and a wide aperture that makes it great for shooting in low light, whether you're taking pictures of sports, people, or events.

Key Features:

- **Focal Length**: 70-200mm
- **Aperture**: Constant f/2.8
- **Image Stabilization (IS)**: Yes, with up to **5 stops** of stabilization
- **Autofocus**: Dual Nano USM motors for fast and accurate autofocus
- **Weight: 1070g (2.36 lbs)**

What's Great About It?

- **Constant f/2.8 Aperture**: One of the main reasons this lens is so famous is its f/2.8 aperture, which stays the same. It remains the same across the whole zoom range, so you can shoot in low light and get beautiful backgrounds blurred (bokeh), which is great for portrait and sports photos. You can shoot at faster shutter speeds when you have a fast lens, which is important for freezing action that moves quickly.
- **Exceptional Image Quality**: The RF 70-200mm f/2.8 from the L-series takes pictures that look great. It has high-tech lens elements and layers that lower distortion, chromatic aberration, and flare. This makes sure that your pictures are clear all the way around. It works great for photographers who need the best optical performance.

- **Compact and Lightweight**: One thing that makes this lens stand out is that, for a 70-200mm f/2.8, it's not too big. Usually, lenses in this class are big and heavy, but Canon surprised everyone by making the RF 70-200mm f/2.8 surprisingly small and light. This makes it easier to carry around and use with one hand.
- **Fast and Accurate Autofocus**: You can quickly and accurately focus on your subject thanks to the two Nano USM motors inside the lens. This makes it great for taking pictures of moving subjects because you can quickly lock focus. It's also very quiet, making it great for video work.

Ideal for:

- Portrait photographers who want creamy bokeh
- Sports photographers who need a fast telephoto lens
- Event photographers who work in low-light environments
- General-purpose photographers who want a reliable, high-quality telephoto zoom

3. **Canon RF 70-200mm f/4 L IS USM Lens**

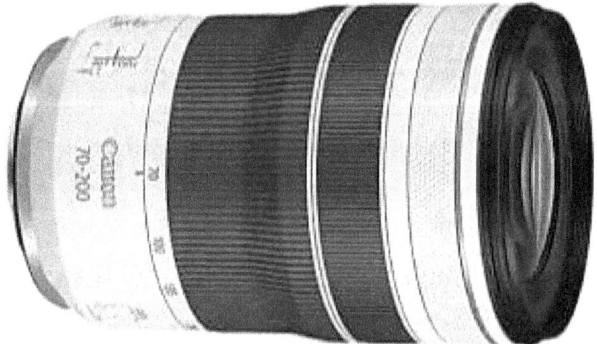

The Canon RF 70-200mm f/4 L IS USM is a lighter and less expensive version of the f/2.8 version. It has many of the same benefits, but its maximum aperture is smaller. For photographers who don't need the faster f/2.8 aperture but still want a high-quality, flexible telephoto zoom lens, this is the answer.

Key Features:

- **Focal Length**: 70-200mm
- **Aperture**: Constant f/4
- **Image Stabilization (IS)**: Yes, with up to **5 stops** of stabilization
- **Autofocus**: Nano USM motors for smooth and quick autofocus
- **Weight**: 695g (1.53 lbs)

What's Great About It?

- **Lightweight and Portable**: The RF 70-200mm f/4 is a lot smaller and lighter than the f/2.8 version. This makes it a great choice for photographers who need to carry their gear for long periods or for people who are traveling. It's not too big to fit in most bags, which is great for people who are always on the go.
- **Constant f/4 Aperture**: The constant f/4 aperture is still fast enough for most cases, especially when there is enough light. It won't blur the background as much or work as well in low light as the f/2.8, but for many photographers, it's more than enough.
- **Superb Image Quality**: Even though the aperture is smaller, the picture quality is excellent. The lens still has the sharpness, color accuracy, and clarity that Canon's L-series is known for. This makes it a great telephoto zoom lens for professional work in general.

Ideal for:

- Travel photographers who need an easy-to-carry lens
- Portrait photographers who don't need a super-fast aperture
- General photographers who want an option for the f/2.8 version that costs less

4. **Canon RF 100-400mm f/5.6-8 IS USM Lens**

The Canon RF 100-400mm f/5.6-8 IS USM is a great choice for photographers who want a long telephoto zoom lens but don't want to spend a lot of money on one. It has a wide zoom range and is great for artists or anyone else who wants a small, light telephoto lens for shooting wildlife, sports, or just being outside in general.

Key Features:

- **Focal Length**: 100-400mm
- **Aperture**: Variable f/5.6-8
- **Image Stabilization (IS)**: Yes, with up to **5.5 stops** of stabilization
- **Autofocus**: Nano USM motor for smooth and fast focusing
- **Weight: 635g (1.4 lbs)**

What's Great About It?

- **Affordable Telephoto Zoom**: This is one of Canon's RF telephoto zooms that isn't too expensive, so more photographers can use it. It has good picture quality even though it's cheaper, and it's a great lens for beginners or people on a budget.
- **Compact and Lightweight**: This telephoto zoom lens is very portable, especially given its 400mm reach, as it only weighs 635g. It's great for photographers who want to bring a telephoto lens with them but don't want to carry a heavy one.
- **Impressive Image Stabilization**: This lens has up to 5.5 stops of image stabilization, which means you can get sharp pictures even at slower shutter speeds. This is especially important when shooting at 400mm. It works well with the in-body image stabilization on the EOS R5 Mark II to make steadiness even better.

Ideal for:

- Beginners and hobbyists looking for a cheap telephoto zoom lens
- Travel photographers who need a long-reach lens that is light
- Wildlife photographers who don't need top-tier aperture speeds

The Best Standard Prime Lenses for the Canon EOS R5 Mark II

1. Canon RF 50mm f/1.2 L USM Lens

One of the best lenses in Canon's RF line is the RF 50mm f/1.2 L USM. It is made for professionals and serious photographers who need the best picture quality, performance, and durability. It is part of the L-series. This is a high-end, fast prime lens with beautiful sharpness, smooth bokeh, and great performance in low light.

Key Features:

- **Focal Length**: 50mm
- **Maximum Aperture**: f/1.2
- **Autofocus Motor**: USM (Ultrasonic Motor) for fast and quiet focusing
- **Lens Elements**: Advanced optics with aspherical and UD elements
- **Weather Sealing**: Yes
- **Weight**: 950g (2.1 lbs)

What's Unique About It?

- **Incredible Sharpness**: One of the best things about the RF 50mm f/1.2 is how sharp it is, even when shot wide open at f/1.2. It takes pictures that are very clear and have great detail all over the frame. This makes it ideal for photos, fine art, and other professional work that needs to be very clear.
- **Ultra-Wide Aperture**: The f/1.2 aperture is very fast, so you can shoot in low light without having to raise the ISO. This wide aperture also gives you a very small depth of field, which makes your subject stand out against a background that is beautifully blurred. This lens makes bokeh that is soft and creamy. It gives your pictures a feeling of luxury and depth, which is great for portrait photographers.
- **Professional Build Quality**: This lens is part of the L-series, so it's professionally made and built to last. Because it's weatherproof, you can use it in bad weather like rain or dust without thinking about damage. It is built to last and can handle the wear and tear of expert use. For people who shoot outside or in places that aren't always stable, this is a big plus.
- **Fast and Quiet Autofocus**: It has fast and quiet autofocus thanks to the USM (Ultrasonic Motor), which is important for both still photos and videos. It focuses quickly and stays focused even when there isn't much light, which makes it great for events and street photos where things move quickly.
- **Large Size and Weight**: This lens's only real flaw is that it is big and heavy. At 950g, it's pretty heavy for a prime lens, so people who want to carry their gear around

with them might not want to get this one. If picture quality is the most important thing to you, though, the trade-off is well worth it.

People who should buy it:

- **Portrait photographers**: Photographers who take portraits will love the f/1.2 aperture, which gives you beautiful subject separation and bokeh.
- **Wedding photographers**: The fact that it can work in low light is a big plus for event and wedding photographers who often work inside or in dim light.
- **Professional photographers:** This lens is made for you if you need the best quality images and can handle the weight and cost.

Ideal for:

- Portrait photography
- Weddings and events
- Low-light shooting
- Fine art and editorial work

2. Canon RF 50mm f/1.8 STM Lens

The Canon RF 50mm f/1.8 STM is often called the "nifty fifty" because it takes great pictures at a price that most people can afford. For beginners or artists who want a small, light, and inexpensive prime lens that still takes beautiful pictures, this is a great choice. Even though it's not very expensive, the RF 50mm f/1.8 is a great lens that can be used in a lot of different situations.

Key Features:

- **Focal Length**: 50mm
- **Maximum Aperture**: f/1.8
- **Autofocus Motor**: STM (Stepping Motor) for smooth and silent autofocus
- **Lens Elements**: Aspherical element to reduce aberrations
- **Weight**: 160g (0.35 lbs)

What's Unique About It?

- **Compact and Lightweight**: This lens weighs only 160g, making it very portable and easy to carry. This is a great choice for photographers who don't want to carry around heavy gear, whether they're going on a trip or just strolling around town. It's small enough to fit in most bags, and you won't feel heavy carrying it around for street photos or casual shoots.
- **Affordable Price**: One of the best things about the RF 50mm f/1.8 is that it's not too expensive. Since it's one of the RF lenses with the lowest price, it's great for beginners or photographers on a budget. Even though it's cheap, the quality of the pictures it takes is very good, making it a great deal for anyone who wants to add a multipurpose prime lens to their collection.
- **Sharpness**: Even though it's not quite as sharp as the f/1.2 version, the RF 50mm f/1.8 is still very sharp, especially when the aperture is slowed down to f/2.8 or f/4. This lens is more than good enough to take clear, detailed pictures for everyday use or even semi-professional work.
- **f/1.8 Aperture**: The f/1.8 aperture is still fast enough to get good low-light performance and small depth of field, but it doesn't give you as much bokeh as the f/1.2 aperture. But the difference isn't always clear-cut, and the f/1.8 is still great for pictures because it lets you blur the background and separate the subject from it nicely.
- **STM Autofocus**: The STM (Stepping Motor) autofocus is quiet and smooth, so it works well for both film and stills. It's not as quick or accurate as the USM in more expensive lenses, but it's fine for most general shooting tasks.

People who should buy it:

- **Beginners and hobbyists**: This is a great choice if you're new to shooting and want a versatile prime lens that won't break the bank.
- **Budget-conscious photographers**: This lens has a great price-to-performance ratio, making it a great choice for anyone who wants to get the most for their money.
- **Travel and street photographers**: Its small size and light weight make it perfect for times when you don't want to carry around a lot of stuff.

Ideal for:

- Everyday photography

- Portraits on a budget
- Travel and street photography
- Video work

Comparison: Canon RF 50mm f/1.2 L USM vs Canon RF 50mm f/1.8 STM

Both of these lenses serve a similar purpose: these two lenses are standard prime lenses with a 50mm focal length, which is very close to the human eye's natural field of view. But even though they have some things in common, they are aimed at different groups:

- **Image Quality**: When it comes to image quality, the RF 50mm f/1.2 L is the clear winner. Because its aperture is wider (f/1.2), it's sharper, has better bokeh, and works better in low light. The RF 50mm f/1.8 still takes very good pictures, especially considering how cheap it is.
- **Aperture**: The L-series lens's f/1.2 aperture gives it an edge in low light and lets you separate subjects even more dramatically. The f/1.2 is a great lens to buy if you often shoot in dim light or want the best background blur. That being said, the f/1.8 aperture is still fast enough for most cases and blurs the background nicely.
- **Build and Durability**: The RF 50mm f/1.2 is built to last. It's made to look like an expert tool. It can stand up to bad weather and is built to last for a long time. The RF 50mm f/1.8, on the other hand, is made of plastic and doesn't seal against the weather, so it's not as good for rough places.
- **Size and Weight**: The RF 50mm f/1.8 is much smaller and lighter than the other lens, so it's a better choice for photographers who want to carry their gear around with them or travel light. The f/1.2 version is bigger and heavier, but that's to be expected since it has a bigger aperture and is made for professionals.
- **Price**: There is a big price change. The RF 50mm f/1.2 is a high-end lens that costs a lot. The RF 50mm f/1.8, on the other hand, is much cheaper and can be used by more photographers.

Best Standard Zoom Lenses for Canon EOS R5 Mark II

1. **Canon RF 24-70mm f/2.8 L IS USM Lens**

Professional photographers often use the Canon RF 24-70mm f/2.8 L IS USM as their main zoom lens. It can be used in a lot of different situations, is reliable, and is known for having great image quality at a lot of different focal lengths. As part of Canon's L-series, this lens is made to work well in tough shooting situations and give you stunning pictures, whether you're taking pictures of people, places, events, or anything else.

Key Features:

- **Focal Length**: 24-70mm
- **Maximum Aperture**: f/2.8 constant throughout the zoom range
- **Autofocus Motor**: USM (Ultrasonic Motor) for fast and precise focusing
- **Image Stabilization**: Yes, up to 5 stops of stabilization
- **Weather Sealing**: Yes, fully weather-sealed for dust and moisture resistance
- **Weight**: 900g (2 lbs)

Why the Canon RF 24-70mm f/2.8 L IS USM Stands Out

- **Versatile Focal Range**: The 24-70mm focal length is a popular choice for a standard zoom lens because it can be used for both wide-angle and short-telephoto shots. Because of this, it can be used in a huge range of shooting scenarios. At 24mm, you can take pictures of wide scenery, buildings, or people in their natural environments. When you zoom in to 70mm, you can get closer shots, pictures, or more details in scenes. This lens is great for people who shoot a lot of different things, like wedding photographers, trip photographers, or people who just like to take pictures of different things.
- **Constant f/2.8 Aperture**: The **f/2.8** maximum aperture is constant across the zoom range. This means that at 70mm, you can control the depth of field and exposure just as well as at 24mm. That makes it easier to shoot indoors or in poorly lit places without losing quality, which is especially helpful when there isn't much light. Because the aperture is f/2.8, you can blur the background and separate the subject beautifully, which makes it perfect for pictures.
- **Advanced Image Stabilization**: The 5-stop image stabilization that's built-in is amazing, especially when shooting handheld in low light. With the in-body stabilization on the EOS R5 Mark II, you can get very steady shots, even when the shutter speed is slow. With this, you can shoot inside, in low light, or when you don't have a stand with you.

- **Superb Optical Performance**: This lens is part of the L-series and is made to have great sharpness, contrast, and color rendering. It has high-tech lens parts like aspherical and ultra-low dispersion (UD) glass that help lower chromatic errors, distortion, and other optical problems. Even when shooting wide open at f/2.8, the pictures are clear and full of detail to the edges.
- **Weather-Sealed and Durable**: The RF 24-70mm f/2.8 is built to last, just like all L-series lenses. It's fully weather-sealed, which means it can handle dust, water, and rough conditions. This makes it perfect for taking pictures outside and on trips. You don't have to worry about hurting your lens when you shoot in the rain, snow, or dust.
- **Fast and Quiet Autofocus**: The USM autofocus motor is quick and quiet, which makes it great for both photos and videos. It locks on to things quickly and correctly, even when the lighting is bad. For people who take videos, silent focusing is very helpful because it keeps your recordings from being broken by noisy lens movements.

People who should buy it:

- **Event photographers**: This lens is great for weddings, concerts, and other events because it has a wide focus range and a fast aperture.
- **Travel photographers**: The 24-70mm range is great for general-purpose needs and is great for traveling when you want to bring as little stuff as possible.
- **Portrait photographers**: The f/2.8 aperture blurs the background and separates the subject beautifully, making it great for taking professional portraits.
- **Professional photographers**: For professional photographers, this lens is made to be used a lot. Its image stabilization, weather sealing, and high optical quality make it an essential part of any professional kit.

Ideal for:

- Weddings and events
- Portraits and lifestyle photography
- Travel and landscape photography
- Street photography

2. **Canon RF 28-70mm f/2 L USM Lens**

There is no other lens like the Canon RF 28-70mm f/2 L USM. It goes beyond what a normal zoom can do. It has an aperture of f/2 through the zoom range, which makes it one of the fastest regular zooms ever made. When it comes to low light, shallow depth of field, and overall picture quality, this lens is made for photographers who want the best. While it's bigger and heavier than the RF 24-70mm f/2.8, many people find that the extra weight is worth it.

Key Features:

- **Focal Length**: 28-70mm
- **Maximum Aperture**: f/2 constant throughout the zoom range
- **Autofocus Motor**: USM (Ultrasonic Motor) for quick and accurate focusing
- **Weather Sealing**: Yes, fully weather-sealed
- **Weight**: 1430g (3.15 lbs)

Why the Canon RF 28-70mm f/2 L USM Stands Out

- **Ultra-Wide f/2 Aperture**: This lens's f/2 aperture is what makes it stand out. It works better than any other zoom lens in low light, so you can shoot in darker situations without having to raise your ISO. The f/2 aperture also makes the depth of field very small for a zoom lens, which lets you get a look that you can usually only get with prime lenses. For portrait photographers who want smooth bokeh and subject separation, this is a big plus.
- **Exceptional Image Quality**: The picture quality is great, as you would expect from an L-series lens. Even when shooting wide open at f/2, the RF 28-70mm f/2 takes pictures that are very sharp and have a lot of detail. There are special lens elements in the advanced optical design that reduce distortion, chromatic errors, and flare. This makes sure that your photos always look professional. As fast as f/2, the whole frame is sharp, which is one of the best things about this lens.
- **Unique Focal Range**: The focal range for the 28-70mm lens is a little different from the range for the 24-70mm lens. Even though it's not as wide as the 24-70mm range, it's still good for most everyday shooting situations, from panoramas and portraits in natural settings to closer portraits. This focus range won't feel too narrow if you don't use ultra-wide angles a lot.
- **Solid Build and Weather Sealing**: This lens, like the RF 24-70mm, is fully weather-sealed, which makes it a durable choice for shooting in any weather. The lens is

very well made, and it feels solid in your hand. It was made to last years of professional use.
- **Fast, Silent Autofocus**: The USM autofocus motor lets you focus quickly and quietly, which makes it great for both picture and video work. Even though it's big and has heavy glass parts, the autofocus is quick and accurate, so you don't miss important times.
- **Heavy and Large**: This lens weighs 1430 grams, which is a lot. It takes amazing pictures, but it can be heavy, especially for photographers who like being able to carry their gear around. It's not as good for traveling or long shooting sessions because of its size and weight, but for professionals who care about picture quality, the trade-off is often worth it.

People who should buy it:

- **Portrait photographers**: The f/2 aperture gives you a bokeh that looks like a prime lens, which is great for portraits.
- **Low-light photographers**: The f/2 aperture lets you use faster shutter speeds and get better results.
- **Professional photographers**: This lens changes everything for pros who need the best picture quality and don't mind carrying a heavier lens.

Ideal for:

- Portraits and portraits
- Low-light photography
- Weddings and events
- Fine art and editorial work

Comparison: Canon RF 24-70mm f/2.8 L IS USM vs Canon RF 28-70mm f/2 L USM

Some photographers will love both of these lenses, but they are best for different types of photographers:

- **Aperture**: The RF 28-70mm's f/2 aperture makes it better in low light and small depth of field. This lens is great if you often shoot in low light or want to have

complete control over the depth of field. The f/2.8 of the RF 24-70mm, on the other hand, is still very fast and works very well in low light, but it is lighter and more useful overall.
- **Focal Range**: When it comes to focal range, the 24mm lens at the wide end of the RF 24-70mm is more useful, especially for landscapes and buildings. The 24-70mm is a better choice if you need that extra width. The 28-70mm f/2, on the other hand, takes amazing pictures if you don't mind starting at 28mm.
- **Portability**: The RF 24-70mm f/2.8 is lighter and easier to carry, which makes it a better choice for long shoots or trips. Most of the time, the extra weight of the RF 28-70mm f/2 is worth it for people who need the f/2 lens.

Last Thoughts:

- The Canon RF 24-70mm f/2.8 L IS USM is the better choice if you want a lightweight, flexible lens that can be used for a wide range of tasks. It's great for events, trips, portraits, and more, and the image stabilization makes it even better.
- For those who don't mind the extra weight, the Canon RF 28-70mm f/2 L USM is the best choice for getting the best picture quality and performance in low light. It has the picture quality of a prime lens in a zoom lens and is great for portraits, weddings, and art.

Best Wide-Angle Zoom Lenses for Canon EOS R5 Mark II

1. Canon RF 15-35mm f/2.8 L IS USM Lens

With a wide focal range and great optical performance, the Canon RF 15-35mm f/2.8 L IS USM is one of the best wide-angle zoom lenses on the market. It's part of Canon's L-series and is made for pros and serious hobbyists who need high-quality pictures in a tough, weatherproof package.

Key Features:

- **Focal Length**: 15-35mm
- **Maximum Aperture**: f/2.8 constant throughout the zoom range
- **Autofocus Motor**: USM (Ultrasonic Motor) for fast and precise focusing
- **Image Stabilization**: Yes, up to 5 stops of stabilization
- **Weather Sealing**: Yes, fully weather-sealed
- **Weight**: 840g (1.85 lbs)

Why the Canon RF 15-35mm f/2.8 L IS USM Stands Out

- **Fast f/2.8 Aperture:** This lens's f/2.8 aperture across the whole zoom range makes it great for low-light photos and making a shallow depth of field, which isn't often possible with wide-angle lenses. When you're shooting indoors, at dusk, or in other low-light situations, the f/2.8 aperture lets you keep your ISO low and still get sharp pictures.
- **Exceptional Image Quality**: The 15-35mm range takes pictures that are very sharp all the way around, even when the aperture is set to f/2.8. Canon's L-series lenses are known for having great optics, and the 15-35mm is no different. Aspherical elements, UD (Ultra-Low Dispersion) glass, and Air Sphere Coating (ASC) work together to cut down on chromatic errors, ghosting, and flare, so your pictures are clear and colorful.
- **Image Stabilization**: Up to 5 stops of image stabilization make this lens great for shooting by hand, even when there isn't much light. When you need to shoot video or at slower shutter speeds without a tripod, the IS system comes in handy.
- **Versatile Focal Range**: The focal length of 15–35mm is good for a lot of different wide-angle needs. At 15mm, you can take pictures of very wide scenery, buildings with lots of lines, or creative points of view. A focal length that is longer, like 35mm, gets you closer to your subject. This makes it a more versatile focal length that can be used for both environmental portraits and street photography.
- **Durable and Weather-Sealed**: The RF 15-35mm is fully weather-sealed, just like all L-series lenses. This makes it perfect for photographers who need to shoot outside in bad weather. This lens will work whether you're outside in the rain, dust, or snow.

People who should buy it:

- **Landscape photographers**: This lens's 15-35mm focal range and f/2.8 aperture make it great for shooting bright, detailed landscapes in any light.
- **Real estate photographers**: the ultra-wide 15mm lens length lets you take pictures of whole rooms, which makes them look bigger and more open.
- **Event and wedding photographers**: The fast f/2.8 aperture is great for shooting inside in low light, like in churches or reception halls. It also gives you a wide field of view for group shots or photos in natural settings.

Ideal for:

- Landscapes and nature photography
- Real estate and architecture
- Wedding and event photography
- Street photography

2. **Canon RF 14-35mm f/4 L IS USM Lens**

The Canon RF 14-35mm f/4 L IS USM is a slightly slower lens with an aperture of f/4. However, it has an extra millimeter of reaching power at the wide end, making it the broadest L-series zoom lens in Canon's RF range. This lens is great for photographers who don't need the f/2.8 aperture but still want a high-quality wide-angle lens that is small and light.

Key Features:

- **Focal Length**: 14-35mm
- **Maximum Aperture**: f/4 constant throughout the zoom range
- **Autofocus Motor**: USM (Ultrasonic Motor) for quick and quiet focusing
- **Image Stabilization**: Yes, up to 5.5 stops of stabilization
- **Weather Sealing**: Yes, fully weather-sealed
- **Weight**: 540g (1.19 lbs)

Why the Canon RF 14-35mm f/4 L IS USM Stands Out

- **Amazing Focal Range:** The 14mm focal length has an incredibly wide field of view, making it perfect for taking pictures of wide-open scenery, tall buildings, and small rooms inside. At 35mm, it still has enough reach for more general shots, which makes it a useful camera for everyday use.
- **Lightweight and Compact**: The 14-35mm is much lighter than the 15-35mm f/2.8, weighing only 540g. This makes it a great choice for trips or long shooting sessions. If you care about travel, this lens gives you great performance without adding extra weight.
- **Constant f/4 Aperture**: f/4 isn't as fast as f/2.8, but it's still fast enough for most wide-angle work, especially when the light is good. Because the aperture stays the same, your exposure settings won't change as you zoom, so they'll be the same across the whole range.
- **5.5-Stop Image Stabilization**: This lens is great for shooting by hand because it has up to 5.5 stops of image stabilization, even at slower shutter speeds. For very steady shots, you don't need a stand when you use the EOS R5 Mark II's built-in stabilization.
- **Excellent Sharpness and Low Distortion**: Even when shooting at its widest focal length, the 14-35mm lens has great sharpness across the whole picture. This lens is great for shooting in low light because Canon's advanced lens elements and optical coatings help reduce distortion, flare, and chromatic aberration.
- **Weather-Sealed and Durable**: The 14-35mm is made to last in harsh shooting conditions, just like the other lenses in the L line. Since it's fully weather-sealed, dust, water, or high temperatures won't be able to hurt the lens.

People who should buy it:

- **Travel photographers**: This lens is great for traveling, hiking, or just walking around towns because it is small and light.
- **Real estate and architecture photographers**: the 14mm focal length is great for getting a full picture of a room or building. It also gives you the freedom to shoot in tight spaces or wide-open outdoor scenes.
- **Landscape photographers**: The 14-35mm f/4 is a better lens for landscapes if you don't need the f/2.8 aperture. It's also lighter.

Ideal for:

- Travel and street photography
- Real estate and architecture
- Landscape photography
- General wide-angle shooting

3. Canon RF 10-20mm f/4 L IS STM Lens (Hypothetical Lens)

With an ultra-wide 10mm focal length, the Canon RF 10-20mm f/4 L IS STM lens would give you an even bigger view than the first two choices. Canon hasn't released a 10–20mm lens for the RF line yet, but this kind of lens would be great for extreme wide-angle photography because it would let photographers record a really wide field of view. It would work especially well for real estate, building, and astrophotography.

Key Features:

- **Focal Length**: 10-20mm
- **Maximum Aperture**: f/4
- **Autofocus Motor**: STM (Stepping Motor) for smooth and silent focusing
- **Image Stabilization**: Yes, expected up to 5 stops
- **Weather Sealing**: Likely to be weather-sealed, as part of the **L-series**
- **Weight**: Estimated around 500g

Why the Canon RF 10-20mm f/4 L IS STM Would Stand Out

- **Ultra-Wide Field of View**: A 10mm focal length gives you a surprisingly wide field of view, which is great for architectural shots where you want to show the whole room or building, or for creative wide-angle compositions in nature photography.
- **STM Autofocus for Video**: If this lens uses STM technology, it would be great for video work because it would be able to focus without making any noise that would be annoying.
- **Lightweight and Versatile**: A 10–20mm lens would probably be very portable and light, making it great for photographers who need an ultrawide-angle lens without the bulk.

Ideal for:

- Architecture and interior photography

- Real estate photography
- Creative landscape photography
- Vlogging and video work

Best Wide-Angle Prime Lenses for Canon EOS R5 Mark II

1. **Canon RF 16mm f/2.8 STM Lens**

The Canon RF 16mm f/2.8 STM Lens is an ultra-wide-angle prime lens made for the Canon RF mount. It gives photographers a small and light way to capture scenes with a lot of space. Landscape, building, and astrophotography are all great things that you can do with it thanks to its fast f/2.8 maximum aperture and wide focal length.

Key Features:

- **Focal Length**: 16mm
- **Maximum Aperture**: f/2.8
- **Autofocus Motor**: STM (Stepping Motor) for smooth and quiet focusing
- **Weight**: Approximately 165g (0.36 lbs)
- **Close Focusing Distance**: 0.13m (5.1 inches)

Why the Canon RF 16mm f/2.8 STM Stands Out

- **Ultra-Wide Perspective**: This lens has a field of view that is very wide at 16mm, making it great for taking pictures of wide landscapes, tall buildings, and the night sky. It lets you add a lot of detail to your designs, which makes it great for dramatic views.
- **Compact and Lightweight**: The 16mm is one of the lightest lenses in the RF lineup, weighing only 165g. This makes it a great choice for travel photographers or people who need to keep their gear light while they're on the go. This little thing is small enough to fit in your bag or carry around without any trouble.

- **Fast f/2.8 Aperture**: The f/2.8 aperture is good for taking in low light because it lets you get clear pictures when it's dark. It also gives you some artistic freedom when you want to isolate subjects against a soft background.
- **Macro Capability**: With a close focusing distance of 0.13m, you can get clear pictures of small objects, making it useful for both landscape and close-up photos. This function is great for capturing textures or small details in nature.
- **Affordable**: The 16mm f/2.8 is a great deal for photographers who want to add to their wide-angle lens collection without spending a lot of money.

Who Should Buy It:

- **Landscape photographers**: These people love taking pictures of big views and dramatic skies.
- **Travel photographers**: It's perfect for people who want a high-quality wide-angle lens but don't want to carry around a lot of weight.
- **Astrophotographers**: The f/2.8 lens works well in low light, so you can use it to take pictures of stars and night scenes.

Ideal for:

- Landscapes
- Travel photography
- Night sky and astrophotography

2. **Canon RF 35mm f/1.8 Macro IS STM Lens.**

It's easy to use the Canon RF 35mm f/1.8 Macro IS STM Lens, which has a normal focal length and macro features. This lens is great for photographers who want to try both wide-angle views and close-up features. It's also a great choice for a lot of other situations.

Key Features:

- **Focal Length**: 35mm
- **Maximum Aperture**: f/1.8
- **Autofocus Motor**: STM (Stepping Motor) for smooth and silent focusing
- **Image Stabilization**: Yes, up to 5 stops
- **Weight**: Approximately 405g (0.89 lbs)

- **Close Focusing Distance**: 0.17m (6.7 inches)

Why the Canon RF 35mm f/1.8 Macro IS STM Stands Out

- **Versatile Focal Length**: The 35mm focal length is a standard choice for street photography, portraits, and shots of nature. It's a good mix of wide-angle and normal perspective, so you can make creative compositions with it.
- **Fast f/1.8 Aperture**: The f/1.8 maximum aperture works well in low light and creates a beautiful blurred background (bokeh), which makes it a great choice for portraits and artistic shots with a shallow depth of field.
- **Macro Capability**: The 35mm lens can focus up to 0.17 meters away, so you can get very close to flowers, insects, or other small objects to catch their fine details. This makes it a useful tool for both wide-angle and close-up shots.
- **Image Stabilization**: The built-in image stabilization helps keep the camera from shaking, so you can take better pictures with your hands, especially when there isn't much light. This is especially helpful for macro photos, where even the smallest movement can blur the picture.
- **Compact Design**: Weighing in at about 405g, this lens is still pretty light and portable, making it easy to bring with you for long shoots.

People who should buy it:

- **Street photographers**: The wide range of focal lengths and fast aperture make it a great choice for casual and natural shots.
- **Macro enthusiasts**: the close-focusing feature lets you take detailed close-up pictures.
- **Portrait photographers**: The f/1.8 aperture works well in low light and blurs the background beautifully.

Ideal for:

- Street and environmental photography
- Macro and close-up photography
- Portraits

3. **Canon RF 24mm f/1.8 Macro IS STM Lens.**

For photographers who want a wide-angle view and the extra benefit of macro capabilities, the Canon RF 24mm f/1.8 Macro IS STM Lens is another great choice. This lens is flexible enough to be used for both wide-angle and close-up photography.

Key Features:

- **Focal Length**: 24mm
- **Maximum Aperture**: f/1.8
- **Autofocus Motor**: STM (Stepping Motor) for smooth and silent focusing
- **Image Stabilization**: Yes, up to 5 stops
- **Weight**: Approximately 325g (0.72 lbs)
- **Close Focusing Distance**: 0.14m (5.5 inches)

Why the Canon RF 24mm f/1.8 Macro IS STM Stands Out

- **Wide-Angle Flexibility**: The 24mm focal length is great for taking pictures of scenery, buildings, and city streets. It gives you a wide view without the severe warping that most ultra-wide lenses have.
- **Fast f/1.8 Aperture**: The 24mm lens has a fast f/1.8 maximum aperture, just like the 35mm lens. This makes it great for low-light situations and lets you use depth-of-field effects in creative ways. It's great for blurring the background and focusing on a subject.
- **Macro Capability**: This lens has a close focusing distance of 0.14m, so you can get very close to your subjects. This makes it great for capturing small items, flowers, or textures with fine details. This extra closeup feature makes it more useful as a prime lens.
- **Compact and Lightweight**: The 24mm lens is only 325g, which makes it easy to carry around. This makes it a great choice for travel and everyday use.
- **Image Stabilization**: The built-in stabilization helps make sure that pictures are clear, especially when there isn't much light, which gives you more trust when shooting handheld.

People who should buy it:

- **Landscape and nature photographers**: The 24mm lens length is great for taking pictures of wide views.
- **Street photographers**: This lens can be used for both wide-angle shots and close-up work.
- **Macro enthusiasts**: The macro features let you take detailed close-ups as well as regular photos.

Ideal for:

- Landscapes and architecture
- Street photography
- Macro photography

Best Portrait Lenses for Canon EOS R5 Mark II

1. Canon RF 85mm f/1.2 L USM Lens

The Canon RF 85mm f/1.2 L USM Lens is a top-of-the-line portrait lens made just for the Canon RF mount. This lens is popular among portrait photographers who want to make stunning pictures with a soft, dreamy background because it takes beautiful pictures and has beautiful bokeh.

Key Features:

- **Focal Length**: 85mm
- **Maximum Aperture**: f/1.2
- **Autofocus Motor**: Ring USM (Ultrasonic Motor) for fast and quiet focusing
- **Weight**: Approximately 1,195g (2.63 lbs)
- **Close Focusing Distance**: 0.85m (2.79 feet)

Why the Canon RF 85mm f/1.2 L USM Stands Out:

- **Exceptional Image Quality**: Even at wide apertures, the 85mm f/1.2 lens produces stunningly sharp and clear images. Because of this, it's perfect for getting clear colors and fine features in a person's face.
- **Beautiful Bokeh**: This lens's widest aperture (f/1.2) creates a smooth, creamy background blur (bokeh) that makes the subject stand out from the background

beautifully. This effect gives your pictures more depth and dimension, which makes the people in them stand out.
- **Fast Autofocus**: The Ring USM autofocus system lets you focus quickly and accurately, so you can confidently record fleeting moments. This lens works well whether you're taking a posed picture or a natural shot.
- **Versatile for Various Settings**: The 85mm is mainly a portrait lens, but it can also be used for other types of photos, such as fashion, events, and product shots. Its focal length makes face features look good, so it can be used for both portraits and full-body portraits.
- **Weather-Sealed Design**: The 85mm f/1.2 lens from Canon's L line is made to work in harsh conditions, which makes it a good choice for portraits taken outside.

People who should buy it:

- **Professional portrait photographers**: The great picture quality and bokeh make it a great choice for professionals who want to make portraits that stand out.
- **Wedding photographers**: As a wedding photographer, you can use this lens to capture both casual times and formal portraits.
- **Fashion photographers**: The lens's ability to blur the background beautifully makes clothes and accessories stand out more.

Ideal for:

- Portraits
- Weddings and events
- Fashion and editorial photography

2. **Canon RF 135mm f/1.8 L IS USM Lens**

The Canon RF 135mm f/1.8 L IS USM Lens is also a great portrait lens. It has a longer focal length that makes it perfect for taking beautiful, close-up photos. This lens has great sharpness and image stabilization, which makes it a useful tool for any portrait photographer.

Key Features:

- **Focal Length**: 135mm

- **Maximum Aperture**: f/1.8
- **Autofocus Motor**: Ring USM for fast and quiet focusing
- **Image Stabilization**: Yes, up to 5 stops
- **Weight**: Approximately 1,020g (2.25 lbs)
- **Close Focusing Distance**: 0.8m (2.62 feet)

Why the Canon RF 135mm f/1.8 L IS USM Stands Out

- **Longer Focal Length**: The 135mm focal length lets you get closer to your subject without blurring the image, which makes it perfect for taking stunning photos of the whole body or just the face. This space gives the face a flattering view without the distortion that can happen with wider lenses.
- **Fast f/1.8 Aperture**: The f/1.8 aperture isn't as wide as the 85mm f/1.2 aperture, but it still works well in low light and allows for beautiful bokeh. It gives you enough space to get that desired out-of-focus background look.
- **Image Stabilization**: The built-in image stabilization helps keep the camera from shaking, which makes pictures clearer, especially when the shutter speed is slow. This feature comes in handy when there isn't much light or when the lens isn't attached to a tripod.
- **High Image Quality**: The lens gives the picture great sharpness and clarity all the way around, so your photos will look clear and full of detail. It also fixes chromatic aberration and distortion, which makes clear pictures.
- **Versatile for Various Photography Styles**: The 135mm lens is useful for more than just photos; it can also be used for sports, wildlife, and event photography.

People who should buy it:

- **Professional portrait photographers**: This lens is a top choice for pros because it can make portraits look great.
- **Event photographers**: The longer focal length lets them take pictures of natural moments from afar.
- **Wildlife photographers**: Because it can do so many things, the longer reach also makes it good for wildlife photos.

Ideal for:

- Portraits

- Events and candid shots
- Wildlife photography

Best Macro Lenses for Canon EOS R5 Mark II

1. **Canon RF 100mm f/2.8 L Macro IS USM Lens**

For serious macro photographers, the Canon RF 100mm f/2.8 L Macro IS USM Lens is the best macro lens out there. It has great picture quality and a lot of useful features. Because this lens is made to catch fine details very clearly, it's great for everything from taking close-ups of bugs to taking detailed pictures of products.

Key Features:

- **Focal Length**: 100mm
- **Maximum Aperture**: f/2.8
- **Autofocus Motor**: Ring USM (Ultrasonic Motor) for fast and quiet focusing
- **Image Stabilization**: Yes, up to 5 stops
- **Weight**: Approximately 505g (1.11 lbs)
- **Close Focusing Distance**: 0.26m (10.2 inches)
- **Maximum Magnification**: 1.0x (life-size)

Why the Canon RF 100mm f/2.8 L Macro IS USM Stands Out

- **Great Magnification:** This lens can magnify up to 1.0x, so you can get pictures of your objects that are life-size. You can get very close to flowers, bugs, and other small things to photograph them and see features that might not be visible to the naked eye.
- **Superb Image Quality**: This lens is famous for having great optical performance. It makes pictures that are sharp, contrasty, and have few artifacts, so your macro shots will be clear and colorful. The glass and build quality are in line with Canon's L-series standards, so the camera will last and work reliably.
- **Effective Image Stabilization**: The built-in image stabilization changes the game when it comes to macro photos because it lets you shoot at slower shutter speeds without blur from the camera shake. This feature comes in handy when working with natural light or taking pictures of delicate objects.

- **Versatile for Various Applications**: The 100mm f/2.8 is mainly a macro lens, but it can also be used for portraits and other types of photography. A good working distance is provided by the focal length, which is especially helpful when taking pictures of moving objects like insects or animals.
- **Weather-Sealed Design**: This lens is part of Canon's L series and is weather-sealed to protect it from dust and water. Because of this feature, it's a good choice for outdoor shooting because you can take macro shots in a variety of settings.

People who should buy it:

- **Professional macro photographers**: The lens is great for professionals who want to take high-resolution pictures because it is well-made and can be used in many ways.
- **Nature and wildlife photographers**: The ability to focus close up and the longer lens length make it easier to get pictures of subjects without scaring them.
- **Product photographers**: It's great for showing off textures and goods because it's sharp and captures lots of detail.

Ideal for:

- Macro photography
- Nature and wildlife photography
- Product and commercial photography

2. Canon RF 85mm f/2 Macro IS STM Lens

There is also the Canon RF 85mm f/2 Macro IS STM Lens, which is smaller but still has great macro powers. If you want a flexible and light way to capture details, whether you're at home or in nature, this lens is made for you.

Key Features:

- **Focal Length**: 85mm
- **Maximum Aperture**: f/2
- **Autofocus Motor**: STM (Stepping Motor) for smooth and quiet focusing
- **Image Stabilization**: Yes, up to 5 stops
- **Weight**: Approximately 500g (1.1 lbs)

- **Close Focusing Distance**: 0.35m (1.15 feet)
- **Maximum Magnification**: 0.5x

Why the Canon RF 85mm f/2 Macro IS STM Stands Out

- **Compact and Lightweight**: The 85mm f/2 lens is easier to carry around than its longer counterpart, which makes it a great choice for photographers who like to keep their gear light. This feature comes in handy when working in the field or moving.
- **Decent Magnification**: This lens can only magnify things by 0.5x at its biggest, but it still lets you take great close-up pictures. You can get great features in flowers, small items, or any other subject where you want to draw attention to texture and detail.
- **Good Low-Light Performance**: The wide f/2 aperture makes it possible to shoot in poorly lit areas without having to raise the ISO too much. This is very helpful for closeup work inside or in shady places.
- **Smooth Autofocus**: The STM autofocus motor makes focusing smooth and quiet, which is good for both macro photos and video work. It is easy to switch between autofocus and manual focus on this lens, which gives you more control over your shots.
- **Versatile for Different Photography Styles**: This lens's 85mm focal length makes it good for portrait photography as well, thanks to its nice compression that makes face features look better. If you want to try both macro and portrait photos, this is a great lens for you.

Chapter 2

Initial Setup: Charging the Battery and Attaching the Lens

Charging the Battery

1. Take off the protective cover of the battery.

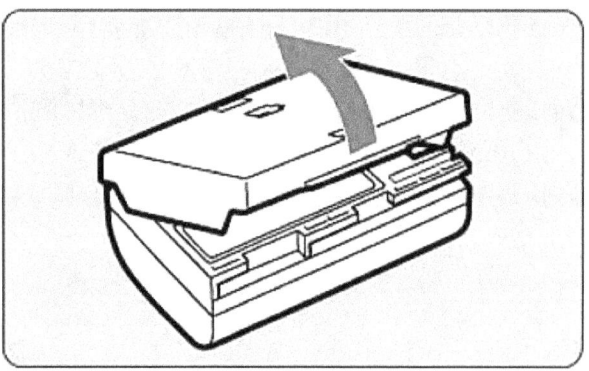

2. Fully place the battery into the charger.

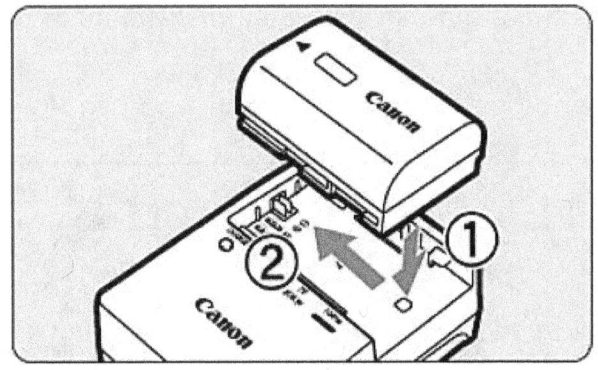

Do the reverse of what you just did to take out the battery.

3. Get the battery charged.

LC-E6

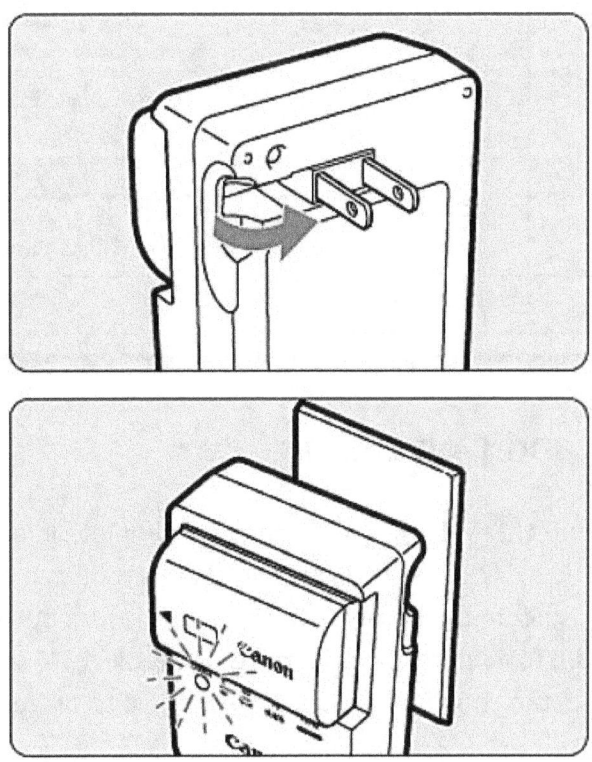

- Flip the prongs out as shown and plug the charger into a wall port.

LC-E6E

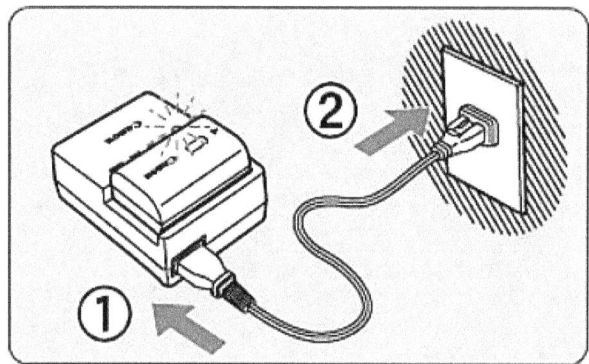

- Connect the charger's power cord to a power source.
- The charging starts automatically, and the charge lamp blinks orange.

Charge Level	Charge Lamp	
	Color	Display
0–49%	Orange	Blinks once per second
50–74%		Blinks twice per second
75% or higher		Blinks three times per second
Fully charged	Green	Turned on

Charge Time and Conditions

- It takes about three hours to charge a completely dead battery at room temperature (23°C/73°F). However, the charge time can change based on how much power is left in the battery and the temperature outside.
- It could take up to 4 hours to charge when it's cooler (5°C to 10°C or 41°F to 50°F). When it's cold, the charging speed can slow down to protect the battery.

Pre-charging requirements

- **Battery condition at purchase**: The battery will not be fully charged when you buy it for the first time. To get the best results right away, always charge the battery up before using it.
- **Charging recommendations**: Charge the battery the day before or the day you plan to use it. Batteries lose their power over time, even when they're not being used. If you charge them right before you use them, they will be fully charged for the shoot or session.

Safety and Battery Maintenance Tips

- Take the battery out of the charger and disconnect it from the power outlet when it's fully charged. This keeps the charger and battery from overcharging and using too much power, which makes both last longer.
- **Battery Charge Indicator:** The protective cover is a good way to keep your batteries in order. You can connect the cover in different ways to show whether a battery is charged or not. This makes it easy to see when you're working in the studio or out in the field.

Putting in the Battery.

1. To release the cover, slide the Battery Compartment Cover Lock. Once it's unlocked, open the cover to get to the battery area.

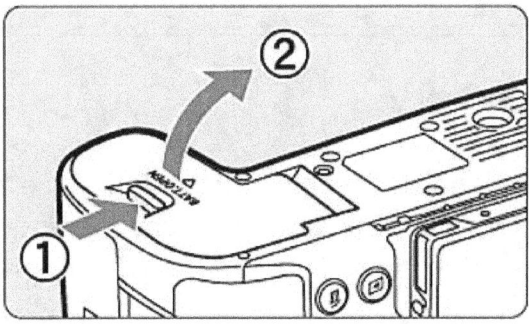

2. **Insert the Battery**: To insert the battery, place your LP-E6P Battery Pack that has been fully charged into the slot.

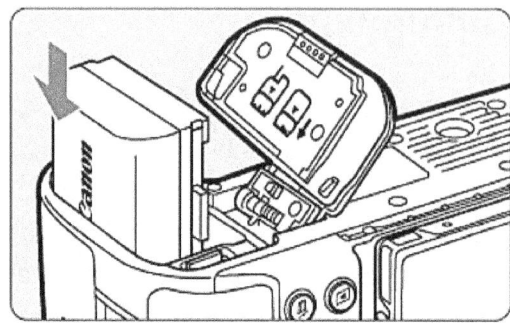

- Orientation: Insert the battery with the electrical connections first.
- Carefully push the battery into place until it clicks, which means the lock is secure.

3. **Close the lid:** Put the battery in and press the compartment lid until it snaps into place. This makes sure the cover is tightly closed, which protects the battery from being exposed to air or taken off by accident.

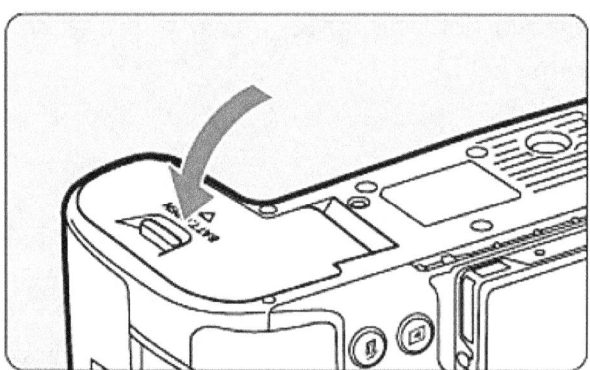

Removing the Battery.

1. To get to the battery, slide the compartment lock and open the cover.
2. After taking off the cover, find the battery lock lever inside the compartment and press it. Press the lever in the direction shown by the arrow (usually outward) to release the battery.
3. Once the lock lever is pressed, gently pull the battery out to remove it. Be careful when you handle the battery, especially where the electrical points are.

4. **Attach the Protective Cover:** As soon as you take the battery out, quickly put the cover back on to stop damage and short circuits.

By following these steps, you can make sure that you safely and correctly enter and remove your camera's battery, which will protect both the performance of your camera and the battery's life.

Chapter 3

Camera Setup

Step 1: Inserting the Battery and Memory Card

Putting the memory card and battery into your Canon EOS R5 Mark II camera is the first step in setting it up. The slot for the memory card is on the side of the camera, and the battery section is at the bottom.

With the connections facing the camera, insert the battery into the battery compartment after opening it. Once you're sure the battery is in place, close the chamber.

Before you put the memory card in and open the cover for the memory card slot, make sure that the label is facing the camera. Before you close the lid, make sure the memory card is in place tightly.

Step 2: Charging the Battery

Make sure the battery in your Canon EOS R5 Mark II camera is fully charged before you use it for the first time. The battery will start to charge as soon as you plug the battery into the charger and a power source. When the battery is filled, the charger will let you know.

Step 3: Putting the Lens On

The lenses that come with the Canon EOS R5 Mark II mirrorless camera can be interchanged. Make sure the lens mount on the camera and the lens mount on the lens are lined up. Then, turn the lens clockwise until it clicks into place. Make sure the lens is attached to the camera properly before you use it.

Step 4: Turning on the Camera

The power button on top of the Canon EOS R5 Mark II camera is what you press to turn it on. It will take a little while for the camera to turn on.

Step 5: Choose the Language and Time Zone

You will be asked to choose the language and time zone when the camera turns on. Use the touch screen to pick the language and time zone you want to use.

Step 6: Put in the Time and Date

The next thing you need to do is set the time and date on your Canon EOS R5 Mark II. Make sure the time zone is set properly when you use the touch screen to enter the date and time.

Step 7: Configuring the Camera's Settings

Once the time and date have been set, you can change the camera settings to suit your needs. You can change a lot of things about the Canon EOS R5 Mark II, like the autofocus, image quality, and shooting modes.

The menu button is on the back of the camera. Press it to see the settings. You can use the touch screen or the camera's control knobs to move through the menu. Here are some important camera settings to consider:

- **Shooting mode**: This mode controls how the camera takes pictures and movies. The Canon EOS R5 Mark II can shoot in program mode, manual mode, aperture priority mode, and shutter priority mode.

- **Autofocus options**: Autofocus options let you choose how the camera will focus on the subject. The Canon EOS R5 Mark II has a lot of different focus settings, such as single-point AF, zone AF, and face recognition AF.
- **Image quality settings**: These settings control the resolution and compression of the photos and videos that the camera produces. The Canon EOS R5 Mark II has many settings for picture quality, such as RAW, JPEG, and HEIF.
- **Custom functions**: You can change the camera's settings to suit your needs with the custom functions. The Canon EOS R5 Mark II has some features that can be customized, such as buttons, shot modes, and white balance which can all be changed.

Step 8: Customizing the Quick Control Screen

The Canon EOS R5 Mark II's Quick Control Screen is one of its best features. It lets you quickly change important camera settings like ISO, shutter speed, aperture, and more. When setting up the camera, making this screen unique speeds up the shooting process and increases the output.

These steps can be used to customize the Quick Control Screen

1. To get to the Quick Control Screen, press the **Q** button on the back of the camera.
2. In the top right corner of the screen, click the "Customize" icon.
3. You can add settings to the Quick Control Screen by using the joystick or touch screen.
4. To add the changes you made, click the **Set** button.
5. You can change the order of the settings on the Quick Control Screen by using the joystick or touch screen.
6. Press the **Menu** button to leave the Quick Control Screen customization screen.

You can skip the camera menu and quickly get to the settings you use most often by customizing the Quick Control Screen. This will help you fire faster and more accurately.

You can also quickly switch between up to three different Quick Control Screen setups that the EOS R5 Mark II lets you store, based on what you need to shoot. Just choose **Save/Load Settings** from the customization menu and enter the right setup number to save a customized Quick Control Screen setting.

The Set-up Menu

The Set-up Menu on the Canon EOS R5 II is where you can change how the camera works and what settings it has. It has basic settings like formatting the memory card, changing the date and time, controlling the camera's power-saving features, and changing how the information is displayed on the camera. You can change the screen brightness and connection to the internet via Bluetooth or Wi-Fi. You can also update the software. The main goals of the Set-up Menu are to make the camera work the way you want it to and to keep it running smoothly.

Set-up Menu Options

Five amber-coded Set-up menu screens let you change how your camera works while you're taking pictures or videos. Please do not mix this up with the Shooting menu, which changes how photos are taken. These are some of the options:

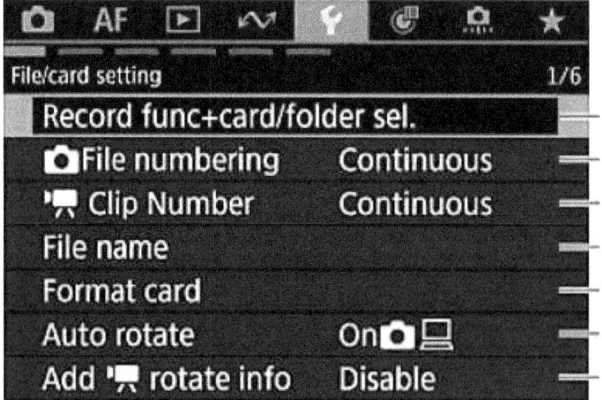

Record Functions+Card/Folder Sel.

This is the first thing on the Set-up 1 menu. When it comes to the EOS R5 II, there are (sometimes) too many choices for the card and folder that will hold your pictures and videos. You can pick which card is more important than the others, store movies on one card and photos on another, and change how folders are named by default. You can even automatically swap between the cards.

Record Stills/Movies Separately

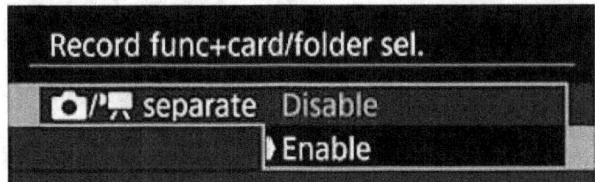

You can choose to either Enable or Disable this sub-entry. When enabled, strict storage and playback separation will happen, with photos and movies always being kept on Card 1 and Card 2, respectively.

That kind of file can't be recorded if a spot is empty or a certain card is full. When the camera is in movie mode, Playback will only show movie files. If you press the Playback button while the camera is in still photo mode, it will only show the pictures on Card 2 and not any movies.

These steps are good if you want to keep your picture and video files separate. One bad thing is that there are no backup or extra options. If one card is full, the camera won't switch to the other, and you can't make a copy of every file on the other media. If you pick this option, put your fastest memory card in Slot 1. This is particularly important if you want to record 4K or 8K video. Make sure you have a fast card in Slot 2 so you can keep shooting at high speeds.

When this sub-entry is activated, the two Recording options and the Record/Play options are not available.

Recording Options

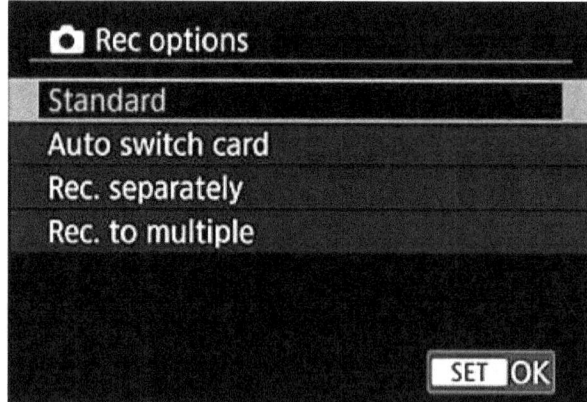

This setting tells the computer how to handle still photos. There are four choices;

- **Standard.** Any card picked in the Stills Record/Play field is where the still shots will always be saved in this mode. If the card is full, you can't take a still picture anymore.
- **Auto switch card (overflow).** The card where stills are recorded is named by the Stills Record/Play entry. If the recording stops because one card is full, stills will be saved on the other card when you start the recording again. With this helpful automatic overflow feature, you can take more pictures without having to **reload** your camera with a new card. The only bad thing is that your photos and movies are no longer kept separate.
- **Record separately (backup).** With this backup option, you can keep two pictures, one on each memory card, and set the quality of each one differently. The two files will have the same file number, so it's easy to tell which pairings they belong to. When you use this function, the Image Quality entry in the Shooting 1 menu changes.

This option is very adaptable. To keep Cards 1 and 2 separate, you could pick RAW for Card 2 and JPEG for Card 1. If you want two identical copies, you can pick JPEG twice or RAW twice. Along with a full-resolution RAW or JPEG file, you can also make a smaller S1 or S2 version for emailing over slow connections.

- **Record to multiple (backup).** One of the above backup options boiled down to its simplest form: Cards 1 and 2 make exact copies of your photos with the same level of Image Quality. When this option is used with the Record Separately option, the number of pictures that can be seen will depend on how much space is left on the card. In either case, you have to put in a new card if the first one gets full to keep recording.

Movie Recording Options

In this setting, you can change how movie clips are handled. There are three choices for the R5 II, but only two for the R5:

- **Standard.** In this mode, movies are always saved to the card that is picked in the Movies Record/Play entry. Once the card is full, you can't record any more video clips.
- **Auto switch card (overflow).** Movies are recorded on the card that has the entry for **Movie Record/Play**. If the recording stops because the card that was given to you is full, movies will be saved on the other card in a new folder when you start recording again.
- **Main Proxy.** The main and proxy movies are saved to cards with the same file name. The proxy movies are marked with _Proxy. You can change the file name in the [Movies] setting under [🌹 : File name].
- **Rec. to multiple.** Cards 1 and 2 always record the same movie. When you use an SD or SDHC card, remember that you can't record video.

Recording/Playback Selection with Two Cards Inserted

Movies are saved to Card 2 by default, and stills are taken on Card 1. You can move these labels around and make one of them stand out if you'd like to. You can pick a priority and pick which card is used to record stills with the **INFO** button. These are the options:

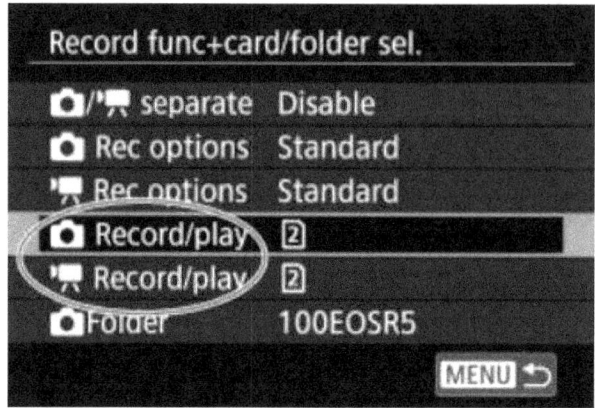

- **Standard/Auto Switch Card modes.** You can choose which card records and plays back the video if the Standard or Auto Switch card is set for Still Recording or Movie Recording. Press the **INFO** button to give the chosen card priority. When Priority is turned on, the camera instantly switches to the priority card whenever a card is added or removed.
- **Record Separately/Record to Multiple/1 Main 2 Proxy.** If you choose Record Separately/Record to Multiple (or, with the R5, when 1 RAW and 2 MP4 are chosen), you can only see playback options. Pick either Card 1 or Card 2 and then click **INFO** to give a card priority. When Priority is turned on, the camera instantly switches to the priority card whenever a card is added or removed.

Folder Settings

Choose this menu option to create a new folder or navigate between existing ones on your memory card where the photos and videos you take will be saved. By default, each folder is given a three-digit number and five letters (**CANON**). A folder can hold up to 9999 pictures. When a folder is full, a new one is made immediately. You can make folder numbers from 100 to 999. You can make folders on a memory card that has been formatted properly inside the main DCIM folder. Follow these simple steps:

1. **Pick Folder.** To access the option, use Record Function+Card/Folder Sel.

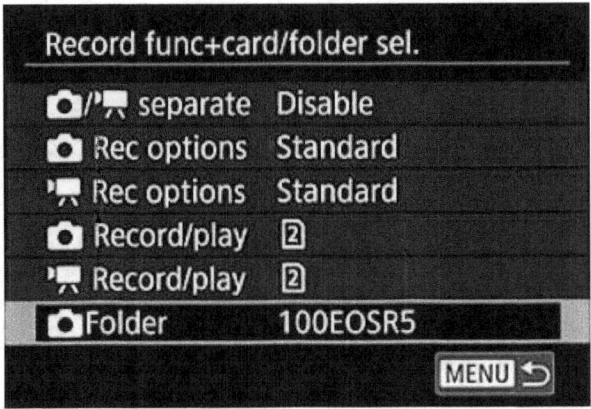

2. **View the list of available folders.** On the Select Folder screen, you can see a list of all the folders that could be on your memory card. The folder names are things like 100EOSR5, 101CANON, and so on.

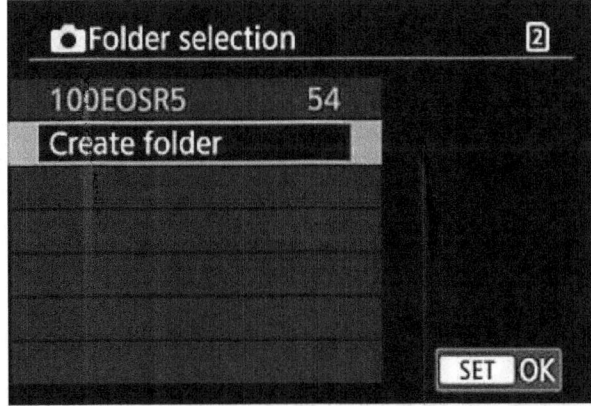

3. **Select a different folder.** You can choose the label of the folder you want to use with the directional keys or the touch screen. Then, save any more photos in that folder. When a photo folder is picked, two thumbnails of the images in that folder show up on the right side of the screen.
4. **Confirm the folder.** Press **SET** to confirm that you want to choose an existing folder.
5. **Create folder.** Highlight Create Folder in the Select Folder box and press **SET** to make a new folder. You can change the Folder Name, Cancel, or OK (which makes the folder) after seeing the name of the folder that will be made. Press **SET** to confirm your choice.

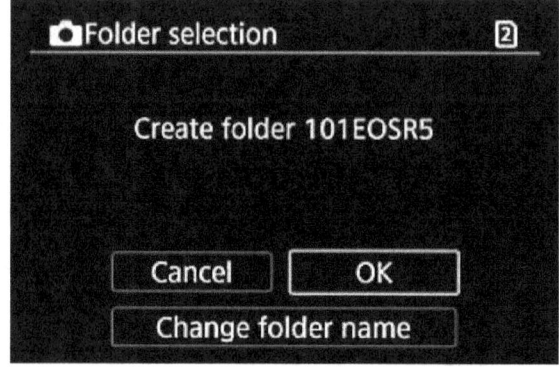

6. **Change folder name (optional).** If you choose "**Change folder name**," you can give the folder a new name, like 101EOSR5. Besides big and small letters, you can also use the underscore character.

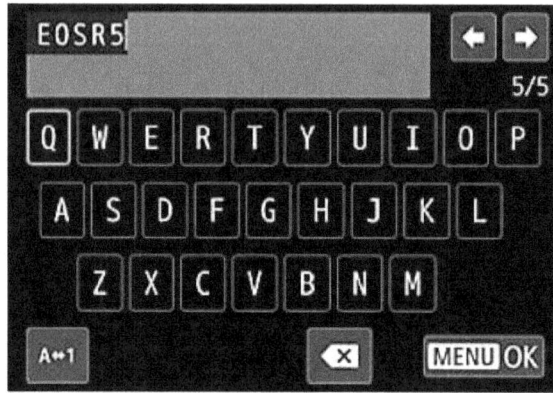

7. **Exit.** Press **MENU** to go back to the Set-up 1 menu.

A little creativity can help you come up with some creative and easily changing folder names, but be careful not to make **bad** folder names. This function is especially helpful when working with very large cards because it lets me arrange things a lot right on the card. I might use some pictures from a certain folder to make a **slideshow** that I can watch on my camera's LCD screen. I could also put the pictures in order by date or location.

File Numbering

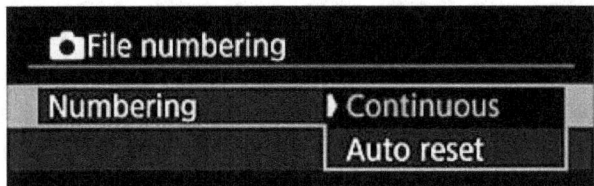

A file number will be given to every picture you take immediately. This numbering will stay the same for all of your pictures taken over a long time and on multiple memory cards. It will reset itself if you put in a new card or change the numbers manually. You can put anything from 0001 to 9999 in folder 100. The numbers will start over in folder 101. Numbers are applied from 0001 to 9999. After that, the camera creates a new folder on the card: 100, 101, 102, and so on.

Its internal memory stores the last number that was used by the camera. That could lead to some strange things that you should be aware of. Numbering might start with the number that comes after the highest number that the previous camera used. This could happen if you put in a memory card that was used with a different camera before. When I first got a new Canon camera, the files it saved would start to number in the 8,000 range.

At first glance, the numbering system seems simple: from the menu, you can choose Continuous, Automatic Reset, or Manual Reset. This is how each one works:

Continuous. It will use a number that is one higher than the number stored in the camera's internal memory if the memory card is blank or has been formatted. If the card isn't blank and has pictures on it, the next number will be one more than the largest number on the card or in the main memory. In other words, if you want to use continuous file numbering regularly, you must always use a blank card or a card that has just been made. Here are some examples:

- You put in a new, empty memory card after taking 4,235 shots with the camera. The number 4,236 will be given out next based on the amount that is stored in internal memory.
- You put in a memory card with a photo with the number 2,728 after taking 4,235 pictures with the camera. The next picture will be number 4,236.

- The camera took 4,235 pictures, and you put in a memory card with a picture that had the number 8,281 on it. The next picture is the number 8,282, which will be used as the **high** shot number when you put in a blank card in the future. It will also be saved in the menu of the camera.

Automatic Reset. If you're using a blank memory card or one that has just been formatted, the next picture you take will be numbered 0001. If you use a card that isn't blank, the next number will be one more than the highest number that can fit on the card. The number after the first one on a memory card will always be 0001 or one more than the card's highest number when you put it in. Please keep in mind that you won't be able to shoot again until you replace the card with a new one when the Folder number hits 999 (that could mean you have a lot of folders on one card!) and that folder has 9999 photos.

Manual Reset. The file numbers start over at 0001, and a new folder is made with a number one higher than the old one. When you put in a different memory card, whether it's blank or not, the camera uses the numbering system that was set up before, either Continuous or Automatic reset. You can change the usual **CANON** folder name to any other name you want, or you can use the five characters you picked out before you do a manual reset.

Movie Clip Numbering

Movies that are saved in a folder are given a clip number between 001 and 999. You can change how the clips are numbered.

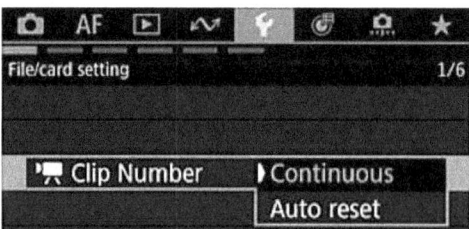

Continuous

For continuous file numbering regardless of switching cards

The clip numbering keeps going until 999, even if you change the target card (like in 1→2) or replace a card. This comes in handy when movies with numbers from 001 to 999 on different cards are being saved to a single folder on a computer.

Keep in mind that the numbering can go on after the number of any previously released movies on cards that you want to use. For continuous movie numbering, you might want to use a card that has been formatted from scratch each time.

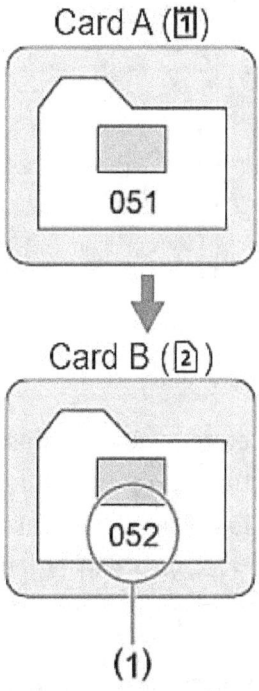

(1)

Auto Reset

To restart clip numbering from 001 after switching cards

The clip numbering goes back to 001 if you change the target card (as in 1→2) or add a new card. This is helpful if you want to put movies in order based on cards.

It's important to remember that the numbering can go on after the number of any previously released movies on cards that you want to use. If you want the file numbering to start at 001, use a brand-new card every time you want to save a picture.

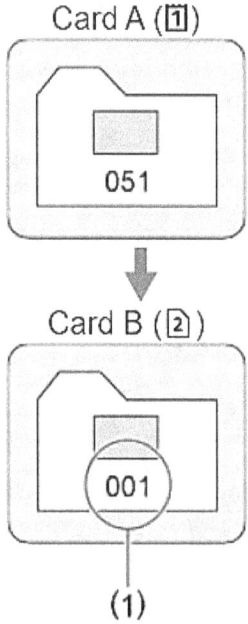

(1)

File Name

Like other Canon cameras, the R5 II gives your picture files a four-digit alphanumeric string as their file name as soon as it makes them. For example, **BE3B0001.jpg**, **BE3B001.hif**, or **BE3B0001.cr3** are the file names. The first four characters are unique to your camera and are set at the factory. As an alternative, you can set up two personal User Settings, numbered 1 (containing four characters of your choice) and 2 (with three).

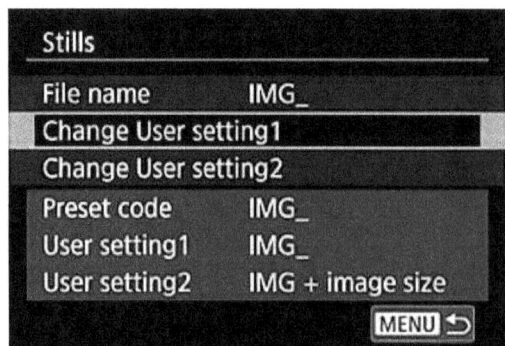

You can change the names that are linked to your pictures using this menu option, but there are some tight limitations.

DCF limits file names made with complying digital cameras to eight characters max, plus a three-character extension (like .jpg, .hif, or .cr3) to show what type of file it is. The eight-plus-three (sometimes written as 8.3) length limitation comes from a bad and annoying computer operating system called D.O.S., which we senior photographers would like to forget but which still lives on as a file-naming convention.

Four out of the eight characters are used to show what kind of camera was used to take the shot. Canon uses the first four characters that were specified by the manufacturer.

When you reach the limit of 9999 numbers, your numbering **rolls over** to aaaa4000 again because the last four are used for numbers from 0000 to 9999. As soon as the camera leaves the factory assembly line, it is set up to offer three different ways to name files:

- **Factory Preset Code.** This camera is not like the others. Each camera comes with its preset code. The names of your pictures will be something like aaaa 0001.jpg if you use the sRGB color space. As a standard, when you switch to Adobe RGB, the first letter is changed to an underline. This means that names like _EOS0001.jpg or _EOS001.cr3 are created. Even though you can't change the factory preset code, you can change it to one of the other naming systems.
- **User Setting 1.** Two different naming schemes may be defined by the user. The camera is set to IMG_0001.jpg/cr3/mov for video or _IMG0001.jpg, etc., for Adobe RGB if you're using sRGB color space. If you're using sRGB, you can enter all four initial characters for this choice to get EOSR0001.jpg instead. The underscore still takes the place of the initial characters of the file name when you use Adobe RGB. If you choose OHIO, you will get _HIO0001.jpg for Adobe RGB and OHIO0001.jpg for sRGB.
- **User Setting 2.** In this second user-definable setting, you can choose to identify only the first three of the four initial characters. IMG is what those characters are set to by default. The code for the image recording quality is stored by the camera in the fourth place. This means that if your first three letters are ABC, you might end up with file names like _BCL0001.jpg or ABCL001.jpg. Here is the list of codes in the way they appear:

    - **L.** You can choose RAW, Large Fine JPEG, or Large Standard JPEG.
    - **M.** You can choose M RAW, Medium Fine JPEG, or Medium Standard JPEG.
    - **S.** You can choose Small 1 Fine JPEG, Small 1 Standard JPEG, or S RAW.

- **T**. Small 2 JPEG.
- **_ (underscore).** The file is a movie, and there is no quality setting shown.

Redefining User Settings 1 and 2

You can change the two User Settings from their default values by going to the File Name. After that, do these things:

1. **Access menu entry.** After choosing the setting you want to change, press **SET**.
2. **Delete old entry.** To get rid of the previous item, press the Trash button in the bottom right corner of the camera's back panel or tap the <x (backspace icon) at the bottom right corner of the screen several times. The cursor point will display a vertical line.

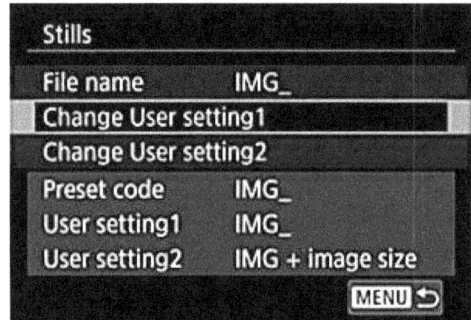 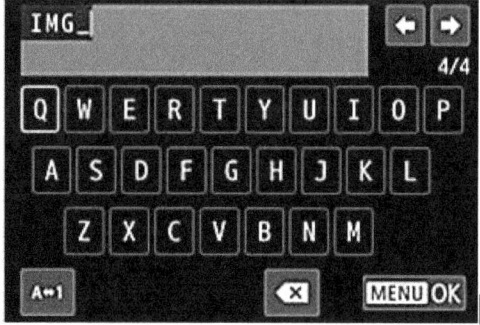

3. **Choose characters.** You can use the Multi-controller joystick or the touch screen to choose the first character you want to use. You can only type numbers, capital letters, and an underscore. One more thing you can do is move the pointer with the Main Dial and pick characters with the QCD-2 or QCD-1. Either press the character or SET to input the highlighted character.
4. **Choose the remaining characters.** You can repeat Step 3 to input the remaining characters (four for Setting 1 and three for Setting 2). After that, the pointer will move to the next location. In case you put a character or characters wrong, you can always use the Trash button to delete them. The camera is the only thing that can use an underscore. Every other character can't use one either.
5. **Finish.** Press **MENU** to confirm what you typed, and press **INFO** to cancel.
6. **Review.** The newest definitions are shown at the bottom of the screen.

Movie File Name Settings

You can set the names of movie files (clips).

Movie file name structure

	Item	Description
(1)	Camera index	Two letters in the range A–Z. An underscore (_) can also be used as the second character. Identifies the camera used.
(2)	Reel number	A 4-digit number from 0001 to 9999. A different number is automatically assigned to identify the card used. You can set the default value. Advances by one when the first recording on a new card* is made. * Newly purchased or formatted card
(3)	Clip number	A 3-digit number from 001 to 999 preceded by C, as in C001–C999. After C999, D is used at the beginning. Automatically assigned to each clip (movie file). You can set the default value.
(4)	Codec identifier	"A" (as in AVC) is automatically set for H.264 main movies, "H" for HEVC, and "X" for RAW.
(5)	Recording date	Year, month, and day, set automatically based on when recording began.
(6)	Recording time	Hour, minute, and second, set automatically based on when recording began.
(7)	Random component	Two characters, from A to Z and 0 to 9, randomly set for each clip (movie file).
(8)	User-defined field	Five characters, from A to Z and 0 to 9. Default: CANON.
(9)	Proxy identifier	_Proxy is automatically appended to proxy movie files.

Format Card

You can erase everything on your memory card and make a new, useful file system with this item. When you click Format Card, a screen comes up that lets you choose between Card 1 and Card 2. After you choose your card, the screen below shows how much room is currently being used on the card and gives you two choices at the bottom: Cancel or OK (continue with the format). Click the Trash button to do a low-level style. If a card seems to be moving slowly, this easier format can speed it up by erasing all of its sectors and creating new ones (because the camera has to skip over **bad** sectors left over from previous uses). An orange bar shows up on the screen to show how far the formatting step is.

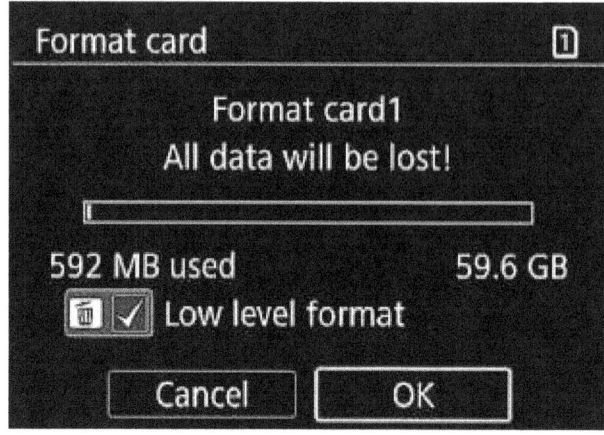

Auto Rotate

You can choose to have this option on or off. If you turn this feature on, you can see pictures taken in a vertical position without having to turn the camera. The images on the screen will rotate. Despite this, this arrangement also shows the picture with the smallest viewing dimension, which makes the picture smaller. You can do three things. You can set your photo-editing or viewing program to automatically rotate the picture when you look at it in the camera and on your computer screen. This feature is shown by two icons; the camera and the computer screen.

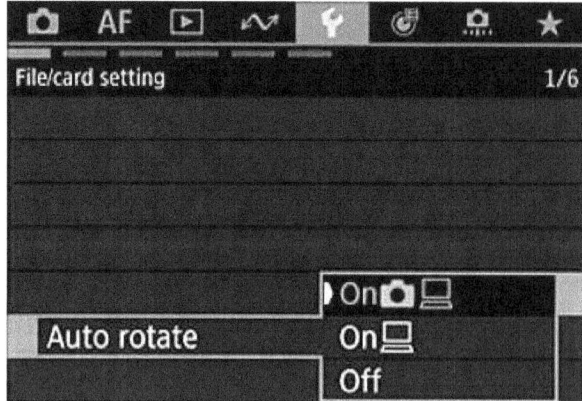

You can't mark an image to auto-rotate until you've looked at it in an image editor or viewing program (a computer screen icon is used). This feature lets you make the picture from the camera look its best on your screen while still rotating it when you're on your computer.

The third choice is **off**. The picture won't be turned whether you view it on your computer or the camera. It is important to know that if you turn off Auto Rotate, any pictures you take during that time will not be automatically rotated when you turn it back on. Autorotation is enabled or disabled based on the data that is stored in the picture file at the time of capture.

Add Movie Rotate Information

Cell phones have changed the way movies are shown so they are not only horizontal. People who use smartphones and tablets like to twist them to record movies in both horizontal and vertical modes, even though video has usually been recorded in landscape mode. You can set up your video clips to automatically include information about which side is up. This way, when people play them again on their devices, they will show up in the same way. This setting doesn't change the video that you see on the camera or on an external screen that is linked via an HDMI cable.

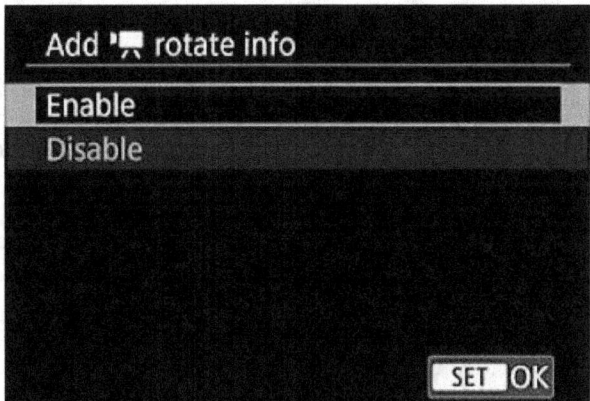

Date/Time/Zone

This option lets you set the time and date. These details will be saved in the image file, along with exposure and other information.

1. To get to this menu entry, use the Set-up 2 menu.
2. Turn the QCD-1 to move the highlight to the Date/Time field.
3. The SET button is in the middle of the QCD-1. Press it to see the Date/Time setting screen.

4. Turn the QCD-1 to pick the number you want to change. When the gold box shows the month, day, year, hour, minute, or second format you want to change, press the SET button to use the number that shows up. Two triangles with points up and down can be seen above the value.

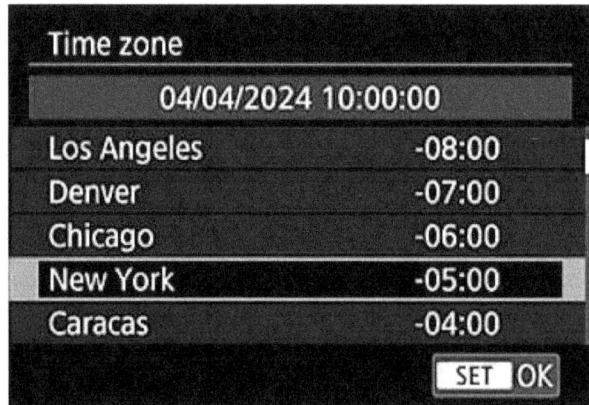

5. Turn the QCD-1 up or down to change the number. To make sure the number you entered is correct, click the **SET** button.
6. Follow steps 4 and 5 again for any other number you want to change. You can change the date style from mm/dd/yy to yy/mm/dd or dd/mm/yy. You can also pick the right time zone and turn Daylight Savings Time on or off.
7. Turn the QCD-1 around to select OK (if the changes are good) or Cancel (if you want to go back to the Set-up 2 screen and not make any changes). Press **SET** to confirm your choice.
8. You can stop by hitting the shutter release or pressing the **MENU** button after you've chosen the date and time.

Language

To switch between 29 different languages for the menu display, turn the Quick Control Dial 1 or use the Multi-controller joystick. After that, the language you want will be marked. Press the **SET** button to turn it on.

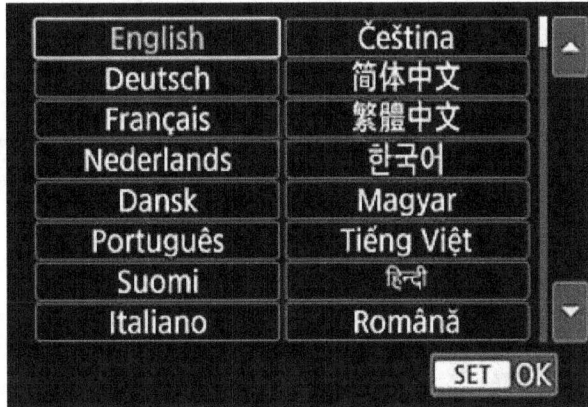

System Frequency

Any television used for display should have its video system set. It is this setting that controls the frame rates that can be used to record movies.

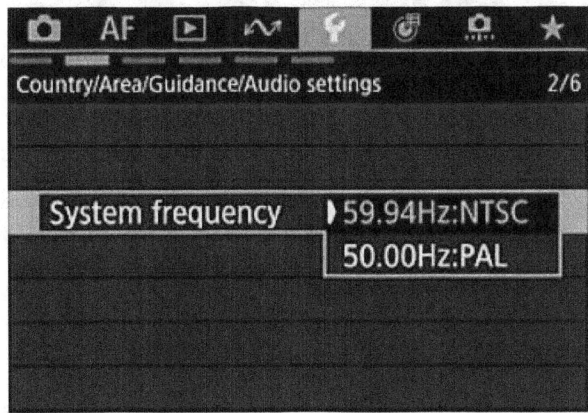

- **59.94Hz:NTSC**

For places where the TV system is NTSC, like North America, Japan, South Korea, Mexico, and so on.

- **50.00Hz:PAL**

For places where PAL is the TV system, like Europe, Russia, China, Australia, and so on.

Help Text Size

When you turn on your camera for the first time, the **INFO Help message** might show up behind a menu. You'll need to press the **INFO** button to see it. When you press it, a screen will show up with directions on how to choose options for that menu item. You won't need this help after a while with your camera, but while you do, you might as well have it shown in a big, easy-to-read style. You can move around in the help text window by pressing the up and down arrow keys.

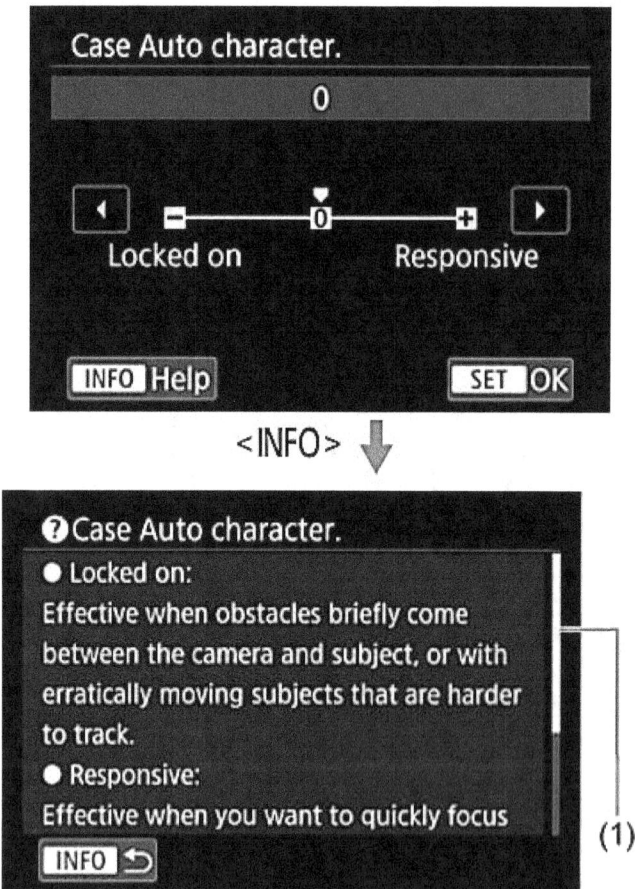

Beep

An internal beeper makes a useful chirp to let you know about several things, such as when the self-timer on your camera is counting down, when a picture is in focus, and when you touch something. You can turn off the beep totally for any reason, like if it's annoying, rude, or distracting (at a concert or museum), or for any other reason. On the Beep screen, choose the choice you want: Enable to turn on, Disable to mute all beeps, or Touch To Silence to only mute the sound when you're using the touch screen. Press **SET** to make your choice take effect and to leave.

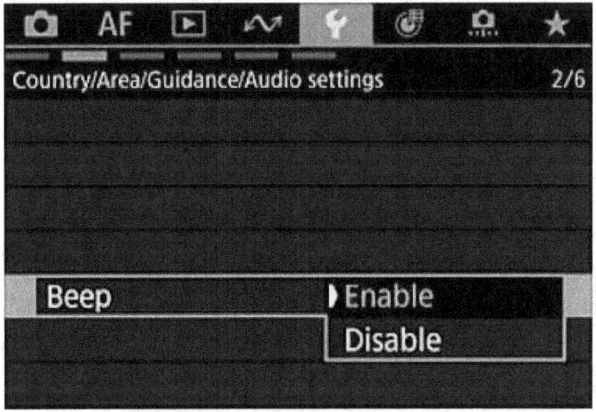

Volume

You can change the volume of the sound going to headphones through the camera's headphone port by spinning the QCD-2 or QCD-1 or using the Multi-controller joystick. The levels range from 0 to 15, with 16 to choose from. Headphones are a great way to check the sound quality of recordings made with either an external microphone or the camera's built-in microphone when Sound Recording is on and the High Frame Rate is off. You can find both of these in the Movie Shooting 1 menu.

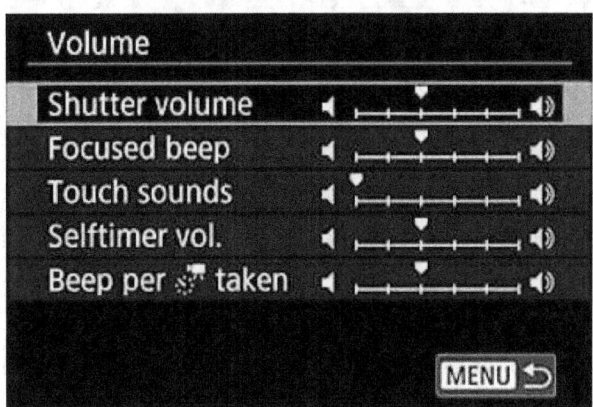

Screen Brightness/Viewfinder Brightness

The next two entries both do the same thing: they let you change the LCD screen and the viewfinder. In general, you will have to change the LCD screen more often to make it easier to see outside or less clear inside. When I'm at a concert, I usually use the electronic viewfinder to look over my shots. If I want to show a friend a picture, I turn down the LCD screen's brightness to the lowest setting so as not to bother other people who might not be as interested in my shots.

Use the example picture and the highlighted gray areas to check if the brightness is right. You can **calibrate** your screen to the way you're shooting by looking at the thumbnail of the most recent picture you saw while the video was playing back. It's important to keep all the steps in the middle and still be able to see the lightest and darkest steps at the top and bottom of the grayscale. When the brightness is turned up, you can see the LCD screen outside in full sunlight, but it drains the battery faster. To lock in the brightness you picked, press the **SET** button. Then, go back to the menu.

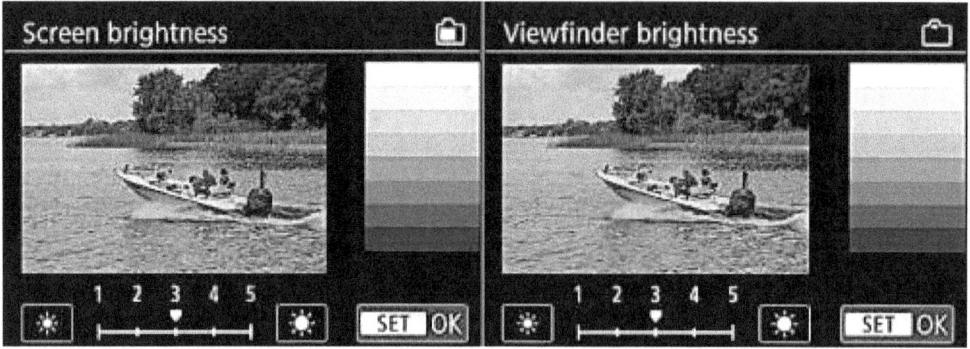

Screen/Viewfinder Color Tone

With this setting, you can fine-tune the color balance of the LCD screen and the camera to your liking. It works the same way as the Display Brightness entry: hold the camera up to your eye to adjust the viewfinder and look at the LCD screen to change the color tone. You should choose this choice if you want a preview image that looks a little more like the real thing and your photos are often warmer or colder than what you see. (Neither display will exactly match the final picture, especially if you shoot in RAW; the screen will always show a JPEG version, no matter what format you choose.)

To change the color, turn this entry on. It will show the most recent picture you played back. The lighting conditions in the room that you want to be consistent should be used. Choose 1 for warm tone, 2 for standard, 3 for cool tone 1, or 4 for cool tone 2. Then press **SET**.

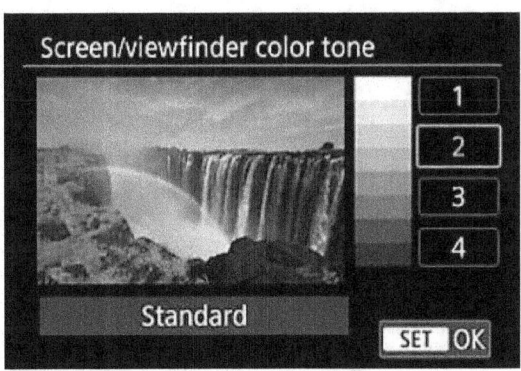

Fine-Tune Viewfinder Color Tone

This item lets you change the viewfinder's color tone in the same way that color balance settings do. It does this by changing the bias along the blue/amber and green/magenta axes. There are four ways to move the Multi-controller joystick to change the color balance to zero point while looking at the video picture in the viewfinder. A grayscale is shown at the bottom of the screen as a reference. To make sure you're happy with the settings, press **SET**.

Screen and Viewfinder Display

You can choose whether to use the screen or the viewfinder for viewing so that you don't turn on the viewfinder sensor by accident when the screen is open.

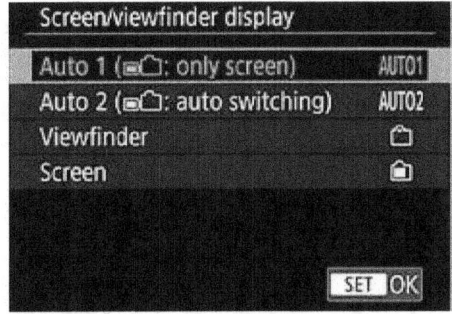

This item is the first thing that comes up in the Set-up 3 menu. One problem that a lot of mirrorless camera users had was that the display would suddenly switch between the LCD screen and the viewfinder. Canon fixed this problem. The eye sensor under the viewfinder window can turn on the lens when your face (or, unfortunately, anything else) comes close to it. If your camera is on a stand, you can turn on the switch with simple movements like pressing the **MENU** button.

This setting has four useful modes:

- **Auto1:** When the LCD screen is swiveled out from the camera body, Auto1 mode is always on. This is true even if something is close to the eye sensor. Once the screen is back to its normal shape and your eye gets close to the sensor, switch to the viewfinder. In practice, this means that you can only switch to the EVF when the screen is swiveled out.
- **Auto2:** Use the LCD to show whether the screen is swiveled out or in its normal space. If your eye or something else touches the camera/eye sensor, though, you should switch to the viewfinder. In other words, the image changes no matter where the display is.
- **Viewfinder:** Always use the viewfinder for display.
- **Screen:** Always use an LCD screen when displaying info. The Customize Button option in the Custom Functions 3 menu lets you make a button that can switch between this setup and the last one.

UI Magnification

If the regular user interface (UI) sometimes makes it hard for you to see menus in less-than-ideal viewing conditions, you can turn this option on to make menu screens twice as big. After that, to make the LCD screen bigger, just double-tap it. If you double-tap it again, it will be fine. When the user interface is expanded, you can't use other touchscreen features, so you have to use the camera controls to change the settings.

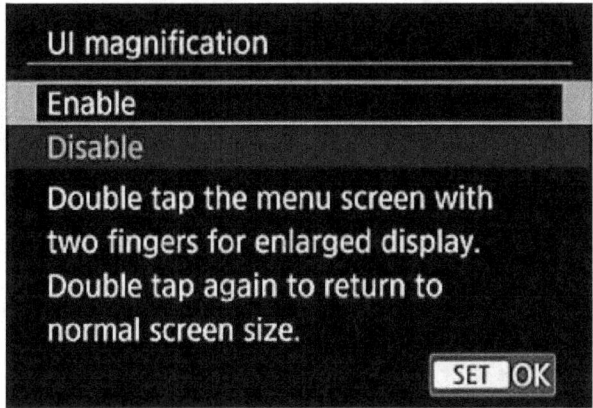

HDMI Resolution

An HDMI Mini-C connector on one end of the cable connects to the camera, and a normal HDMI connector on the other end connects to your device. This lets you send the video to an external monitor or recorder. If you set this to **Auto**, the camera will try to figure out the size of the device you connect it to and then output in that format. If you know your gadget can handle it, you can skip the time lag by picking 1080p video. While it gets the right resolution, there may be a short wait.

The biggest problem with this method is that you can't pick the right resolution by hand. This makes it harder for the system to figure out that some devices need a different resolution. Some devices, like my BlackMagic Intensity Shuttle capture device, need a setting that Canon doesn't let you change by hand, and the camera can't figure out what those settings are either. I called Canon for help, but they couldn't help because there was no way to choose a format other than 1080p by hand. In the end, I used the $20 MavisLink USB-to-HDMI video capture device and the free OBS Studio app to record the displays.

Cooling Fan Settings

- Fan
- Fan Rotation Speed

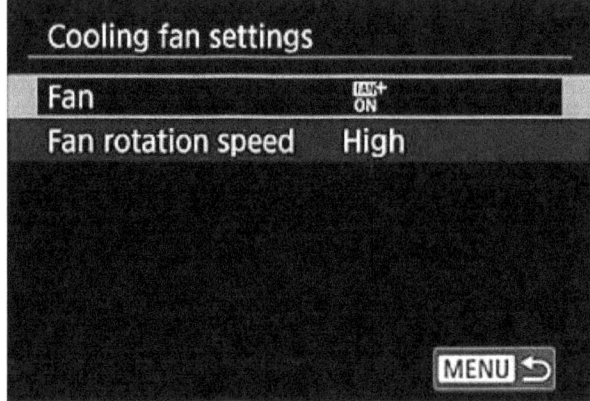

When an optional cooling fan is used, the camera can be used to change how the cooling fan works. Connect the cooling fan before you change the settings.

Shutter at Shutdown

Some people get nervous when they take off the lens on their first compact camera and see the image sensor that isn't covered or protected. Those people don't have an EOS R5 II because Canon cleverly stops the shutter when the camera is off so that dust or other bad things don't fall on the sensor. I only turn off this great feature when I'm shooting acoustic shows or other places where silence is important, and the camera turns off every so often to save battery power. You will only hear the very faint whirring of the autofocus motor if you leave the camera open and use the electronic shutter.

Sensor Cleaning

The automatic sensor cleaning method is very helpful because it reduces or eliminates the need to clean your camera's sensor by hand with brushes, swabs, or bulb blowers. Canon has coated the sensor and other parts inside the camera body with anti-static material to stop charge buildups that bring in dust. Ultrasound waves move a separate filter above the sensor every time the camera is turned on or off. This shakes off any dust that is stuck to a sticky strip below the sensor.

You can choose to have the sensor cleaned automatically when the camera is turned on (Auto Cleaning) or during a shooting session (Clean Now) using this menu choice.

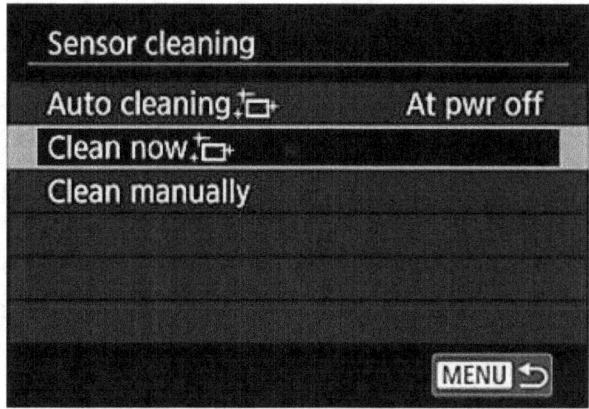

You can also use the Clean Manually option to open the shutter and use a cleaner, brush, or swab. The camera will let you know if the battery level is too low to safely finish the cleaning process, and it won't go any further unless you use the extra AC Adapter Kit ACK-E6N with the DC Coupler DR-E6.

Power Saving

When the camera is not being used, you can change when the screen dims and then turns off, when the camera turns off, and when the viewfinder turns off (Screen dimmer, Screen off, Auto power off, and lens off).

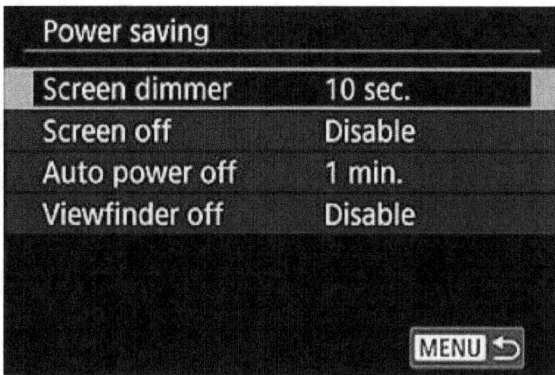

- **Auto Power Off.** This setting changes how long the camera will wait before turning off. When you touch the shutter button, the system will restart. I usually leave this setting at five minutes, but when I'm taking sports or street scenes and need the camera to be ready for a quick shot, I leave it at a longer time.

- **Viewfinder Off.** It doesn't save much power to turn off the electronic viewfinder, that's why there are only three choices: 1 minute, 3 minutes, and Disable. The screen turns back on when you bring the camera up to your eye, no matter what setting you're using, so it makes sense to wait three minutes.

Reset Camera

This gives you options that let you return most settings to their original settings. If you want to go back to the way the camera and menus were set up by default, you can choose **Basic Settings**. If you don't change anything about your camera, it will automatically go to One-Shot AF mode, Evaluative metering, Single Shot drive mode, JPEG Fine Large image quality, Automatic ISO, sRGB color mode, Automatic White Balance, Auto Lighting Optimizer Off, and Standard Picture Style. You can undo any changes you've made to white balance, exposure compensation, or flash exposure compensation. You also lose any bracketing you used for exposure or white balance. Custom white balances and Dust Delete Data will be deleted.

Root Certificate, Communications Settings, Shooting Information Display, Custom Shooting Modes, Copyright Information, Custom Functions (Customize Buttons and Customize Dials will be retained), Custom Controls (clears Customize Buttons and Customize Dials), and My Menu. are some of the other settings that can be reset here.

Custom Shooting Mode (C1–C3)

Custom shot modes can't be turned off with the reset camera commands. You can save your current camera settings in C1, C2, or C3 using this item. You can then get to them by pressing the **MODE** button. This replaces any numbers that were saved there before. You can also clear the settings for all three MODE positions to return them to the way they were when the camera was first made.

Save your preferred settings so that you can use them in certain situations. It has settings for sports, portraits, and landscapes that I saved. If you go to C1, C2, or C3 and forget the settings you saved for that spot, press the **INFO** button to see what they are. Remember that the settings for my Menu are not saved separately. For each Mode Dial position, you can only have one list of My Menu items that can be used.

There are only three options in this menu: Clear Settings, Register Settings, and Auto Update Settings. Register Settings saves your current settings to C1, C2, or C3. Clear Settings deletes the settings from C1, C2, or C3. If that option is set to "Enable," any changes you make to your settings in C1, C2, or C3 modes will be saved in that memory spot. If you choose **Disable**, your registered setting will stay the same, regardless of any changes you made while you were in that Custom Shooting mode. To clear your choices, you must use this menu item.

Simply follow these steps to finish these tasks:

1. **Make your settings.** Set the camera to a different exposure mode than Scene Intelligent Auto.
2. **Access Camera user settings.** In the Set-up 5 menu, choose Custom shooting mode. Then press SET.
3. **Choose function.** If you want to save the current settings for your camera in C1, C2, or C3, choose Register Settings. If you want to delete the settings from any of those locations, choose Clear Settings. To get to the settings screen you want, press **SET**.

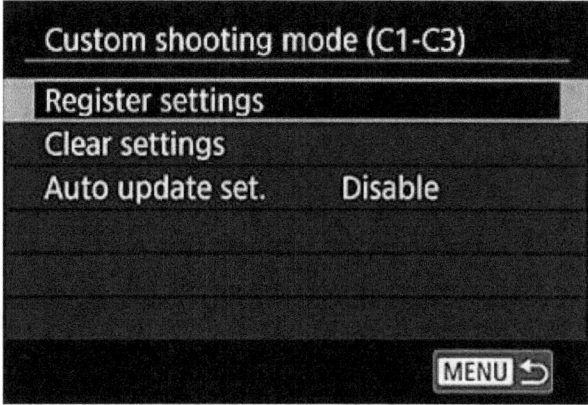

4. **Store/Clear settings.** The screens for saving and clearing are very similar to each other. Pick among Custom Shooting Mode: C1, Custom Shooting Mode: C2, or Custom Shooting Mode: C3 on the QCD-1, then press **SET** to save or clear the settings for that spot. (You will first be given the choice to go ahead or stop.)
5. **Auto update.** Remember that if you change a setting in one of the custom shooting modes and want to keep it, you can quickly update your saved settings

to reflect the change. Click on Auto Update Set. Click on **Enable** to turn this choice on. Pick **Disable** instead of **Update** if you'd rather keep your custom settings until you choose to do so.
6. **Exit.** You will be taken back to the Set-up 5 menu after you confirm. To get out of the menu system for good, press the **MENU** button or the camera release button.

Save/Load Camera Settings On Card (R5 II only)

With this item, you can save your current settings, like shooting modes, menu settings, and Custom Function settings, on a memory card as a specific file that can be put back into your R5 II or moved to another R5 II. There are two options: Save to Card and Load from Card. You can use the standard text-entry screen and the **INFO** button to give these settings a unique 8-character name while you're saving.

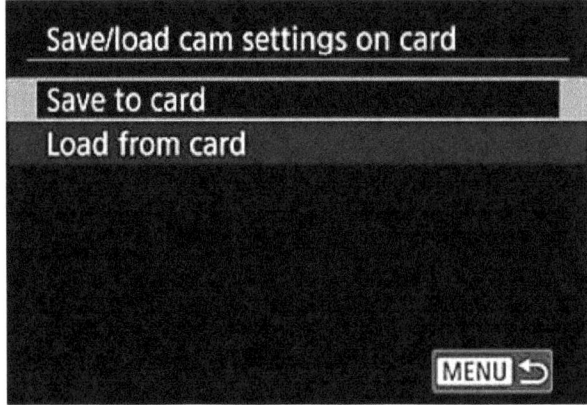

Keep in mind that you can only load settings to an R5 II or another R5 II. Other Canon cameras that can save settings will not work. When you update the software on this or any other camera, the settings can't be brought back. The camera needs to have the same firmware as before for the settings to be saved. Up to ten sets of settings can fit on a memory card.

Battery Information

This is a very important tool that lets you keep an eye on the state and performance of batteries and keep track of data from multiple batteries.

Each LP-E6, LP-E6N, or LP-E6NH battery has its serial number, so your camera can keep an eye on more than one. Each battery you use is "registered" with the camera, which reads the serial number and stores information about it.

Usually, I say to have at least two batteries, and three or more is even better. This is very important when you use a power grip. I have other Canon cameras that use the same battery, so it makes sense for me to use four batteries to power various cameras.

This tool lets you keep an eye on how each battery is doing, switch them around to make sure they all use the same amount of power, and figure out when a battery needs to be replaced. When you choose this menu item, details about both LP-E6/E6N packs will show up if you use two of them in a grip, like the BG-R10.

- **Battery position.** On the second line of the screen, there is an icon that shows where the battery being looked at is plugged in.
- **Power type.** Next to the position icon is a symbol that shows the model number of the battery that is inserted or a DC power adapter that is being used.
- **Remaining capacity.** When the Battery check icon shows up, it shows both the amount of power left and a percentage that reads in 1-percent increments. You can use this to get a rough idea of how much power you still have. If you need to keep shooting, you might want to switch to a fully charged battery that's between 25 and 33 percent charged to avoid interruptions.
- **Shutter count.** It shows how many times the shutter has been opened with the fully charged battery. The following details can help you figure out how much certain functions cost in electricity. For example, if your battery is only half full but you've only taken a few dozen pictures, you know that the power is being used up by reviewing the pictures, using autofocus a lot, and image stabilization a lot because the shutter speed is slow, or (most likely) that flip-up flash you've been using. Knowledge is usually power, but in this case, it can help you save power by telling you to use fewer functions that drain the battery quickly if you need to make the current battery last as long as possible.
- **Recharge performance.** This indicator shows how well your battery pack can take a charge and hold it. Three green bars mean that the pack is working well; two bars mean that it's not working as well when it's being charged. If the light turns red, it means that your pack is almost dead and needs to be changed. If you want

your batteries to last longer, you might want to use different packs at different times so that they all **age** at about the same rate.

Registering Your Battery Packs

The camera can **remember** up to six LP-E6 battery packs and send updates on their state for each one. Follow these steps to register your camera's current battery level:

1. Access the Battery Information Screen.
2. On the left of the LCD panel, press the **INFO** button.
3. There will be a new screen that shows details about the current battery, like the date and serial number.

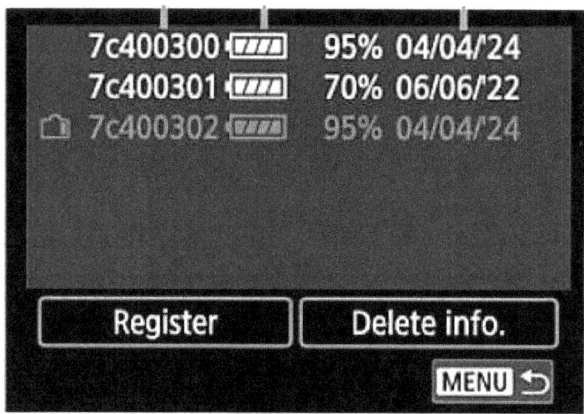

4. To log the battery, you can choose Delete Info instead of Register if the pack has already been registered. Remove the battery from the list (This is what you'd do if you already entered up to six batteries and want to add more.)
5. Press **SET** to add the battery to the register.
6. The camera shows Battery Info when you delete a battery. Delete the screen instead. You can delete a battery pack even if the battery is not in the camera. This is helpful if you lose one. Just pick the battery by its serial number and click **Delete**.
7. To get out of any of the Battery Info screens, press **MENU**.
8. You can check the Battery Info page at any time, even if the battery isn't in the camera, to see how much power it still has left after registering it. The camera keeps track of and updates its state every time a registered battery is added. It also shows the date of the last time the battery was used.

TIP: Take this information with a grain of salt, because a battery may have fully charged since the last time it was put in the camera, or it may have self-discharged a lot while being stored. But this information can help you keep track of how much power is left in a lot of battery packs during a single shooting session or over a few days if the packs aren't charged between sessions.

Copyright Information

This is where you can praise yourself for the great pictures you take with your camera:

- **Display Copyright Info.** Turn on or off the ability to insert copyright information in image files. If you're a double-naught agent who wants to share spy photos without being caught, you should turn off copyright information.
- **Enter the Author's Name.** You can put your name (up to 63 characters) on each picture file.
- **Enter Copyright Details**. You can give more information when you use the extended character set. You have 63 characters to use. Keep in mind that there is no copyright sign. Some people put a lowercase c in braces, but (Copyright) or (Copr.) is the correct way to write it.
- **Delete Copyright Information.** This deletes all the information you've entered, leaving you with a clean slate.

Manual/Software URL

You can enter the URL in this item to get to the page with your camera's instructions and software. There is also a QR code on this item that you can scan with your phone to get to the same page.

Certification Logo Display

With a software update, Canon can add certification data (like what's shown on the camera's bottom panel) to this information-only screen, so they don't have to make new stickers for the bottom of the camera.

Firmware

In the menu listing, you can find the most recent firmware release for accessories that work with the camera. To get a new version of the software, put in a memory card with the binary file on it and press the SET button to start the process.

Chapter 4

Working with the AF System

You can now move on to the settings and options that are available to you since you have a basic understanding of how the autofocus system works. To get tack-sharp focus every time, you need to know how to use focus modes and how to choose the area of focus that you want to look at.

AF Operation

The AF Operation focus modes tell the camera when to focus, but not where. Other focusing features take care of that. These modes let you choose whether the camera locks focus once when you press the shutter halfway down or track moving objects and change focus all the time. The camera has two AF modes: One-Shot AF (single autofocus) and Servo AF (continuous autofocus). You can focus manually with a zoom of up to 10X. Picking the right autofocus setting and focus point is important for getting clear pictures of the subject you want to capture. As I learned from my first mistake when taking pictures of sports, using the wrong setting can lead to sharp pictures of the wrong subject.

If you don't choose Continuous AF in the AF 1 menu, the focus will only show up when you partly depress the shutter button. Autofocus doesn't happen automatically; you can change the settings to have more control. Pressing the Q button will bring up the Quick Control menu. From there, go to AF Operation and use the dial to choose the mode you want to use. Make sure the AF/M switch on the lens is set to AF to switch between focusing modes.

One-Shot AF.

When the camera is in single autofocus mode, the focus is locked once and stays there until the shutter button is fully pressed to take a picture or removed without taking a picture. Because it lowers the chance of out-of-focus shots, this mode works best with subjects that aren't moving. This makes it great for photography that isn't related to action. But you can't take a picture while the camera is still trying to find focus. You have to lock the focus first before you can shoot, which is why it's also called **focus priority**.

Even though it uses less battery power than other autofocus settings, this small delay can cause shutter lag.

If the Beep feature is not turned off, the camera will beep and the focus point will light up green on the screen. When you use Evaluative metering, the exposure locks at the same time. If you half-press the camera button, you can move the picture around while keeping the focus and exposure the same. The AE/FE Lock buttons can also be used to lock brightness while reframing. If the camera can't find focus, the focus point turns orange, and you can't take a picture even if you press the shutter button down.

To switch to release priority, press the shutter button more quickly. This is useful if you need to take quick pictures and want to capture the moment more than getting perfect clarity. This setting, which can be found in the AF 4 menu under **One-Shot AF Release Priority**, lets the camera take a picture even if it hasn't checked for crisp focus yet.

Servo AF.

Continuous autofocus, also known as Servo AF, works well with continuous video modes and is good for things that move quickly, like sports. Once you press the shutter button halfway, the camera focuses on the spot you choose and keeps an eye on the subject, adjusting if you or the subject move. The focus point glows blue when it's in focus, but there are no buzzer sounds because they would be confusing while refocusing over and over again.

Focus and exposure are not locked until you fully press the camera button while taking a picture, unlike single autofocus. With Servo AF, there is almost no flash-lag, so as soon as you press the button, the camera starts shooting. It takes more power, though, because the autofocus system works even when the shutter button is only partly pressed in this mode. In Scene Intelligent Auto mode, the camera turns to Servo AF as soon as it senses motion.

With Servo AF, the camera can take a picture even if the focus isn't right. This is called **Release Priority**. This method uses predictive AF to figure out the right focus as the subject moves closer or farther away from the camera. The camera is always making changes to keep things clear, whether the focus point is chosen automatically or by hand.

When you set the release priority, the camera will take the picture even if the focus isn't fully on it. This doesn't mean that you will get a lot of out-of-focus pictures. The picture will stay sharp or very close to it for the most part during the exposure time.

Manual Focus.

To use manual focus, slide the lens's AF/MF switch to the MF position. This lets you specify the focus by hand. There are some good and bad things about this method. In manual focus mode, your batteries will last longer, but it can be hard to fix the camera every time because it takes longer. Canon does offer help with manual focusing.

- **Focus peaking.** In the AF 2 menu, you can also use MF Peaking to bring out the edges of a picture with a different color. Additionally, you can pick how much peaking to use (High, Medium, or Low) to get the outcomes shown below. Peaking can't be seen on an enlarged screen.
- **Magnified view.** When using the magnified view (which is also available in autofocus modes), manual focusing is a lot easier.

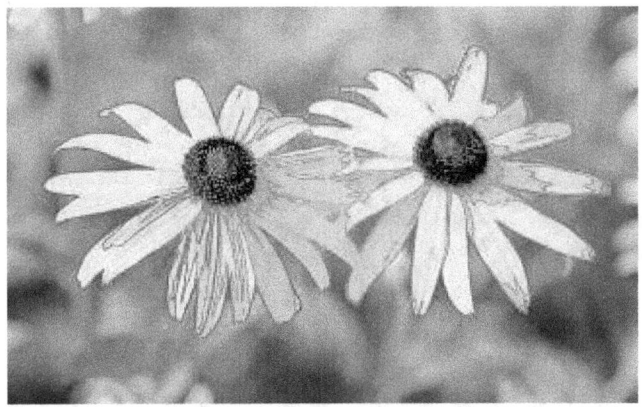

AF Method

Canon's AF Method tool picks which parts of the picture are used to gather information for autofocus. You can pick the starting point or zone of points from seven AF area options. If needed, you can also change what other points will be deployed. Face+Tracking is the eighth mode. This mode lets the camera, not you, choose and track the focus point, giving more weight to the eyes and faces of people, animals, or neither.

It's easy to switch between AF modes: press the AF selection button in the upper-right corner of the camera's back panel, to the right of the * button; then, keep pressing the M-Fn button while the display changes between modes. In the AF 4 menu, there is an item called **AF Method Selection Control**. This lets you change AF methods with the Main Dial instead of the M-Fn button. If you only use a few of the total modes, Canon lets you hide the others by going to the AF 4 menu and choosing the Limit AF Methods option.

Face+Tracking AF

If you choose this mode, the camera will look for faces and focus on them. If it doesn't find any, it will use the whole autofocus area. A box shows up around a face, and that face is tracked as it moves around the screen. You can choose where the Servo AF setting starts when you use it. The camera will first use the AF point you chose. If it doesn't find a face there, it will look at another part of the picture. That could be helpful if you're taking a bunch of pictures and know that the main subject will be in a certain part of the frame but want the camera to refocus as it moves. This helps get rid of AF problems that come up when something else moves in the frame beside the main subject.

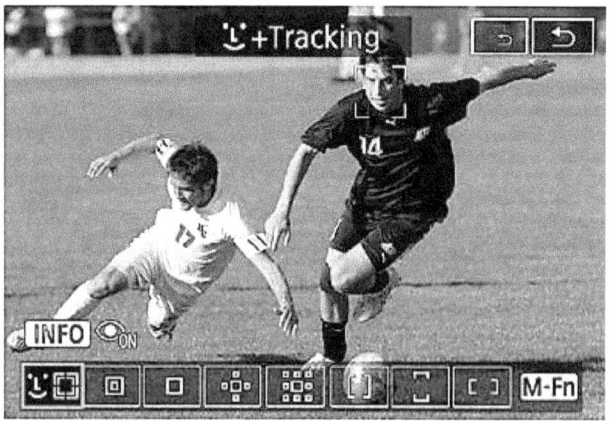

Here are some tips on how to use Face + Tracking AF:

- **Pick a Subject to Detect**. This AF 1 menu entry tells the camera to look for faces or heads of people, animals, or other things. The system is very good at telling the difference between people, dogs, cats, and birds. If faces or heads are hard to tell apart, it will also track bodies or parts of bodies. **Note:** Subject to Detect works in Zone AF or Large Zone AF (horizontal/vertical) mode as well.

- **Enable/Disable Eye Detection.** If Eye Detection AF is turned on, the camera will show an extra small box around an eye when it's in One-Shot mode. You can pick an eye by tapping the LCD screen as well. When Face+ Tracking is turned on, pressing the INFO button will turn eye recognition on and off. By pressing the AF Point Selection button, then the M-Fn button, and finally the **INFO** button while using Face+ Tracking, you can turn on or off eye recognition at any time.
- **Faces Detected.** Any faces or eyes that are found get a box over them. Press the AF Selection button again to move from the face that is marked to another in the picture. The box has arrows on both the left and right sides. You can switch between faces by pressing the Multi-controller key.

To pick a face, press the touch screen. To stop locked tracking, press the **Off** icon in the bottom left corner of the screen. One-Shot AF can be used when a face is selected with a touch, even when the Servo is set to operate in AF mode.

- **Set Initial Focus Point.** If you go to the AF 5 menu and select Initial Servo AF place for Face+Tracking, you can pick a spot on the screen to begin face tracking in Servo AF mode. Make sure that Face+Tracking and Servo AF are already turned on. Press the AF Point Selection button and then tap the screen or use the Multi-controller joystick to choose where to start. After that, press **SET**. If you click the Multi-selector or tap the **return to center** icon on the screen, you can move the starting point to the middle of the frame. The first face+tracking focus point can be one of three things:

    o **A point you specify.** In Servo AF mode, the Initial AF Point for Face+Tracking entry choice lets you choose a specific spot in the frame that will always be used first when Face+Tracking is turned on.
    o **Retain manual point used for 1-Point AF, Expand AF Area, Expand AF Area: Around**. Servo AF will use the AF point you set in one of these three AF modes if you use one of them and then switch to Face+Tracking.
    o **Auto.** When Face+Tracking is turned on, the camera chooses the first AF point for Servo AF. This option is the easiest to use and is the least likely to go wrong.

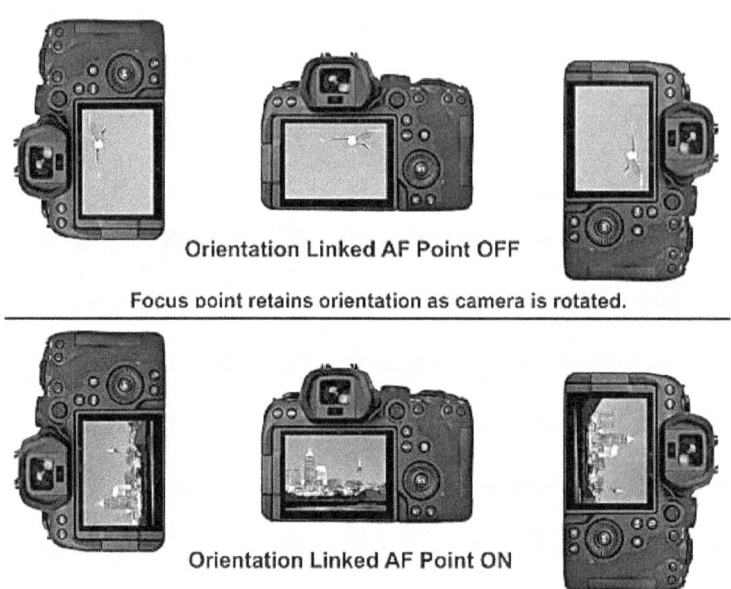

Orientation Linked AF Point OFF
Focus point retains orientation as camera is rotated.

Orientation Linked AF Point ON
Different focus points can be selected for each orientation.

Spot AF

You can focus on and zoom in on a small box on the screen in this mode. The Multi-controller joystick, the Main Dial (for horizontal movement), or QCD-1/QCD-2 (for up/down movement) can be used to move this focus area to almost any place on the screen in very small steps. To move the focus point, press the AF Point Selection button first. Press the Multi-controller button or tap the Return to Center icon in the top right corner of the LCD screen to move the focus point back to the middle.

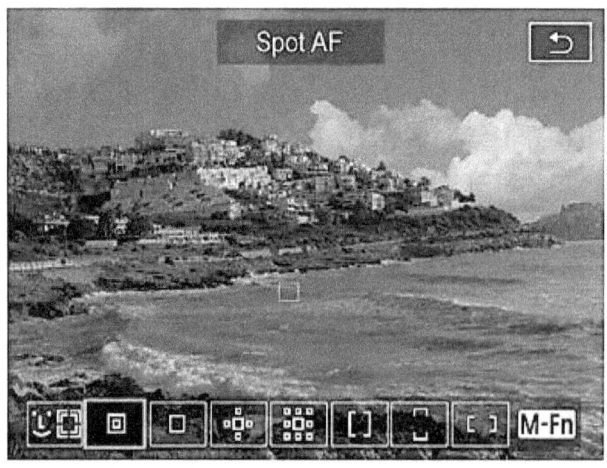

But this level of accuracy can be too much. If you move the camera or the subject, the focus can easily move away from your main subject, especially if you're shooting hand-held or with a front-heavy long lens. This mode may be the best way to focus on a subject surrounded by small details. When you want to focus on a certain spot but your subject is going slowly, this is the best tool for you. You can move the current focus point with the controls. Spot AF can be used for everyday shooting when accuracy is needed and there is enough detail in the image for the sensor to pick up. If such a small part of your subject isn't solid, you should use one of the following selection modes. This will let the AF system look at both the manually chosen spot and the focus points around it.

1-Point AF

You can zero in on and focus on a box that is about three times bigger than the one on the screen in this mode. This is usually the best way to go when speed is important but you still need to be very precise about where the focus point is. In sports, I use it to find people who aren't moving around much, like an infielder guarding third base. As was already said, the attention point can be moved to a new place.

Expand AF Area

In this mode, the main point you choose is used, along with the points above, below, and on either side of it (until the point you chose manually goes to the edge of the array and one or more of the other points scroll off). The bigger effective zone in this mode makes it easier to track items that are moving in the frame, so it's better for tracking things that are moving. Three to four focus points around the subject can pick up and follow the movement as it goes outside the area defined by the chosen focus point. In One-Shot AF mode, the focus point you chose by hand and the expanded point that was used will be shown.

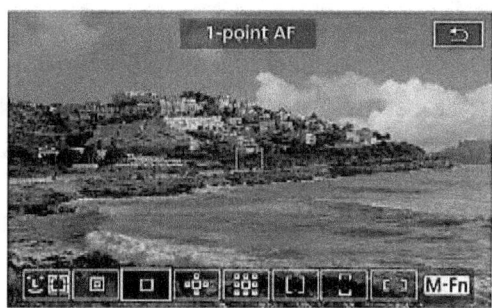

Focus on a part of the frame that is somewhat larger.

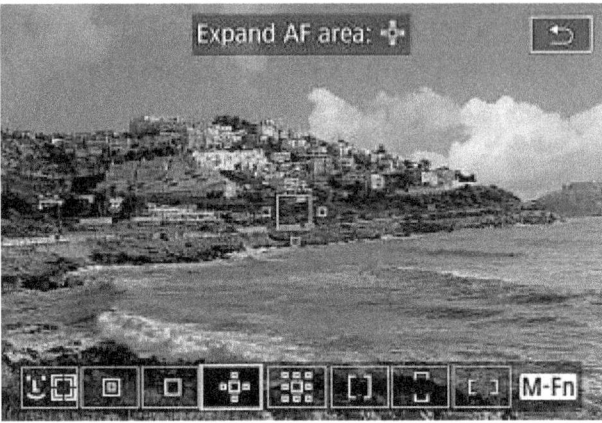

When you use an Expand AF area, a bigger AF area lets moving objects autofocus.

Expand AF Area: Around

This mode is like the last one, but the eight points next to the point that was chosen manually are also part of the focusing array. It works a little better for subjects that don't have a lot of detail at the carefully chosen focus point, and the extra points around the first focus point make the results better. Also, bigger moving things move better in this mode, even though it's not as precise. Always, the active points are shown in the middle of the frame in the figure, but you can move the active area around while you look at the screen.

Zone AF

This is a zone-oriented point selection method. The AF points are spread out in a zone that covers about a sixth of the frame. With the tools, moving the focus point means moving the focus zone from one place in the frame to another. This mode is useful when you have a good idea of where your subject will live and only want to cover a certain area. This mode focuses on the closest subject most of the time, so it's not as accurate as the other AF ways we've talked about so far. The camera will try to focus on any people it finds in the AF frame, though.

Large Zone AF (Vertical)/(Horizontal)

The last two ways use large rectangular zones that are lined up across and down each other. Either one might work well for tall people (basketball) or big areas (motorsports or boat races). The AF points that are needed inside the frame will be chosen automatically. Usually, these will be the ones that cover the closest subject. Both methods will scan the picture for faces and focus on any that are detected.

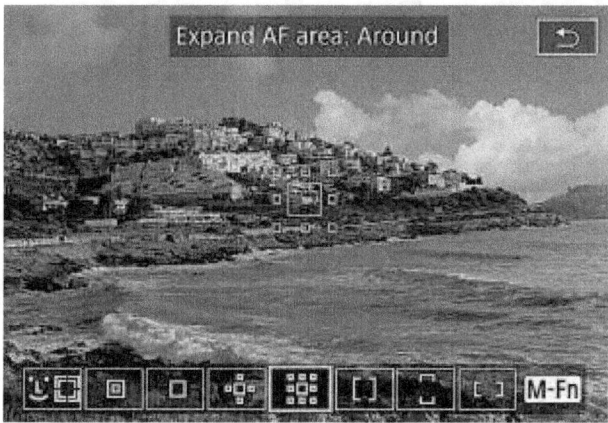

In this mode, four more focus points are active.

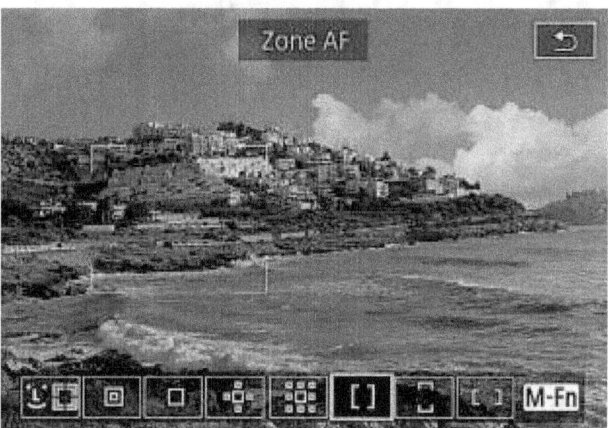

A bigger focus area is used by Zone AF.

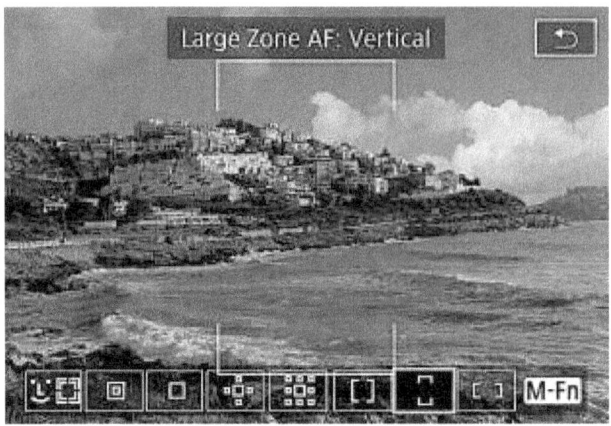

Large zone (vertical).

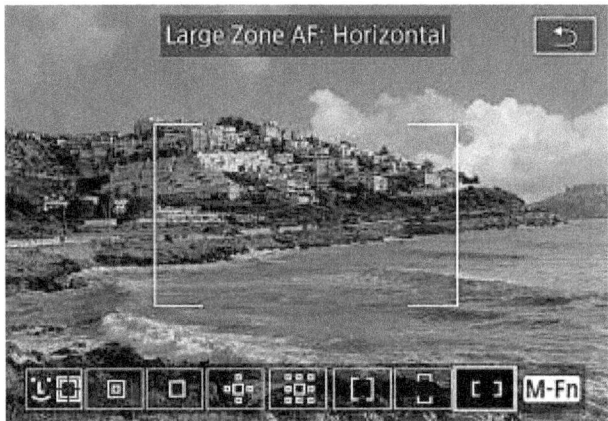

Large Zone (horizontal).

Magnified View

By pressing the Magnify/Reduce button, you can see pictures that are 6X or 15X (R5) or 5X, or 10X (R5) bigger in all modes except Face+ Tracking to make sure you're in focus. To zoom in, just touch the Magnify/Reduce button once or twice. To go back to the normal view, touch it again. The zoom is focused on the AF point when you use Spot AF, 1-point AF, Expand AF Area, Expand AF Area: Around, or Zone AF. In Spot AF and 1-point AF, AF is done on a bigger screen if you press the camera button halfway.

When using other modes, AF is done after the screen is back to normal. When the camera is in Servo mode, it goes back to normal eyesight to focus. In magnified mode, you can't use Continuous AF or Movie Servo AF. It might be harder to concentrate when you are shaking a lot. When the area is zoomed in, use the Multi-controller to move around it. To fix the expanded area in the frame, press the Multi-controller button.

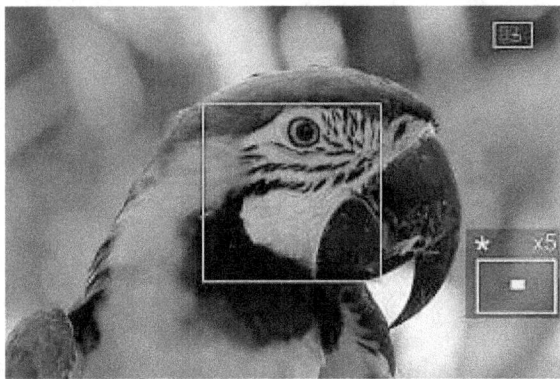

You can use magnified views in any AF mode besides Face+ Tracking or when you focus manually.

Fine-Tuning Your Autofocus

Sometimes all the choices for autofocus can be too much to handle. The bulleted list below has most of the information you need to find the different choices and use them. These are your choices:

- **Continuous AF.** The camera will keep refocusing until you press the shutter release halfway, even when it's in One-Shot mode. Then, the camera will keep refocusing in Servo AF mode until you fully press the shutter release to take a picture. The focus will be locked in One-Shot mode. When this setting is used, the pre-focus action can speed up AF when taking pictures, but it drains the battery faster. In the AF 1 menu, you can find this choice.
- **Touch & Drag.** You can change the focus point on the touch screen while you're still in the viewfinder making your shot. You can also find this item in the AF 1 menu.
- **AF-assist beam firing.** This setting decides whether an external electronic flash or the camera's built-in LED is used to make a pulse of light that makes a subject stand out enough to focus on. This option can be found in the AF 2 menu.

- **Servo AF Characteristics.** You can change how tracking works in Servo AF mode by using the AF 3 settings. There are four pre-set Cases, and each one has conditions that are good for a different type of shooting situation. Instead, you can choose Case A (Auto), which tells the camera to adjust itself to moving things.

Two things about the preset cases can be changed. Just pick out the Case you want to customize and press **SET**. Then, press the **RATE** button and pick one of the two changes that follow. Again, press **SET**, and then use the Multi-controller to make the following changes:

- **Tracking sensitivity.** Here you can change how fast the AF system moves to focus on a new subject. You can choose between -2 (Locked On) and +2 (responsive). Negative numbers make it easier to track because they keep your focus on the original subject even if it quickly moves out of the area covered by the focus points. The bad thing is that you have to wait longer for the right picture to be taken if the camera picks the wrong subject. When a new subject comes in, the AF system responds faster when the number is positive. But because the reaction is so quick, the camera might focus on the wrong thing.
- **Acceleration/deceleration tracking.** This setting controls how the AF system responds to sudden stops, starts, or accelerations. You can choose between 0 (for subjects going at a steady pace) and 2 (for faster responses to people whose speed changes quickly). The camera may be fooled by lower values if an object that has been moving regularly stops all of a sudden. The focus may move to where the object would have been if it had kept moving. If more, things move at a steady speed and might not be in focus evenly.
- **When the focus is difficult.** When there isn't enough contrast or light, the focusing system may not work as well. This is very true for long telephotos and lenses whose widest aperture is small. With the Lens Drive When AF Impossible (AF 4) setting, you can tell the camera to either keep trying to focus or stop.
- **Limit AF methods.** You can hide the AF methods on the selection screen if you don't use them all. This will make switching between them faster. You can let any or all of the methods happen. You can't turn off the 1-point AF mode. These options are part of the AF 4 entry.
- **Orientation Linked AF point.** If you want to use a certain carefully chosen AF point when taking pictures in either vertical or horizontal orientation, you can set that preference with this menu item (AF 4), Separate AF Points: Point Only.

Alternatively, you can say that you want to use the same mode or point in both vertical and horizontal positions. If you want to tell them apart, the Separate AF Points: Point Only choice gives you three orientations to think about one horizontal, two vertical, and one other.

Same for both vertical and horizontal. The AF point or zone that you choose by hand works on photos taken both vertically and horizontally.

Separate AF points: Point Only. In manual point selection modes, you can set the AF point so that it is different for each of the three views. If you switch from one manual selection mode to another, the point you picked will still be there. These are the orientations:

- **Camera held horizontally.** In this position, the camera is set up so that the viewfinder and shutter button are on top.
- **Camera held vertically** with the shutter release and grip are placed above the mode dial.
- **Camera held vertically** with the mode dial is placed above the grip/shutter release.

Initial Servo AF Point for Face+Tracking. The choices are in the AF 5 menu.

Chapter 5

Autofocus Menu

AF Menu Options

Depending on the shooting mode, the AF menus have different entries.

AF Operation

This is the first item in the AF 1 menu, and it lets you set autofocus action without using the QCD-1 or M-Fn buttons. If the AF/MF switch on the lens is set to MF, this entry only shows MF and not the other two. To remind you, the focus point changes color to green or blue (in Servo mode) when it's in focus and orange when it's not. To sum up:

- **One-Shot AF**. The One-Shot AF locks on to a focus point when the shutter button is half-pressed. Green boxes show up when the picture is sharply focused at the active focus points. Orange boxes show up when it is not. When the gaze is locked, you will hear a beep if Beep is turned on in the Set-up 2 menu. The focus will stay where it is until you let go of the button or take a picture. If you can't get good focus, the camera won't take a picture, even if you press the shutter release down.
- **Servo AF**. As you move the subject or the camera in Servo AF settings for continuous focusing, the focus stays on it. There is no sound when the camera is in focus, and the focus area turns blue. When it can't focus, it turns orange. If you press the shutter button down, you can take a picture even if the focus isn't perfect.
- **AI Focus AF** lets the camera automatically switch from [One-Shot AF] to [Servo AF] mode based on the condition of the subject while shooting constantly or in the middle of a shot.

Subject to Detect

This entry tells the Face+Tracking, Zone AF, and Large Zone AF (Vertical or Horizontal) autofocus algorithms how to track objects in the order they should be tracked.

Auto

- Picks the main subject to track automatically from people, animals, or cars in the scene.

People

- Finds and sorts detecting results for people, who are the main things to keep an eye on.
- Faces, heads, or bodies of people are found, and tracking frames are shown over each face or head that is found.
- If the camera can't tell if a face, head, or body belongs to a person, it may focus on another part of the body.

Animals

- Finds both people and animals (dogs, cats, birds, or horses), with animal detection results being used to choose the main subjects to watch.
- When the camera is pointed at an animal, it tries to identify faces or bodies and shows a tracking frame over any faces it finds.
- If the camera can't tell what kind of animal it is by looking at its face or whole body, it may look at a part of its body.

Vehicles

- Finds people and vehicles (sports cars, motorcycles, planes, trains, and more), with results from finding vehicles being used to choose the main subjects to watch.
- The camera tries to find important details on the whole car (or, in the case of trains, just the front half), and a tracking frame is shown over any details that are found.
- If the camera can't find important details or the whole car, it may focus on other parts of the vehicle.
- Press the **INFO** button to turn on or off spot detection for important car information.

None

- Instead of finding subjects, the camera figures out what the main subject is based on how you arrange the pictures. The frames for tracking are not shown.

Eye Detection

Eye Detection AF can be turned on and off with this setting. An AF point shows up around a human or animal eye that is identified. One-Shot AF and the Face+Tracking AF method are the only ones that can find your eyes. Press the AF Point Selection button and then the **INFO** button to turn off Eye Detection AF for a short time. To turn Eye Detection back on, press **INFO** again.

Action Priority

Soccer, volleyball, and basketball players can be put in the same category as priority subjects for recognition and AF tracking when shooting because they move in similar ways in each sport.

MF Peaking Settings

You can only use the MF Peaking Settings when you are focusing in Manual mode. Focus peaking is a method that uses color (red, white, or yellow) to draw attention to the edges of the area that is clearly in focus. At a glance, the colored area shows what will be very sharp if you take the picture at that time.

If you're not satisfied, just change the focused distance (manually focus). It's the color outline that forms around the sharp edges of the picture that are in focus that gets closer to the ideal focus for that area. You can change the amount of peaking (High or Low), pick a color accent (Red, Yellow, or White), or turn off the feature.

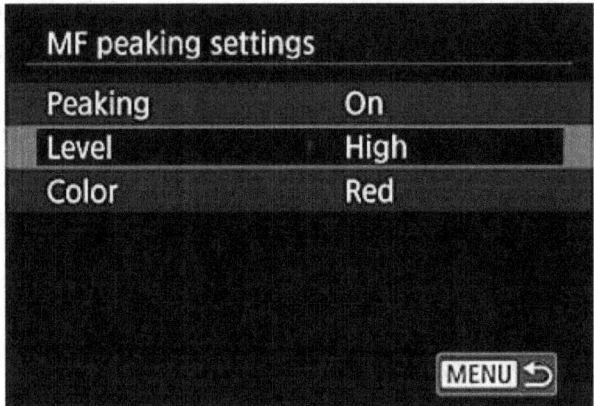

Peaking Color lets you pick the color that shows that you are rising when you are using manual focus. White is the usual color, but you can change it to a more noticeable color, like red or yellow, if it doesn't stand out enough against a subject of the same color. Peaking can't be seen when the view is expanded or when HDMI is used to connect to an external display or recorder. If you use high ISO settings or Canon Log, the lines might be hard to see.

Focus Guide

This is another great tool for manual focus (only). It puts a guide over the picture frame to show you how to move the focus ring and in what direction. If you press the AF Point button and use the directional keys or tap the screen, you can move the focus guide to a certain part of the screen. The guide frame is in the middle when you press the **SET** button or the Return icon in the top right corner of the touch screen.

AF-Assisted Beam Firing

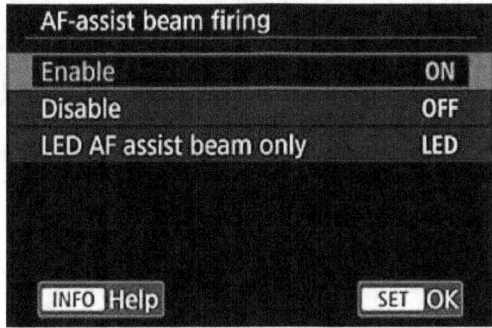

This setting decides whether to use an external electronic flash that is suitable or the camera's built-in LED to make a pulse of light that gives the camera enough contrast to focus on a subject. You can use the camera's LED or a Canon Speedlite that is connected to make a focus assist beam when this setting is enabled. Turn this feature off if it's annoying you. Remember that if you choose **Enable** when the Speedlite's AF-Assist Beam Firing is set to **Disable**, the AF-Assist beam will not be sent out; the flash choice will be used instead.

- **Enable**. When there isn't enough light in the room for proper focusing with just ambient light, the AF-assist light comes from either the camera's LED or a linked, powered-up external flash.
- **Disable**. The lighting for AF-assist is turned off. You might want to use this choice when taking pictures at concerts, weddings, or other dark places where the light might be rude or distracting.
- **LED AF-Assist Beam Only**. An LED AF-assist lamp is built into some Canon flash units. If you choose this, only the Speedlite's beam will be on. The camera's LED will be used if your flash doesn't have one. Again, this function is turned off if you use the external flash's controls to remove its AF-assist beam.

Lens Electronic MF

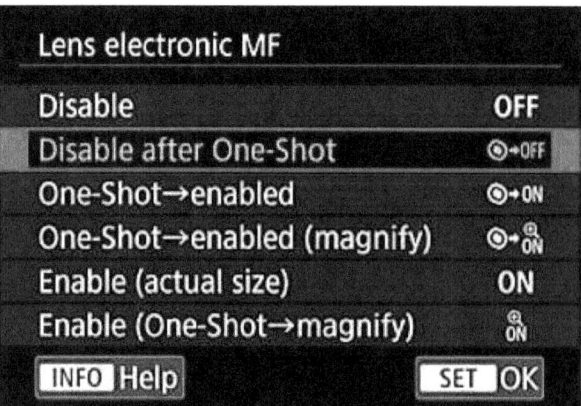

You might need this entry's features if you often use EF- or EF-S-mount lenses with an adapter. You might want to turn off the super-sensitive electric manual focusing rings when using one of the compatible lenses since even a small bump against the ring can cause the focus to shift a lot. Some extra-fast Canon prime lenses and one zoom lens are the only ones that have these rings. They all have USM or STM motors.

- **Disable after One-Shot AF.** This turns off manual focus. Use this if you're happy with how the camera's autofocus sets the focus and don't want to change it by hand. Remember that you can fully turn off the autofocus (AF) system by sliding the lens's AF/MF switch to the MF position.
- **One-Shot AF: Enabled**. When the feature is turned on, you can hold down the shutter button halfway while changing the focus by hand. This helps me get zero focus on a subject sitting diagonally when I'm taking photos with my EF 85mm f/1.2 lens at a wide aperture.
- **One-Shot AF: Enabled (Magnify).** On (Enlarge). When the feature is turned on, you can hold down the shutter button halfway while changing the focus by hand. Turn the lens focus ring to make the area being focused bigger while you're making changes.
- **ON: Enable (actual size):** When the camera is on and certain lenses*1 are attached, you can always change the focus manually. When using other lenses, it works the same way as when [One-Shot] is turned on.

Chapter 6

Exploring Canon EOS R5 Mark II's Video Capabilities

Introduction to the R5 Mark II's 8K Video Recording

The Canon EOS R5 Mark II has several movie shooting choices that let users change the video settings on the camera to their liking. You can get the menus with the camera. We'll talk more about the different ways the Canon EOS R5 Mark II can be used to shoot movies.

1. **Movie Recording Quality**

The first option in the shooting screen is the quality of the movie recording. This is where the user can change the video recording's quality and frame rate. Full HD video can be recorded at 120 fps (fps), and 4K video can be recorded at 60 fps. Users can also pick between taking in Canon Log mode or HDR PQ mode. Both offer more post-production options and a wider dynamic range.

2. **Movie Servo AF.**

When you shoot a video, the movie servo AF choice lets you choose how the camera focuses on the subject. Face recognition and tracking, subject tracking, or human focus are the different ways that the user can choose to focus. When shooting in a mode that supports face recognition and tracking, the camera will find the face of the subject and focus on it, no matter where it is in the frame or how it moves. In the subject tracking mode, users can pick a specific subject to keep an eye on, and in manual focus, users have full control over the focus distance.

3. **AF Method**

The aim of a camera is controlled by a setting called the AF method when shooting video. For their cameras, users can choose between single-point AF, zone AF, and tracking AF. The main difference between zone AF and single-point AF is that zone AF focuses on a bigger part of the frame while single-point AF simply uses a smaller part of the frame.

Tracking autofocus lets the camera follow a moving image and make small changes to the focus as it moves.

4. **Movie Digital IS**

When the camera records video, the movie's digital IS setting controls the technology that keeps the picture steady. The person can pick between the normal, enhanced, and off modes. In regular mode, image stabilization works across the whole frame. In enhanced mode, on the other hand, it works more strongly along the edges of the frame to counteract camera shake.

5. **Movie Crop**

If you are shooting a video, the movie crop setting tells the camera whether to crop the picture or not. The user can pick to shoot in Super 35mm, APS-C, or full-frame mode. The full-frame mode takes a picture of the whole camera, but the APS-C and Super 35mm modes crop the picture before taking it, which makes the field of view smaller.

6. **Movie Sound Recording**

The movie sound recording setting tells the camera how to record sound when it's recording a movie. The user can use either the microphone that comes with the device an extra one, or both. There is a stereo microphone built into the Canon EOS R5 Mark II, and there is also a 3.5mm microphone connector for connecting other mics.

7. **Movie Time Code**

With the movie time code feature, users can give their video recordings a time code. It is possible to sync video footage from multiple cameras and organize video footage during post-production by using time coding. You can use the Canon EOS R5 Mark II in both free run and rec run time code modes.

8. **Movie Recommendation Size**

The movie recording size choice sets the largest file size that can be used for each video recording. Standard settings or automatic settings can be chosen by users. In standard mode, a recorded file can only be 4 gigabytes in size. But in auto mode, the camera can split recordings into as many separate files as it needs to.

9. **Movie Recording Control**

In the movie recording control settings, you can choose when the camera starts recording and when it stops. The user can use the snap or record buttons on the camera or a button on an outside device, like a smartphone app or a remote control.

10. **Movie Playback**

It's up to the camera's movie-playing setting to decide how to show recorded videos when they are played back. People can choose between normal, full-screen, and auto mode.

The Movie Shooting Menu

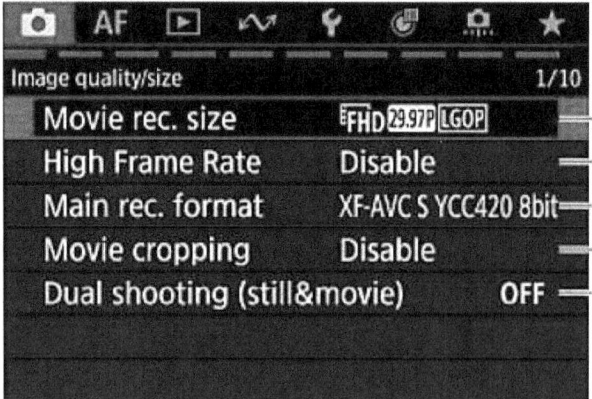

Movie Recording Size

This item is the first choice in the Movie Shooting 1 menu. Your camera lets you change a lot of settings for video clarity. For example, it can record at 4K resolution, which is very high. Here are some of the choices that are out there:

- **Image size**. There are both 4K and HD versions of the movie. The video's resolution and area may be different based on how well it was recorded and how the movie was cropped.

- **Frame rate**. The number of different frames or fields that are recorded in one second. In NTSC mode, which is used in North America, Japan, and other places, these are written as 120 fps, 60 fps, 30 fps, and 24 fps. In PAL-compliant regions, these are written as 100 fps, 50 fps, and 25 fps. It's important to note that the real fps are a little lower than what was said.
- **Compression method**. Each frame is compressed using either the ALL-I or IPB format before it is sent to your storage device. To save room and make the transmission speeds of the collected frames less busy, this is done. An icon with an arrow heading downward shows versions of **IPB Lite** that record at a lower bitrate.

MP4 is the container format for all of your video files, and MPEG4 AVC/H.264 is the codec that is used to encode and decode movies. When recording in the well-known and popular MP4 format, which is also a worldwide standard, progressive scan is used.

Movie files exceeding 4 GB.

- You can't record single movie files that are bigger than 4 GB to SD cards.
- When video files on an SDHC card get bigger than 4 GB, the card creates new ones instantly. When these files are played, they are automatically played in order.
- CFexpress or SDXC cards can record movies in a single file, even if the file size is bigger than 4 GB.

High frame rate.

The camera can record video at 29.97/25.00 fps when set to **Enable**. It can also record at 239.76/200.00 fps or 119.88/100.00 fps.

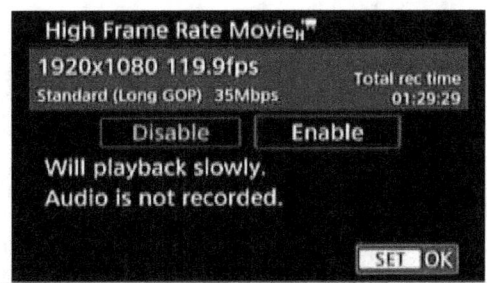

Main Recording Format:

- Supports XF-HEVC S and XF-AVC S movie formats.
- Raw Movies.
- Recording proxy movies.

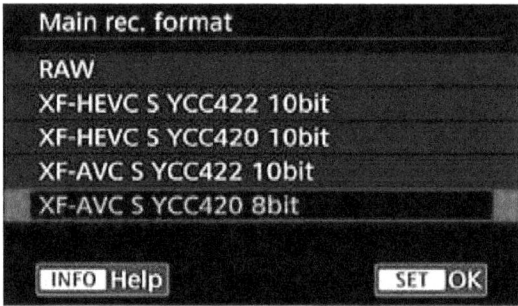

XF-HEVC S and XF-AVC S movies.

Canon video codecs that are extensions of H.265/HEVC and MPEG-4 AVC/H.264 are used for XF-HEVC S movies and XF-AVC S movies. These forms keep the quality of the images while reducing the amount of data that needs to be sent.

RAW Movies

The picture sensor sends raw data in digital form, which is used to make RAW movies.

With EOS Digital Photo Professional, you can watch RAW movies and work on them. Read the Digital Photo Professional instruction booklet to find out more.

Recording Proxy Movies

Main Movie Settings		Proxy Movie Settings (Set Automatically)	
Recording Format	Image Size	Recording Format	Image Size
XF-HEVC S YCC422 10bit XF-HEVC S YCC420 10bit	4096×2160 2048×1080	XF-HEVC S YCC420 10bit	2048×1080
	3840×2160 1920×1080		1920×1080
XF-AVC S YCC420 8bit XF-AVC S YCC422 10bit	4096×2160 2048×1080	XF-AVC S YCC420 8bit	2048×1080
	3840×2160 1920×1080		1920×1080
RAW	8192×4320 4096×2160	XF-AVC S YCC420 8bit	2048×1080

Movie Cropping

When shooting a movie, cropping almost always cuts down on the part of the sensor's full picture size that is captured. Some of the top and bottom of your picture will be cut off because FHD and 4K have 16:9 aspect ratios instead of 3:2 ratios used in still photos. If you choose the movie mode and connect lenses to your camera, the leftover space may be cut down even more. By choosing this choice, you can have some say over how the image is cropped.

Here are the choices you have:

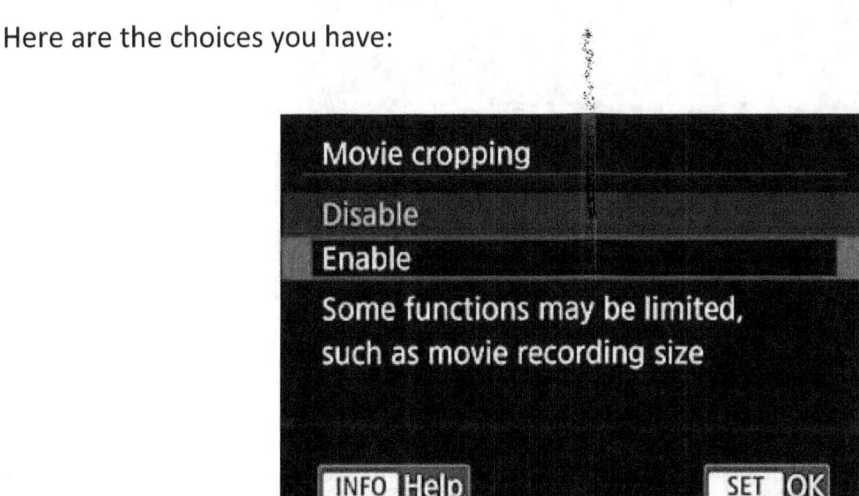

- **Disable**. Lenses with either an RF or an EF mount can be used in this mode with the help of an adapter. These are usually full-frame lenses. Picture area for the R5 Mark II camera when Movie Cropping is not used.
- **Enable**. If you choose this choice, your video will always be cropped, and the image area that is made will be the same as that made by Canon APS-C lenses that are marked RF-S or EF-S. When Movie Cropping is turned on for the R5 MARK II, the green box shows the parts of the picture that were cut out by the camera.

With the R5 MARK II, you can't record movies with a high frame rate if you use RF-S or EF-S lenses or if the Movie Cropping setting is turned on. When you use Movie Digital IS, you will see that an extra, small crop is added.

Dual Shooting (Still Photos and Movies)

By pressing the shutter button down, you can take pictures (single or continuous taking) without stopping the movie recording. This makes it possible to get better picture quality when taking still shots instead of movie frames.

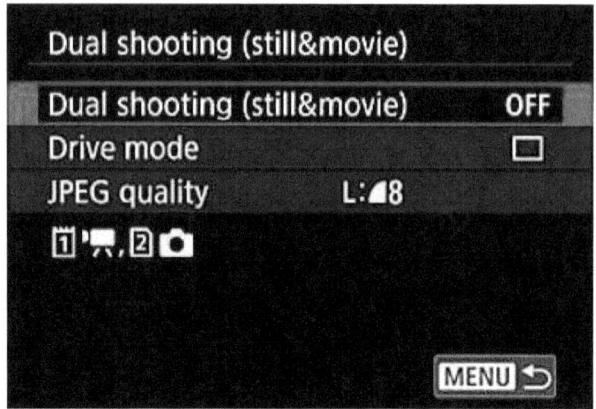

Sound Recording

While recording a movie, press [On] to start recording music. If you don't connect an external microphone, the built-in microphone is used.

Four-channel recording.

It has four sound channels that it can record.

For four-channel recordings, the following sources can be used together.

- Two microphones: one for the multi-function shoe and one for an external microphone.

- Microphone developed for multi-function shoes (2 channels) and built-in microphone (2 channels).
- External microphone (2 channels) and built-in microphone (2 channels).
- Includes two built-in microphones (2 channels each).

When more than one microphone is connected, channels 1 and 2 are given to the microphone with the highest priority, and channels 3 and 4 are given to the microphone with the lowest priority. Microphones are ranked from most important to least important.

- Microphones intended for multi-functional shoes.
- External microphones.
- Built-in microphone.

Audio Format:

When you record a movie, you can choose the audio file.

Audio Settings:

In certain places, set up microphones to catch sound. When using external mics or microphones made for multi-function shoes, look at the microphone's instruction booklet.

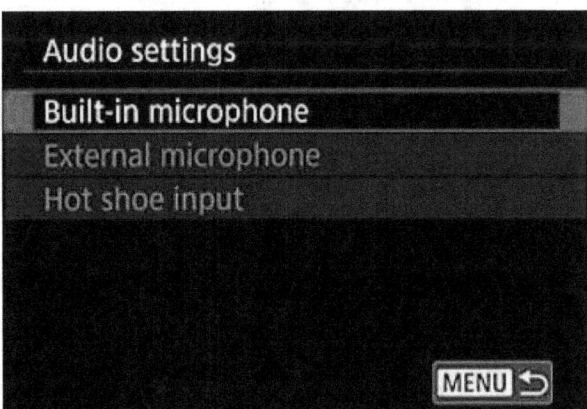

- **Built-in microphone.**

To configure the settings for the built-in microphone.

- **External microphone**.

Use the external microphone IN terminal to set up settings for external mics.

- **Hot shoe input.**

To configure settings for microphones developed for a multi-purpose shoe.

Recording Level

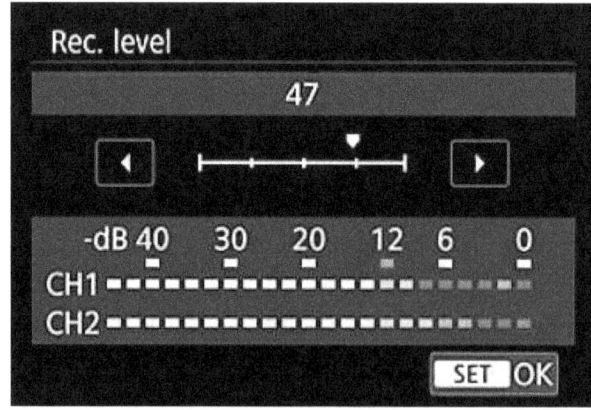

It can be used when the recording mode is set to **Manual**.

Keep an eye on the level meter as you turn the dial to change the recording level. Check the peak hold indicator and make changes so that the level meter sometimes lights up to the right of the **12** (-12 dB) point for the loudest sounds. Any value above "0" will affect the sound.

Wind Filter

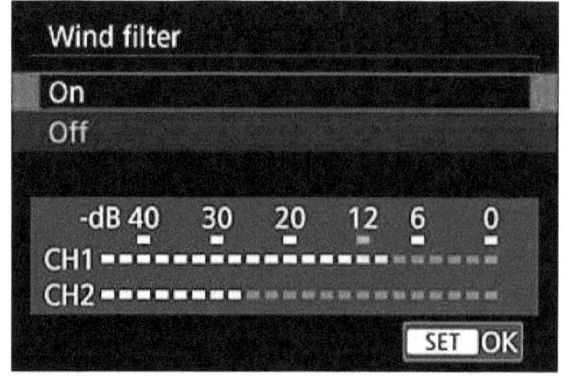

This feature is available when using the built-in microphone or shoe microphones with multiple functions that can work with wind screens.

If there is wind outside, set [Enable] to lower the wind noise. If you use the wind filter tool, some of the low bass sounds will be turned down.

Attenuator

When using mics made for multi-function shoes, the attenuator can be turned on or off. It gets rid of sound distortion caused by loud noises while recording. See the microphone's instruction book for more details.

Microphone Directionality

When using multi-function shoe mics with directional controls, this option is available. See the microphone's instruction book for more details.

Audio Status

Sets the audio status, like an active microphone and headphone volume.

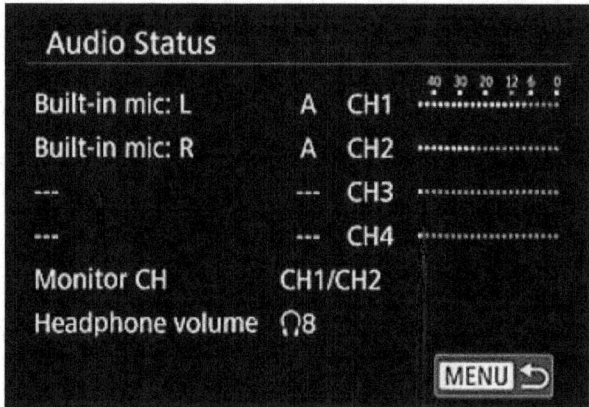

HDR Movie Mode

You can record high-dynamic-range movies that keep details even when the contrast is high.

Shadow Compensation

With Shadow Comp., you can make shadows and other dark parts of a picture brighter.

- On the next screen, pick a choice and see what the results will be.

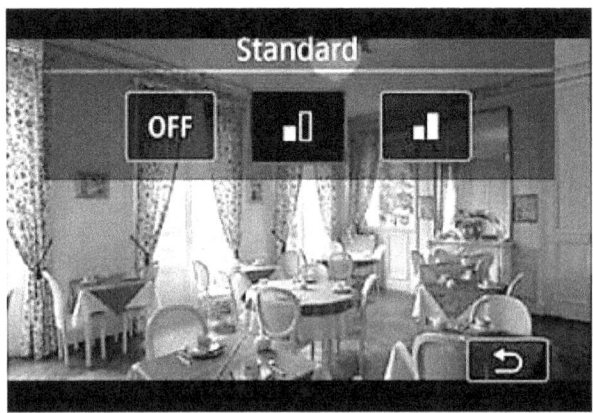

Saturation

You can change how intense a color is generally by changing the saturation.

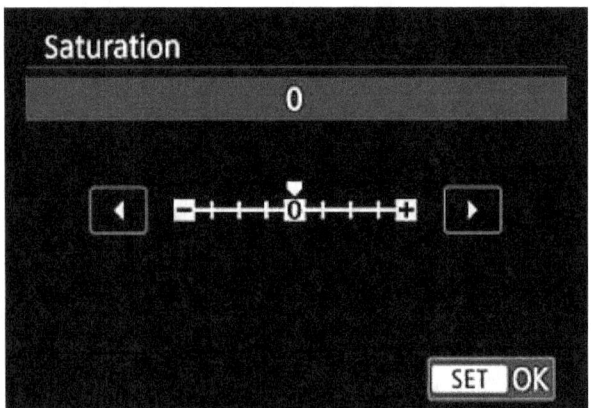

Limiting the Maximum Brightness.

When [🞄: HDR HDR shooting (PQ)] is set to [HDR PQ], this option is turned on.

- When you press [Disable], the highest brightness is not limited. It is suggested that you look at the picture on a computer that has a brightness level of more than 1000 nits.
- The brightest point at [1000 nits] is only about right. 1000 nits.

Time-lapse Movie

A flower bud slowly opening up to its full beauty is something that more than just wildlife photographers can capture with time-lapse photos. Time-lapse photography is becoming more and more popular, and an amazing number of movies and TV shows use it to show how time passes, whether it's the sun moving across the sky during the day or the seasons changing. Canon has given you the chance to try this approach on your own. I'm only going to go over the most important choices with you.

Time-lapse movie. To start the setting process, choose **Enable** or **Disable**.

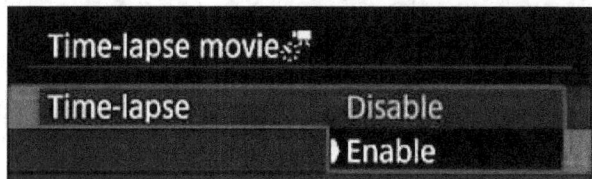

Interval. You can choose how long there should be between pictures. The maximum time is 99 hours, 59 minutes, and 59 seconds.

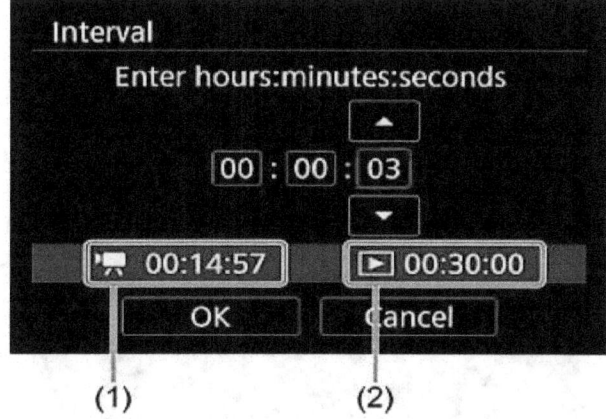

Number of shots. Pick the number of shots you need for the pattern. This number can be between 2 and 3,600. You can get a rough idea of how much time has passed since the beginning of the scene near the bottom of the screen. If the length of time the music is playing is highlighted in red, either the memory card doesn't have enough space or your choices will make the file bigger than 4 gigabytes if the card isn't formatted in exFAT.

If the playback time is highlighted in red, one of the situations below is true. As long as you don't format any SDXC cards before putting them in, the camera will do it for you. The weakness only affects SDHC cards and cards that haven't been formatted in the camera. The record will stop when the memory card is full or the largest file size is reached.

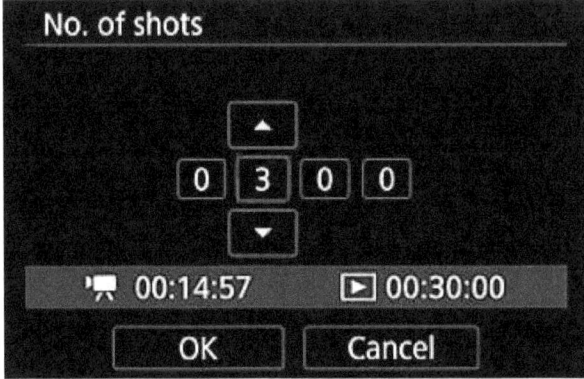

Movie Recording Size. The different movie recording sizes that are available are shown. These sizes are a mix of quality, frame rate, and compression. There are different choices based on the [Main rec. Setting for format.

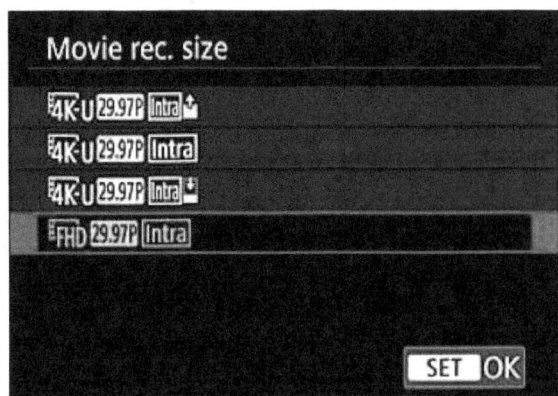

Select [Main Rec.]. Format].

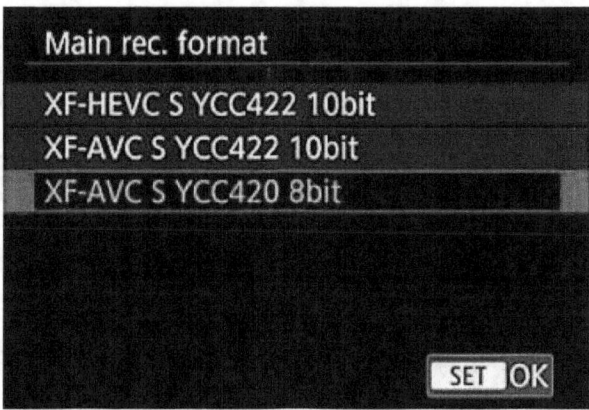

Auto-exposure setting. You can pick:

- **Fixed 1st Frame**. Once the measuring is done, the exposure for the first frame is set and will be used for all frames that follow. This is the mode to use when you want the exposure to stay the same outside, no matter what the light is like.
- **Each frame**. There is a different way to measure each shot in the set. A film that starts at sunrise and ends at dusk and shows the skyline of a city will have the right exposure for each time of day.

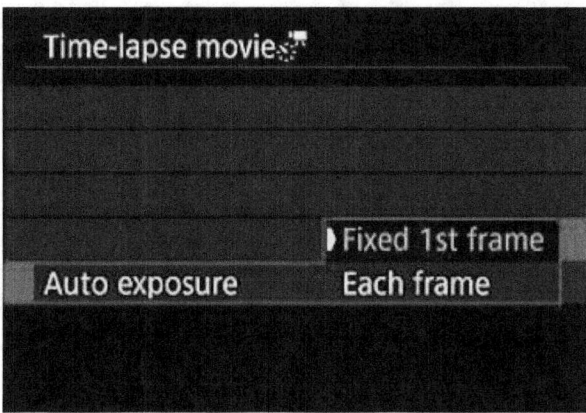

Screen Auto Off. It's going to take some scrolling to see this and the next message. If you choose **Enable**, the screen will go dark 10 seconds after you start shooting. This gives you time to check your exposure and frame before it goes dark on its own after 30 minutes. You can also choose "Disable" to have the screen turn off by itself after about 30 minutes.

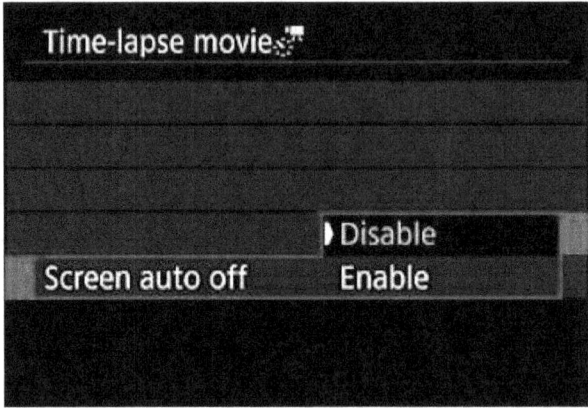

For every encounter, a beep will go off. Change whether the **Beep As Image Taken** feature sounds when an image is taken (the electronic shutter is quiet). You can change how loud the sound is.

Movie Self-timer

This feature is useful because it lets users slow down the start of the video record by two or ten seconds. For 10 seconds, you can choose to comb your hair. For 2 seconds, you can choose to be ready to go and not care about how you look. You have some time to be in front of the camera now.

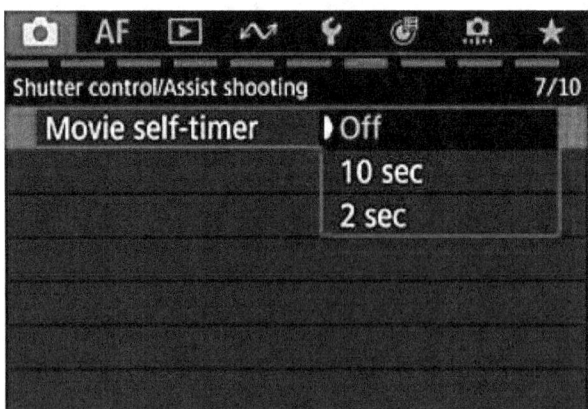

- It beeps and shows you how many seconds are left until recording when you press [●] or tap the video button.

Allow the camera some time to calm down after hitting the Movie button with your index finger. This can also be used if you don't have a remote release. This is helpful if you don't have a remote broadcast.

Some vloggers might not need it, but they could use this feature to record something on the spot. This is because vloggers who are serious about their job enough to use an R5 MARK II instead of a smartphone are probably also good at editing tools that can get rid of the silly sloppiness with which the scene is put together.

Tally Lamp

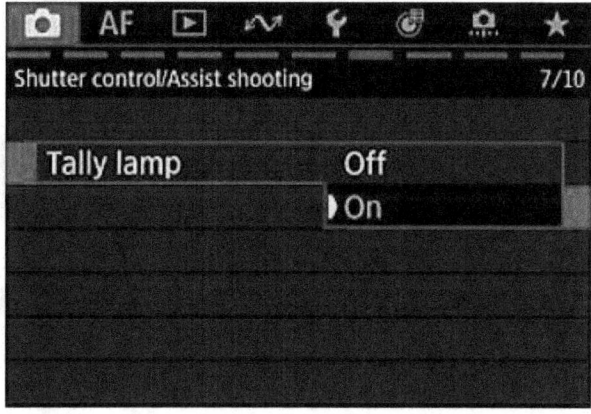

When it is set to [On], this is how the tally lamp blinks or lights up.

Lit	Movie recording in progress
Blinking rapidly	• Cannot record movies, due to a low battery level or insufficient card free space • High internal camera temperature, due to hot shooting conditions or extended movie recording
Blinking slowly	Movie recording is now possible for up to 6 min.

Pre-recording Settings

With pre-recording, you can set your camera to start recording movies at a certain time before you do it yourself.

The name for this first recording is **pre-recording**. The camera takes a pre-roll automatically when it is in standby mode for recording a movie.

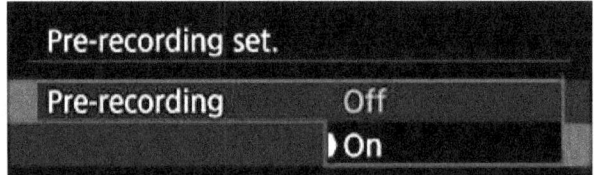

- Press [on].

Select [Recording time]

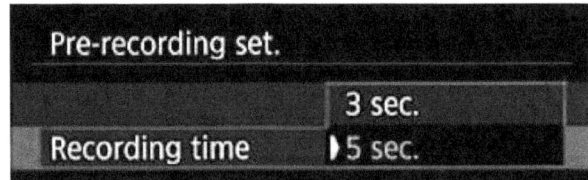

- Choose how long the pre-recording will last before manual recording starts.

Record the Movie.

- Record the movie the same way you would any other movie.
- The pre-recorded part is added to movies while they are being filmed.

IS (Image Stabilizer Mode)

Thanks to the IS mode and movie digital IS features of the camera, shaking is very little when recording.

They can stabilize well even when lenses that aren't IS are used.

When the Image Stabilizer switch on an IS lens is turned on, the stabilizing of both the lens and the camera work together.

Use this feature along with the optical image stabilization that comes with your lenses. If IS is turned off, the camera will tell you to turn it on. When optical and digital image stabilization are combined, Canon makes a system they call **combination IS**. The company also puts out a list of lenses that work with this system. The movie IS shouldn't be used with fisheye, tilt/shift (TS-E), or third-party lenses. It also shouldn't be used with lenses that have a focal length of more than 800 millimeters.

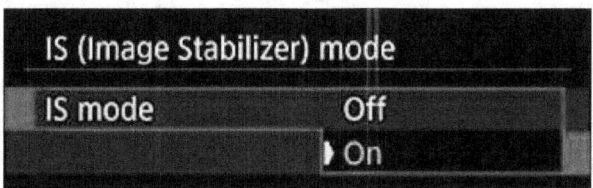

You can do any of the following:

- **IS Mode (On, Off).** This choice will only show up if your lens doesn't have an image stabilization built in. With this button, you can turn the camera's in-body image stabilization on or off. While the camera is on a tripod, you might want to turn it off because the R5 MARK II can still make changes you don't want even when the camera is on a tripod. You should keep using the IBIS even when you're using a small device.
- **Movie Digital IS (Off, On, Enhanced).** This choice is the only one you have if your lens has an image stabilization system built in. You can use it even if your lens doesn't have one.

    - **On**. It will be cropped a little and there will be a lot of motion correction, which will make it look like the picture is bigger than it is. When you use wide-angle glasses with this setting, you get the best results.
    - **Enhanced**. Along with a small increase in size, the camera shake that was already there will be further fixed. You shouldn't do this unless you have no other choice because the noise level might go up and the picture might get fuzzy while you watch it.

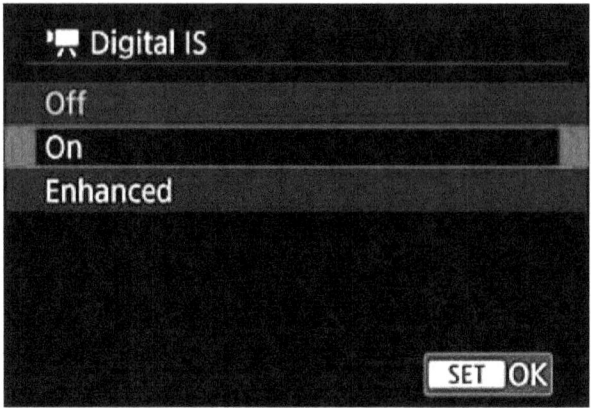

False Color Settings

This is a well-made artwork. You might remember using flashing **blinkies** with older cameras to find underexposed parts of a picture. This works similarly. This setup works a lot like Zebra Settings. Cinematographers have been using false color screens for a long time to check exposure, but this feature may be new to people who are just starting to play around with video.

False color turns different levels of exposure into colors that you can use to get a general idea of which parts of your subjects are too or too little exposed. This has taken the place of the usual black moving lights that you are used to seeing.

When you use False Color, a lot of other exposure features stop working. These include the Zebra display, Auto Lighting Optimizer, and View Assist for Canon Log. False color also changes the color temperature of the picture. You also won't be able to use the manual focus Peaking tool or make time-lapse videos because their colors would clash with the fake color.

False Color Display

The pictures in the viewfinder and on the camera screen are shown in a fake color. [fake color index] also has information about the fake color display.

Color	Meaning
Red	White clipping
Yellow	Just below white clipping
Pink	One stop over 18% gray
Green	18% gray
Blue	Just above black clipping
Purple	Black clipping
Neutral color	Brightness other than above

Zebra Settings

If the highlights in your shot are brighter than the setting you choose from this menu, this feature will let you know. Something like the flashing **blinkies** that digital cameras have been using for a while to let us know after the fact when parts of the picture we just took are blurry. We are taught these things to help us become better photographers.

To use Zebra pattern warnings, go to this menu item, pick the pattern you want, and then enter an IRE brightness number, which could be anywhere from 5 to 100 depending on the pattern you picked. You can change the brightness in your camera's settings to make the highlights less bright after you see the picture on the screen.

Zebra 1 level

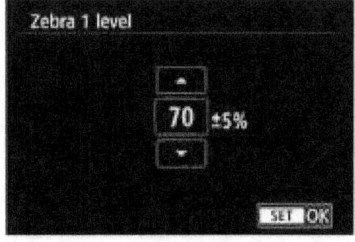

Zebra 2 level

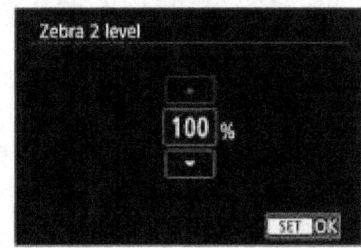

Shooting Information Display

It is possible to change both the details and displays of the information that shows up on the screen or in the viewfinder while a video is being taken.

Standby: Low Resolution

This choice could be thought of as a mode that saves power and keeps the device from getting too hot. Both the sensor and the memory card storage on the R5 MARK II are always on, whether you are previewing video or taking it.

Also, the focusing, exposure metering, and other features are working very hard. Quite a bit of heat can be made when a 4K video is taken and sent at very fast speeds.

This setting helps keep the camera from getting too hot and possibly damaging the sensor when it's not being used by showing the preview picture at a lower quality and refresh rate.

Also, it saves power and could let you shoot for longer, especially if you leave the camera on but in sleep mode for a long time. Even though there is a clear difference between the preview and the recorded video, the picture quality is not nearly as important when the device is in sleep mode.

You won't be able to use this setting when the Pre-Recording mode is on or when Digital Zoom is on. You can change the setting from "On" to "Off" if you don't care about the device getting too hot. The two biggest changes are that it responds faster when you start taking it again and the standby screen looks better.

Canon Log HDMI Output Range

You can choose the output range of the video data when you use an HDMI connection.

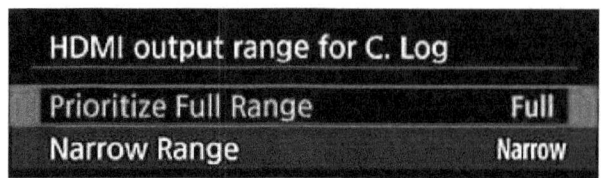

- **Prioritize Full Range**

Full-range audio is used whenever it is possible. Remember that the output range will change itself to fit the needs of the monitor.

- **Narrow Range**

A narrow range of output, or video range, is used.

Time Code

Professional producers find that the time codes that are built into video files and work with SMPTE (Society of Motion Picture and Television Engineers) are useful for editing. In simpler terms, we could say that the time system gives exact hour, minute, second, and frame markers that make it possible to find and sync audio frames.

You may remember that a 30-frame-per-second record gives you 29.97 real frames per second, while a 24-frame-per-second setting gives you 23.976 fps. Dropping frames are part of the time coding method that makes sure the recorded video's fractional frame rate can be matched in real-time.

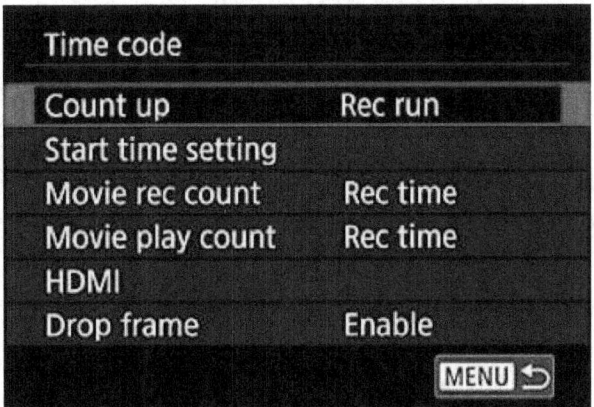

Count Up. You can choose between Rec Run and Free Run, also called Time of Day. In Rec Run, the time code will only go up when you are recording a video. In Free Run, the time code will go up whether you are taking clips or not. This is useful for putting together video clips that were taken at the same event by different cameras.

Free Run lets users change the way their recorded movies look to make it look like they were all taken at the same time, even if the cams were set to record at different times. If you choose Free Run, the time code will stay in the video file no matter how much you change it (except for HFR parts).

Start Time Setting. When the camera first starts to shoot, the frames are set to 0:00, and the hours, minutes, and seconds are found by its internal clock. This is where you can enter the hour, minute, and second frame by hand, or you can set the start time to 00:00:00:00.

Movie Rec. Count. This menu item lets you record video and have the LCD show the Time Code or the amount of time that has passed for the current clip.

Movie Play Count. While the video is playing, you can use the same controls to switch between the Time Code and actual time.

HDMI. If you want to add the time code to the video output, select **Enable**. If you don't want it to be added, select Disable. When the Record Command output is turned on, users can sync the camera's Stop/Start action with an external recording device. When this setting is turned off, the external recording device that is connected decides when the recording starts and stops.

Drop Frame. When you set the frame rate to 30, for example, you get 29.97 actual fps. When you set the frame rate to 60, you get 59.95 actual fps. And when you set the frame rate to HFR, you get 119.9 actual fps. If you choose "Enable," the camera will skip over some time code bits every so often in drop-frame mode to reduce the difference. You can see a change of a few seconds an hour after the feature was taken away.

Other Menu Functions

HDMI Display

If you want to show your output on the recorder or monitor that is linked to the device you are sending the video to, you can. You can also show it on the camera and the device you are sending the video to.

Camera+External. There is a link between the camera and the second device, and both are showing the video at the same time. When the camera is in this mode, you won't be able to record anything on the memory card. HDMI only shows the video itself, with no information on top of it. It can be used for both playing and menus. The screen of the camera shows the video that is being recorded along with any information inserts that can be seen by pressing the **INFO** button. The camera does not show the settings or playback options.

Even if the two devices are far apart and only linked by a long cable, you might want to use this mode so that you can watch the video on both the HDMI device and the camera.

External Only. At this point, the video, data, menus, and playback pictures are only shown on the external device. The camera does not yet show any of these things.

HDMI RAW Output

If you set it to **On**, you can send RAW movies to compatible devices over HDMI at up to 8K quality.

As soon as recording starts, movies are also saved to card 2 in XF-AVC format if it is in the camera.

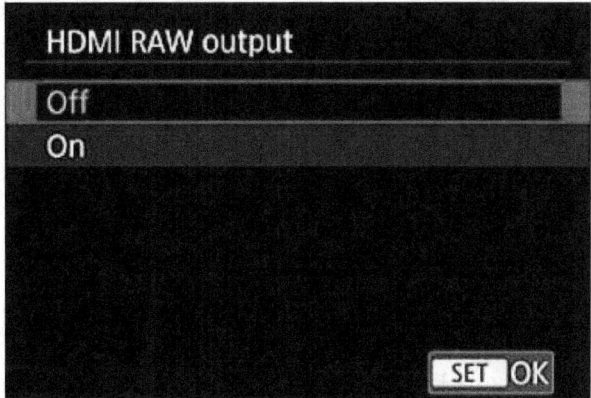

If you turn [Rec Command] to [On], you can only record with external recorders when card 2 is not connected.

Manual Exposure Settings for Video

The camera gives users more control over the picture it records when they record video because it has several brightness settings that can be changed. We are going to talk in-depth about the Canon EOS R5 Mark II's manual video brightness settings.

1. **Aperture**

When you shoot video in custom exposure mode, the aperture is one of the most important settings to change. Through the aperture setting, you can change how much light comes into the camera and how much detail you can record. When the f-number goes down, the aperture gets bigger, which makes the depth of field smaller. This small depth of field can help you focus on one subject and give your photos a movie-like look.

For landscapes or other situations where you want the whole picture to be in fine focus, an aperture with a higher f-number and a smaller diameter will give you a deeper depth of field.

2. **Shutter Speed**

Another important thing to change when taking video in manual exposure mode is the shutter speed. The shutter speed of a camera lets you change the amount of time that light hits its sensor. Motion blur can be created by slowing down the shutter speed, which helps capture movement or take pictures in low light. If you want to take pictures of action scenes or things with a lot of detail, you can stop motion by setting the shutter speed faster.

3. **ISO**

The ISO setting tells the camera how sensitive it is to changes in light. If you choose a higher ISO setting, you can take pictures when there is very little light, but the pictures will have more digital noise. A lower ISO setting will give you a clearer picture, but you might not want to use it when there isn't much light. To get the right exposure, you need to find a mix between the ISO, aperture, and shutter speed settings.

4. **Exposure Compensation**

One way to change the exposure settings in manual mode is to use exposure adjustment. This feature can be very helpful if you want to change the brightness or darkness of a picture without changing the ISO, shutter speed, or aperture. For every stop of exposure adjustments, four or six times as much light can enter the camera. To figure out exposure compensation, stops are used.

5. **Manual Focus**

The Canon EOS R5 Mark II has manual focus settings that let users change the lens's focus by hand. If you want to record in low light or get a certain depth of field, this can be a very helpful tool. Focus peaking is another camera feature that makes it easier to get the focus exactly where you want it by drawing attention to the parts of the picture that are in focus.

6. **Zebra Pattern**

With its diagonal stripes, the zebra pattern draws attention to parts of the picture that are too bright. This might help you find parts of the picture that are too bright, so you can change the brightness settings to make the picture better after you've found those parts. Based on your needs, the zebra's shape can be changed to show different levels of exposure.

7. **Histogram**

A histogram is a type of graph that shows how different amounts of brightness are spread out in an image. It might be easier to see which parts of the picture are too bright or too dark this way, so you can change the brightness settings to get the result you want. When changing the histogram to show different amounts of brightness, the user's needs can be taken into account.

8. **Peaking**

The peaking function can be used to make the edges of an image stand out by using a color that is different from the rest of the image. This feature makes it easy to find the center of attention in a picture. If you want to record in low light or get a certain depth of field, this can be a very helpful tool. You can change the peaking to show different colors and levels of awareness to suit your tastes.

Movie Playback and Editing

1. **Movie Playback Modes**

When people use the Canon EOS R5 Mark II, they can play back their videos in several different ways. Users can play back their movie normally, or they can choose to see it in slow motion, fast motion, or image by image. The camera also has a function called **loop playback** that lets you watch a certain part of the video over and over again.

2. **Movie Editing**

The Canon EOS R5 Mark II has several editing tools that can be used to cut, split, and mix movie videos. Users can also choose to automatically or manually take still shots from their videos. Users can also record short movies with the camera's video clip mode and then put them all together to make a longer movie.

3. **In-Camera Raw Processing**

In-camera raw editing on the Canon EOS R5 Mark II lets users change their raw footage right on the camera. Users can change things like exposure, white balance, contrast, and more. They can also add creative filters and effects. This feature will be especially helpful for people who want to quickly look at and change their film while they're on the go.

4. **HDMI Output**

The Canon EOS R5 Mark II has an HDMI output that can be used to connect to an external display or recorder for better viewing and editing. The camera can make 10-bit 4:2:2 video in both Canon Log and HDR PQ modes to give post-production professionals more choices and control.

5. **Wi-Fi and Bluetooth Connectivity**

With the built-in Wi-Fi and Bluetooth, the Canon EOS R5 Mark II, users can send their video clips to a computer or smartphone to edit and share. The camera can also be controlled from a tablet or smartphone, which lets people change settings and record movies without having to move their bodies.

6. Canon Image Transfer Utility

Anyone can use the free Canon Image Transfer Utility to move video footage from the Canon EOS R5 Mark II to a computer so that it can be edited and saved. The program lets you edit and organize videos in different ways, and it also lets you export them in several different forms.

7. Canon Digital Photo Professional

Canon Digital Photo Professional is a free tool that lets you work with and change Canon camera raw video. The app lets you change photos in some ways, like by adding creative filters and effects and changing the color, exposure, and white balance. The app also lets users export movies in different formats that can be used with other editing programs.

8. Third-Party Editing Software

Editors like Canon Digital Photo Professional, but many people still prefer to use third-party programs like Adobe Premiere Pro or Final Cut Pro X because they give editors more freedom and control, as well as a wider range of cutting-edge features and effects.

Chapter 7

The Photo Shooting Menu

The Photo Shooting Menu is an important part of the Canon EOS R5 Mark II's settings that lets you change many things about how pictures are taken. This part will talk about some of the most important settings from the Photo Shooting Menu and how they affect your pictures.

Image Quality

Image Quality is the first choice in the photo shooting menu. This lets you choose the format in which your photos will be stored. You can pick to shoot in JPEG, RAW, or both. RAW files have all the information that the camera's sensor has picked up, which means you have more editing options after the fact. JPEG files, on the other hand, are compressed, so they take up less room on your memory card.

Picture Size

Another important choice in the Photo Shooting Menu is Picture Size, which lets you change the photograph's resolution. For the Canon EOS R5 Mark II, there are different sizes, from tiny to big. Bigger photos have more details and might be better for printing, but smaller photos are better for sharing online because they take up less room.

Picture Style

With the Picture Style function, you can change your photos' color and contrast to a set of pre-defined choices. As well as Standard, Portrait, Landscape, Neutral, and Faithful, Canon has a few more choices. You can also make and save your Picture Style, which lets you give your photos the look you want.

White Balance

With the white balance choice, you can change your photos' color temperature to make them look more natural and real. You can set Canon's white balance to Auto, Daylight,

Shade, Cloudy, Tungsten, Fluorescent, or Flash. It's also possible to set a custom white balance based on the lighting where you're taking.

Auto Lighting Optimizer

When there is a lot of contrast in a scene, the Auto Lighting Optimizer tool changes the exposure and contrast of your photos instantly. This could be helpful when the camera's metering system is having trouble taking a picture with the right exposure.

High ISO NR

When you shoot at a high ISO setting, the High ISO NR (Noise Reduction) choice changes how the camera handles noise reduction. There may be times when this is especially helpful in dark places where noise pollution is a problem.

Lens Aberration Correction

When you choose the Lens Aberration Correction option, your photos will instantly fix lens distortion, chromatic aberration, and peripheral illumination. This option can make the picture better overall and cut down on the number of changes that need to be made after the fact.

Long Exposure Noise Reduction

The Long Exposure Noise Reduction choice can help you get rid of noise in your photos when you use a long exposure. There are times when you might need to use a slow picture speed to get a certain look.

High ISO Speed Noise Reduction

If you shoot at a high ISO and use the High ISO Speed Noise Reduction setting, your pictures will have less noise. If you need to raise the ISO to get a well-exposed picture in low light, this setting might come in handy.

Multiple Exposure

With the Multiple Exposure preset, you can merge two or more shots into one in the camera. People with this skill can make original, one-of-a-kind pictures that would be hard to make in a single shot.

HDR Mode

Multiple exposures can be put together to make a single picture with a wider dynamic range using the HDR (High Dynamic Range) Mode setting. This could be useful if you need to write down information from parts of a picture that are in dark or bright light.

Interval Timer

You can take a series of pictures at set times if you choose the interval timer choice. With this feature, you can record time-lapse videos or gather a group of pictures that can be processed further.

Time-Lapse Movie

You can make time-lapse movies right from the camera using the Time-Lapse Movie function. This tool is a creative and fun way to keep track of time.

Image Quality

This is the first option in the Shooting 1 menu. You are in charge of all the settings that determine the picture quality used when saving files. When you choose a quality setting, you can pick from the following options:

Resolution. The exact quality of the photos you take is found by adding up all the pixels in a picture. Medium has 3984 2656 pixels, which is 11MP; Large/RAW/C-RAW has 6000 4000 pixels, which is 24MP; Small 1 has 2976 1984 pixels, which is 5.9MP; Small 2 has 2400 1600 pixels, which is 3.8MP; and so on.

HEIF/JPEG compression. The camera uses picture compression to make the photo files you take smaller so that you can store more of them on the memory card. When you scale down the source images, you get smaller photo sizes. You can choose between Fine and Normal compression, but the picture quality may be worse with Normal compression. You will be able to choose between the two, though.

You can remember that the icons will help you remember that the Fine compression level makes the smoothest images and the Normal compression level makes the jaggier images. Indicators that look like quarter-circles show a Fine compression level, while indicators that look like stairs show a Normal compression level. The Small 2 (S2) file choice has a Fine quality, but there is no sign to show which quality was chosen.

JPEG/HEIF, RAW, or both. You don't have to store your pictures as uncompressed, lossless RAW files. You can store them as JPEG or HEIF files instead, which will take up about half of your memory card's space. You can store your pictures with either option. You can also choose to record and save both audio and video at the same time. A lot of photographers choose to keep both a RAW file and a JPEG picture. This lets users save both the original digital negative RAW file and a JPEG or HEIF version that might work just fine. This way, they can store both in case they want to work on the picture later.

This is because JPEGs and HEIFs are lossy formats, while RAW files are not. This makes it much easier to read and work with pictures saved in those formats. If the file has both a JPG extension (which means the picture was taken with a Canon camera) and a CR3 extension (which means the picture is a Canon RAW file), two copies of the same picture will be made.

Open the settings, pick Image Quality, and then press the SET button to pick the amount that works best for you. After that, the screen will show a choice screen with two rows of items that look a lot like the image below. (If you chose HDR recording in the Shooting 2 menu, HEIF will appear at the bottom of the list instead of JPEG.)

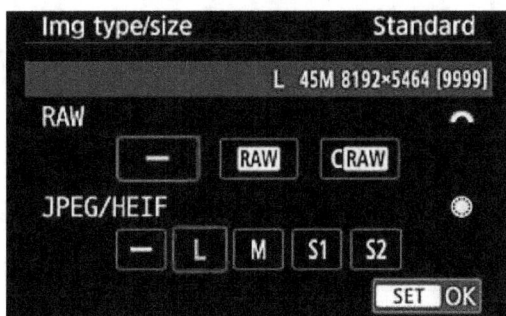

By turning the Main dial, you can now choose (no RAW), RAW, or C RAW from the choices that appear. To choose between JPEG and HEIF, all you have to do is spin the QCD-1 in the way you want. — (no JPEG or HEIF), at the sizes already mentioned: Large, Medium, or Small with Fine or Normal compression (shown by smooth and stepped icons), as well as Small 2 (with Fine compression). A red circle is around the choice that is currently being chosen. In this case, JPEG/HEIF Fine will be the output file if you pick both RAW and JPEG/HEIF. It is always necessary for you to pick an option and then press the SET button to confirm your pick.

Cropping/Aspect Ratio

You can crop out parts of photos right in the camera on your device. If you want to record high-definition or ultra-high-definition video frames, you can pick an aspect ratio of 1:1 (square), 4:3, or 16:9. You could also use a 1.6X APS-C crop with a 3:2 crop ratio that works with the full setting. The frame of the sensor is 36 mm x 24 mm. It's also possible to choose to see the shooting area inside the picture. You can choose to hide it so that only the current crop or aspect ratio can be seen, or you can use blue lines to outline it.

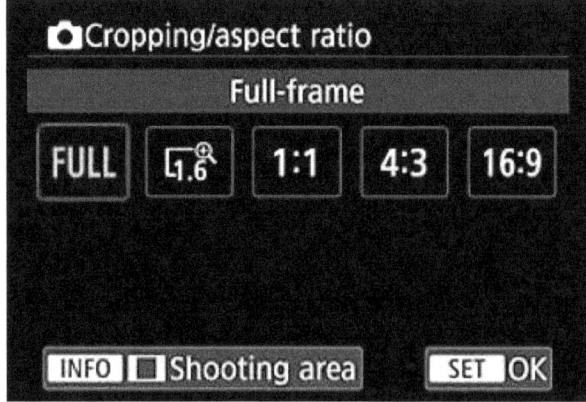

The R5 Mark II needs the 1.6x crop factor so it can work with APS-C format RF-S lenses and, with an EF/EF-S mount adapter, APS-C format EF-S lenses. Both of these abilities are made possible by the 1.6x crop factor. You can make RF and EF lenses reach farther by using the 1.6X crop choice. This will make a photo that is 3744 by 2496 pixels and 9.3 megapixels. If you are using an RF-S or EF-S lens, the 1.6X crop will be picked for you automatically. You won't be able to choose from the other aspect ratios.

Since the aspect ratio of an APS-C image is the same as that of a full-frame image, if you have an RF-S or EF-S lens installed or choose the 1.6X crop, the picture will be blown up so that the reduced area fills the screen. There is a 1.6X sign inside the frame. You can change the aspect ratio by pressing the **INFO** button and selecting Masked or Outlined for the Shooting Area display.

When covered, the screen only shows the part of the picture that was taken. When outline mode is used, the whole frame is shown along with a blue line that marks the area where the picture was taken. Choose **Outlined** if you want to be able to see parts of your subject that aren't in the area that the camera is recording.

When the RAW image is played back, lines will show up in the limited area, and when a slide show is shown, only that area will be seen. If you choose a certain crop when shooting in RAW format, the picture will be saved at its highest quality of 6000 400 pixels. When you play back the RAW picture, however, lines will show you where the cropped image is.

Expo.comp./AEB: 0 –

This is how exposure bracketing or exposure adjustments are set up. Since the big rotary dial on the back of the camera can do the same thing much faster, I wouldn't bother going through the settings to change the exposure compensation.

ISO speed settings

- **ISO speed**: The Auto ISO function is my favorite because it nicely adjusts my shutter speed for different lighting situations.
- **ISO speed range**: When you change the ISO, the ISO speed range of 100 to H changes what you can see. I left the ISO setting at 100-H because I wanted to retain the whole range.
- **Auto range**: 100–12800—this feature is very useful when shooting with the Auto ISO setting. I normally only set the EOS R5 II's highest range to ISO 12800 because I don't like the noise levels above that point.
- **Min. shutter spd**: Auto: If you set this to Auto, the camera will change the shutter speed to match the reciprocal rule. This might be enough to keep your hands steady and your stance straight. But if you have shaky hands, the Auto setting

might not be enough to keep the camera from moving. Moving the slider under Auto to the right toward Faster on the top dial will double the shutter speed setting. If your shots are blurry, this will fix the problem.

Anti-Flicker Shooting

A lot of amateur sports photographers ask me why some stadiums or gyms they shoot in have banding, uneven exposure, or color changes that are very noticeable. The light at the place could be the cause of these issues. This effect can be explained by the fact that some types of artificial lights blink in a way that we can't see but that a camera can record. When this setting is turned on, the camera will measure how often the light source flickers (it works best for 100 to 120 cycles per second). The camera takes the picture at that exact moment when the flashing doesn't hurt the quality of the picture the most. It can't be used to record movies or watch them live.

Anti-flicker shoot: Disable

For taking pictures of sports or other events in artificial light, this is a great feature that can help you get pictures that are properly exposed from top to bottom. Inside, it can be hard to take shots. Once you turn this setting on, the camera will delay the shutter to match the frequency of the light.

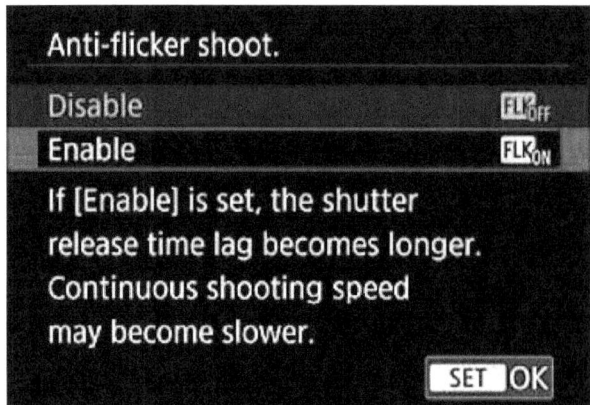

You may notice a small delay in the shutter release as the camera waits for the right moment. This can make it take longer to keep shooting. But you have to use this setting if you want to record sports or other events with a lot of movement because it lets you catch those fleeting moments that you would miss otherwise. If you shoot in P or Av mode, the shutter speed may change between shots to make sure you get the right exposure. Because of this, it can lead to different results. If you want to keep the shutter speed the same, you should use either the TV or M mode.

After this feature has been turned on, you can manually find flicker by pressing the **INFO** button, then pressing the Q button and selecting Anti-Flicker Shooting from the Quick Control menu. Because of this, you will be able to find flicker by hand. It will let you know if the camera has seen the flash or not.

Anti-Flicker is turned off when using Basic Zone modes, and it probably won't work as well when shooting in other situations, like when using wireless flash in a room with a dark background or a lot of light. Canon recommends that you take a few test photo graphs to see if the feature works properly in the given lighting conditions.

High-Frequency Anti-Flicker Shooting

You have never noticed it because you have spent your whole life getting used to the bright, flashing lights of modern society. In 60 Hertz (Hz) circuits, old incandescent lights flash at a rate of 100 to 120 cycles per second, but the amount of light they give off only changes by about 10 percent. Most of the time, it won't be enough to bother you or get in the way of your photos.

The Anti-Flicker Shooting entry does a good job with other types of artificial lighting, even ones with enough intensity change to cause banding. But some newer lighting technologies, like better LED bulbs, can flicker at much higher rates and lower intensities, which means they need more complex ways to fix.

By carefully changing the shutter speed to match the cycle of the flickering light sources, this feature can lessen or get rid of the banding effects that come from them. You can do two things. Just do what's written below:

If you take photos with high-frequency light sources that flicker, the pictures might have banding. High-frequency anti-flicker shooting helps make flickering less noticeable in your photos by letting you take pictures at shutter speeds that are right for high-frequency flickering.

Recommended Tv Setting

The camera shows the right shutter speed for shooting in high-frequency flickering light sources. It can pick up light sources that are flickering between 50 and 8193.7 Hz. Then you can use the camera speed that was given to you.

1. **Choose the shutter speed you want.**

Pick the shutter speed you want to use. It will pick a shutter speed that works well with light sources that flicker at a high frequency that is close to this number.

2. **Click on [Recommend TV set].** After that, click OK.

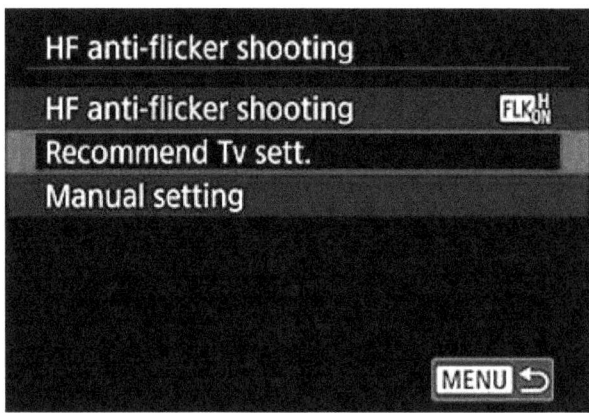

3. Change the shutter speed to the one that's given.

    o Press [Yes] to change to the shutter speed that was given.
    o The [Manual setup] screen will show up when you choose [Yes (go to TV settings)].

For Manual Setting:

1. **Select the Shooting mode.** The Mode dial can be set to either M or Tv, which are two camera speeds that you can choose for your picture.
2. **Pick the shutter speed.** Pick the shutter speed that works best for you.

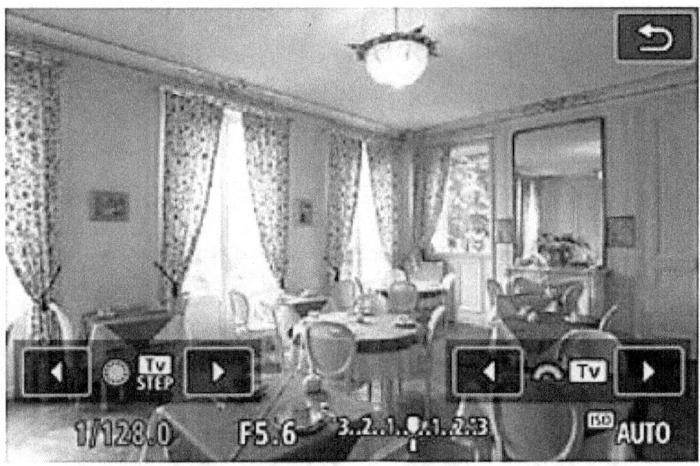

3. **Choose the manual setting.** The first setting that shows up on a setup screen will be the shutter speed which is closer to the speed you want the camera to work at. From 50 Hz to 2011 Hz is the frequency range that the camera can instantly pick up flickering.
4. **View scene.** In addition to looking at the scene as a whole, look at many different parts of the picture for bands.
5. **Adjust the shutter speed.** You can change the shutter speed until the visible banding goes away by turning the QCD-1 and Main dials at the same time.

   - **QCD-1.** This dial lets you choose the shutter speed that gives you the best results. The camera instantly finds the different shutter speeds. As you turn the dial counterclockwise, the shutter speed will try to go faster, going from 2X to 3X to 4X, and so on. If you turn the dial the other way, the shutter speed will slow down by 1/2X, 1/3X, 1/4X, and so on.
   - **Main dial.** As you slowly move the Main dial to the right or left to change the shutter speed, the bands in your picture will become less noticeable.

6. **If the banding remains.** You could use automatic detection or turn the camera around 90 degrees.

When this function is on, you can't switch from HDR Mode to Dynamic Range Mode. Canon says that to keep the same exposure, setting Custom Function 2: Same Exposure for new Aperture to ISO Speed.

This will make sure that the shutter speed doesn't change. When this function is used, the fastest flash sync speed that can be used is 1/181.0 seconds. The shutter speed stays the same when you use a manual safety shift; only the aperture changes.

Flash Function Settings

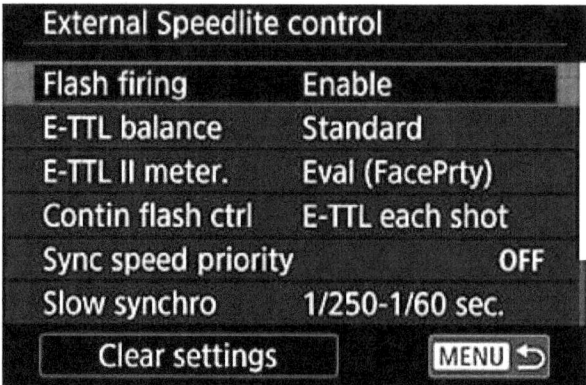

Flash Firing

With this feature, you can turn on or off the light flash that goes with it. Once you have connected the flash to the camera and turned it on, the Enable choice will make it work as it should. If you choose the Disable option, the device's AF-assist beam will still work properly, but the flash will not go off.

For those of you who like to take pictures in low light but still need the extra help that the flash's AF beam gives to autofocusing, the second choice might be worth considering.

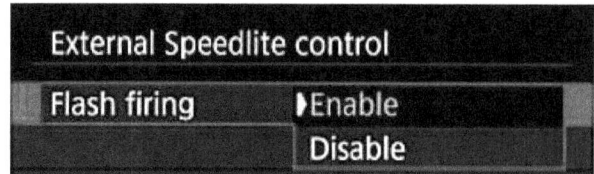

E-TTL Balance

This is an important feature that gives you even more control over how the flash and natural light work together to make the exposure. Standard is the default setting, but you can also choose another one. In this setting, the Speedlite and the existing light are both given the same amount of weight. If you choose the Ambience-priority mode, the flash will only be used as a fill light to lighten up the shadows. If you don't choose this mode, the flash will overpower any other light that is already there.

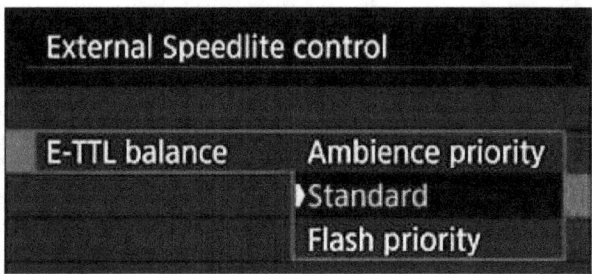

If you change the setting to Flash priority, the Speedlite will become the main light source and light up both the subject and the background of your picture. Low light might be best for this mode when there isn't much additional light around.

E-TTL II Metering

When you use the electronic flash exposure meter, you can pick between the Evaluative (Matrix) and Average metering modes. Evaluative is usually the best choice because it tries to figure out what kind of scene is being shot. Average, on the other hand, reads the whole scene to figure out flash exposure, so it can be a good choice if you want to figure out exposure for the whole scene.

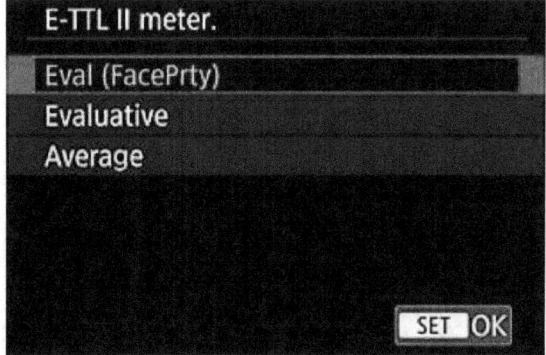

Evaluative (Face-priority) is another choice you have. This option sets the exposure based on the faces in the scene you can picture. Since this process takes a little longer, the constant shooting rates may be a little slower in this mode. That being said, the flash's recycle time is probably going to be the most important thing to think about when choosing a shot speed that lets you shoot continuously.

Continuous Flash Control

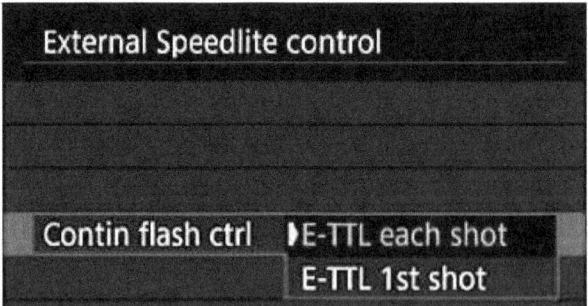

Using a Speedlight to take multiple pictures at once is also changed by this input. If you choose to use E-TTL Each Shot, the camera will check the scene's brightness right before it takes a set of shots. If you choose the E-TTL 1st shot over the other choices, the exposure you choose for the first picture will be used for all the pictures that come after it.

Use this setting when taking continuously at the fastest speed possible. Of course, it works best when you are not rearranging the photo between shots. If the subject moves, the best exposure might change, which means that the setting on the original picture could not have been right.

Sync Speed Priority

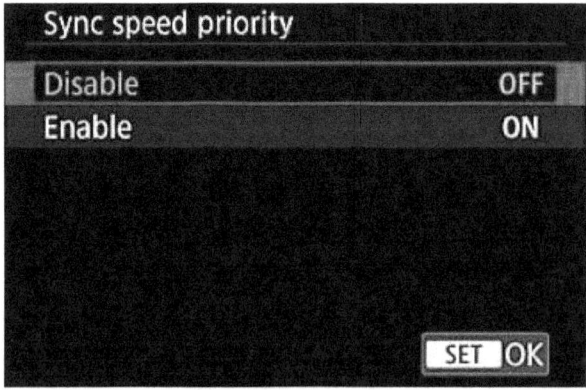

You can use a sync speed that is faster than normal when you use flash photography.

- In case E-TTL II flash metering is selected in Flash mode, accessible.

- When this feature is turned on, Flash sync rates can be different depending on how different camera settings are combined.

Camera Setting		Flash Sync Speed (Fastest)
Shutter mode	Cropping/aspect ratio	
Elec. 1st-curtain	FULL	1/320 sec.
	1.6x*	1/400 sec.
Electronic ES	FULL	1/200 sec.
	1.6x*	1/320 sec.

* Equivalent to APS-C size

Note

- Works with a Speedlite 580EX II or later when Manual flash is chosen in Flash mode.
- If the Flash mode is set to Manual flash and the fastest flash sync speed is used, flash units might not fire at the preset flash output level.
- Doesn't change anything in Mechanical shutter mode.
- The following Speedlites can use Sync speed priority.

   - Speedlite 430EX III, 470EX-AI, 600EX II-RT, EL-5, EL-10, 470EX-AI, and EL-1
   - Macro Ring Lite MR14-EX II / Macro Twin Lite MT-26EX-RT

- When Sync speed priority is set to Enable, there may be times when the picture isn't well exposed.
- If the receiver Speedlites are set to a positive exposure compensation value while shooting wirelessly via radio transmission, then Sync speed priority may not work to get the right exposure.

Slow Synchro

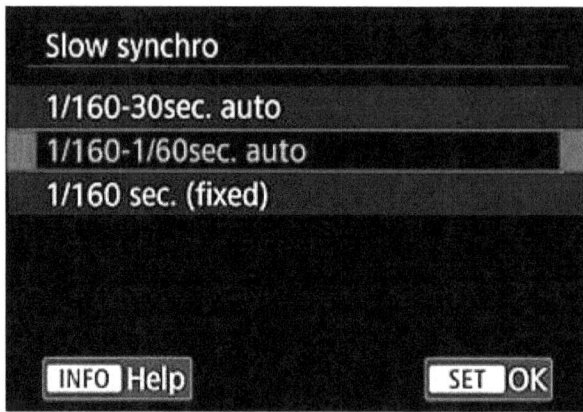

You can pick the speed at which the flash syncs up when the camera is in Av (Aperture-priority) or P (Program) exposure mode. You can do any of these three things:

- **1/*-30sec. auto**

The shutter speed is picked automatically from the following range to adjust for brightness. You can sync very quickly too.

Shutter mode	Cropping/aspect ratio	Shutter Speed
Mechanical	FULL	1/200–30 sec.
Mechanical	1.6×	1/250–30 sec.
Elec. 1st-curtain	FULL	1/250–30 sec.
Elec. 1st-curtain	1.6×	1/320–30 sec.
Electronic	FULL	1/160–30 sec.
Electronic	1.6×	1/250–30 sec.

- **1/*-1/60sec. auto**

This setting stops the camera from setting a slow shutter speed on its own when there isn't much light. Good at keeping the camera from shaking and blurring the subject. The flash's light usually hits the subject, but keep in mind that the background might be dark.

- **1/* sec. (fixed)**

The following shutter speed is constant, which stops blurred subjects and camera shake better than 1/*–1/60sec. auto. But when there isn't much light, the background of the image will look darker than it does in 1/*-1/60sec. auto.

Shutter mode	Cropping/aspect ratio	Shutter Speed
Mechanical	FULL	1/200 sec.
Mechanical	1.6*	1/250 sec.
Elec. 1st-curtain	FULL	1/250 sec.
Elec. 1st-curtain	1.6*	1/320 sec.
Electronic ES	FULL	1/160 sec.
Electronic ES	1.6*	1/250 sec.

Most of the time, you have to choose the f-stop that will be locked in when you use the flash and shoot in aperture-priority mode. The exposure is then changed by the camera by changing the power of the electronic flash. When the camera is in program mode, it sets the aperture number itself. Since the flash gives the primary exposure, the shutter speed has a bigger effect on the secondary exposure, which is based on how much diffuse light is still in the picture.

Flash Function Settings

What's on the screen, where it shows up, and the choices you can use depend on the Speedlite model, its Custom Function settings, the flash mode, and other factors.

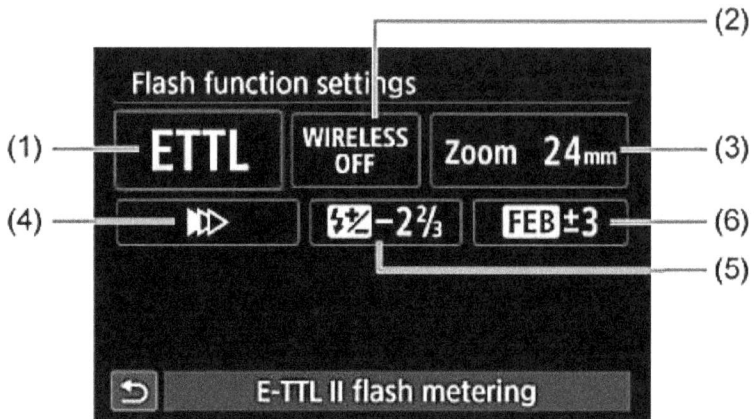

ETTL Flash mode. You can pick from different types of flash exposure, such as manual, multi-exposure (repeating), automatic (E-TTL II), and so on. The second choice saves battery life and lets you keep shooting with the flash on. The ISO speed and flash output are both sped up by one stop to make this happen.

Wireless functions. With radio or optical wireless sharing, you can use wireless multiple-flash illumination to take pictures.

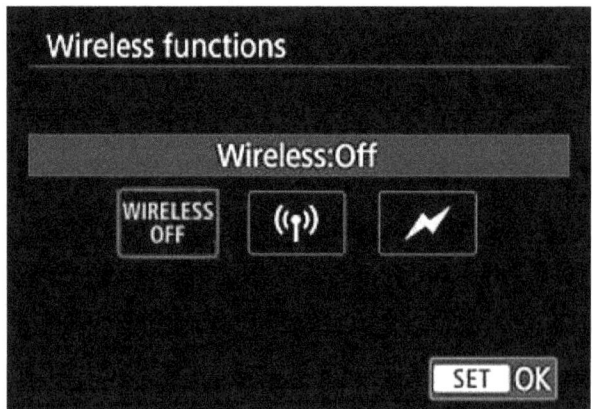

Zoom. You can choose a flash zoom headset to change the area that compatible Speedlites cover.

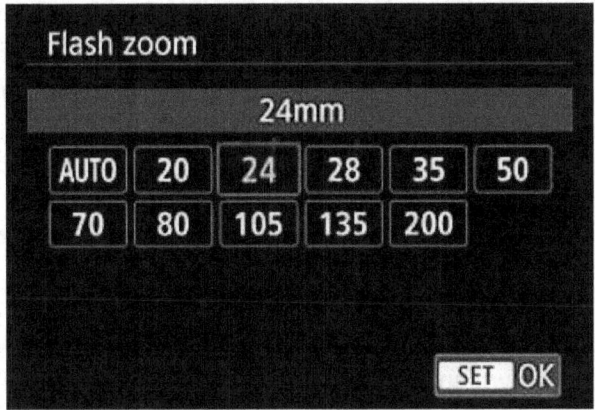

Shutter Sync

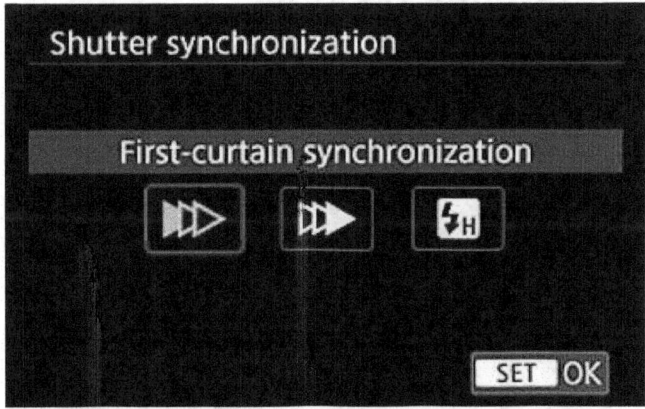

If you pick first-curtain sync, the pre-flash will fire. This sets the exposure right before the shutter opens. As soon as the shutter is fully open, the main flash will go off. When this setting is turned on, which is the default, the pre-flash, and the main flash will look like one burst. You can also use second-curtain sync, which makes the main flash fire in a second burst right at the end of the image, just before the shutter closes after the pre-flash has fired when the shutter opens.

This is done one step at a time. Sharp flash shots at the beginning and end of the exposure make it possible to take pictures of moving objects leaving behind a blurry trail of light. This type of flash exposure is very different from what some other cameras that use a second-curtain sync can do.

- This should be set to First-curtain synchronization by default. This will make the flash work as soon as you start shooting.
- Use slow shutter speeds and set the camera to Second-curtain synchronization to get motion trails that look like they were made by passing cars.
- By setting the shutter speed to High-speed synchronization, you can take flash shots at speeds faster than the fastest flash sync shutter speed. For example, this works well when shooting outside during the day in Av setting with a wide aperture to blur the background behind the subject.

If you use high-speed sync, which you can do through the External Flash Function Setting menu, you can use shutter speeds faster than 1/250th or 1/200th of a second. For this choice to work, you need to have an external Speedlite that is compatible and plugged in.

Flash Exposure Compensation.

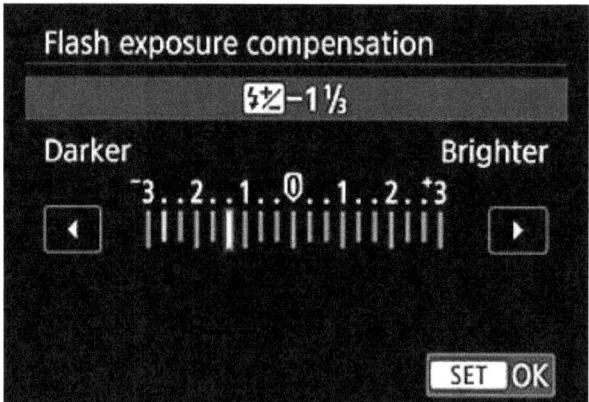

You can change the flash exposure through the menu instead of the ISO/Flash exposure adjustment button if you'd like to. This menu item will be used instead of the value shown by the button if you enter a value with both. To use this option, press the **SET** button to select it and then use the QCD-1 to set the flash EV correction to the right amount. Since it's shown as a blue light, you can quickly go back to the EV you had before you made the change. After making sure your change is correct by clicking **SET** again, you can leave the screen by pressing the screen again.

Flash Exposure Bracketing

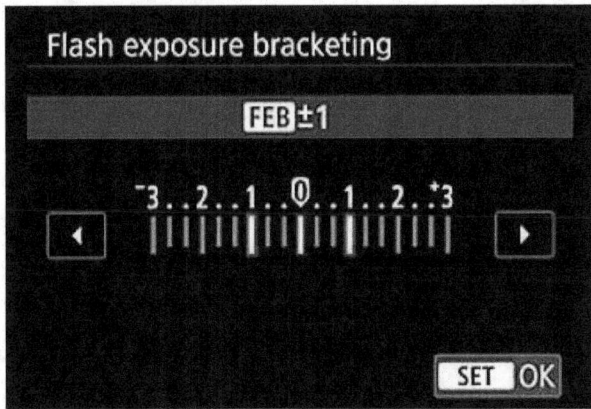

When you use bracketing with an electrical flash that works with your device, these choices will give you the freedom to change the output of your unit.

Flash Custom Function Settings

With many of Canon's external Speedlites, you can set them up to do specific things. These functions let the user set parameters like the flash metering mode and the flash bracketing sequences. They also have more advanced features like modeling light/flash (if available), using external power sources (if connected), and controlling the operations of any slave unit connected to the external flash.

This menu item lets you change the Custom Functions of an external flash unit from within your camera's menu. Based on the model, each flash unit will have certain powers. You can choose from more choices when you have high-end tools like the Speedlite 600EX-RT. Let's look at the Speedlite 320EX. It only has four Custom Functions: 1, Auto Power Off, 6, Quick Flash with Continuous Shot, 10, Slave Auto Power Off Timer, and 11, Slave Auto Power Off Cancel

Clear Settings

You can reset both your Custom Functions and your external flash to their original default settings with this item. This will undo any changes you may have made to those settings. This doesn't work for the C.Fn-00 Distance Indicator Display (if your flash supports it). This number won't change from how it is set up until you change it yourself. To change or restart the Personal Functions (P.Fn) of a flash, you must use the Speedlite's settings. You cannot do this from the camera.

Metering Mode

This item merely provides a menu-based approach to selecting the appropriate metering mode. You can send this function to a user-defined key if you'd rather access it differently. This is because it is mostly stored here.

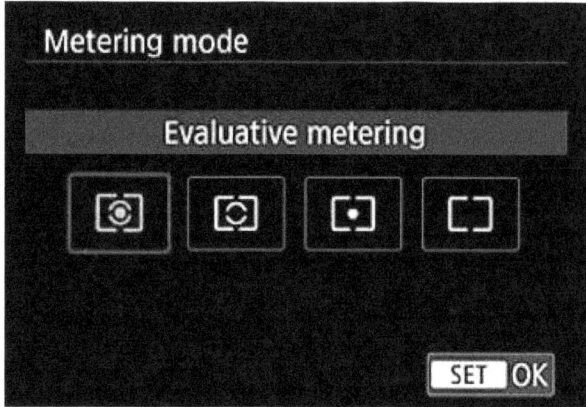

Evaluative Metering

What it Does:

By default, evaluative metering is the camera's main metering mode. It looks at the subject, the background, and the whole scene, and then changes the exposure instantly. It works great in a lot of different situations, even when there is glare or uneven lighting.

When to Use It:

Evaluative metering works well for everyday photos and a wide range of lighting conditions. The camera intelligently chooses the exposure based on what it sees in the frame, whether you're taking a portrait, an event, or a landscape.

Partial Metering

What it Does:

Partial metering can help when there is a big difference between how much light hits your subject and how much hits the background. This could happen if your subject is backlit or surrounded by brighter areas. So that the background doesn't change the brightness too much, the camera only meters a small part of the picture, focusing on the area around the subject.

When to Use It:

This style works well when your theme is very different from the background. This helps keep the attention on the right exposure of the subject while keeping the camera from overexposing or underexposing because of background light.

Spot Metering

What it Does:

Thanks to spot metering, the camera can measure the light in a very small and accurate area of the picture. The screen shows this area, which is usually in the middle of the frame. Using spot metering makes sure that the exposure is set only on this small part of the picture and not on the rest of it.

When to Use It:

This mode is the best for controlling exposure precisely when you are taking pictures of something with strong colors or when you want to be sure that a certain part of the picture has the right exposure. It helps a lot when taking close-ups, portraits, or pictures in dim light, like when you're shooting small things or fine details.

Center-Weighted Average Metering

What it Does:

When you use center-weighted average metering, the exposure is spread over the whole scene, but the middle of the frame gets more attention. Instead of doing a lot of complicated scene analysis, this mode just looks at what's in front of the camera, mostly in the middle of the picture.

When to Use It:

This setting works well for portraits or other shots where the subject is in the middle of the frame. It's also helpful when you want to have a little more control over the brightness in the middle of the frame than the edges, but you want the lighting to be pretty much the same all over the picture.

Practical Tips for Using Metering Modes:

- **Evaluative Metering:** This method works well for most general-purpose photos because it looks at the whole picture.
- **Partial and Spot Metering:** These work well when there is a lot of contrast and you only care about exposing one subject correctly and not the background.
- **Center-Weighted Average Metering:** This method makes sure that people get the right amount of light when they are placed in the middle of the frame, taking into account the background.

If you pick the right metering mode for your Canon EOS R5 Mark II, it will take well-exposed pictures in a range of lighting situations.

AE for Priority Subjects During AF

Metering for detected individuals according to the AF: Subject to detect preset.

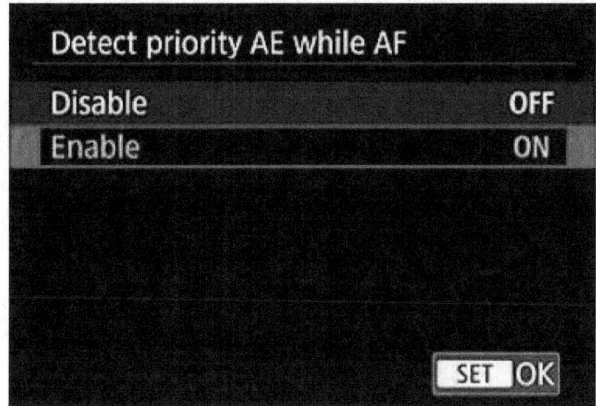

- **Enable:** The AF point or region where the subject was detected is used as a starting place for metering.
- **Disable:** The full screen is used for metering.

Picture Style

That being said, this function is one of the most useful ways to change how your photos are shown. You can improve your pictures with Picture Styles by changing small features in each picture that was taken with a certain Style. Some of the things that can be changed when working with full-color pictures are the amount of sharpness, the level of contrast, the color richness, and the color of skin tones.

You can still change the contrast and sharpness of black-and-white photos, but the two color adjustments that don't do anything for a black-and-white picture have been swapped out for controls that let you add overlays in sepia, blue, purple, or green tones, as well as settings for filter effects (which I will explain in a moment).

There are established Picture Styles for Standard, Portrait, Landscape, Fine Detail, Neutral, and Faithful photos, as well as Auto and three choices that the user can change. These are called User Def. 1. Definition for Users. 2 and User Def. 3. This can be taken to mean any kind of photography setting, like taking pictures of sports, buildings, or newborns. The seventh Picture Style is called Monochrome, and it lets you change the filter effects or add color tones to your black-and-white photos.

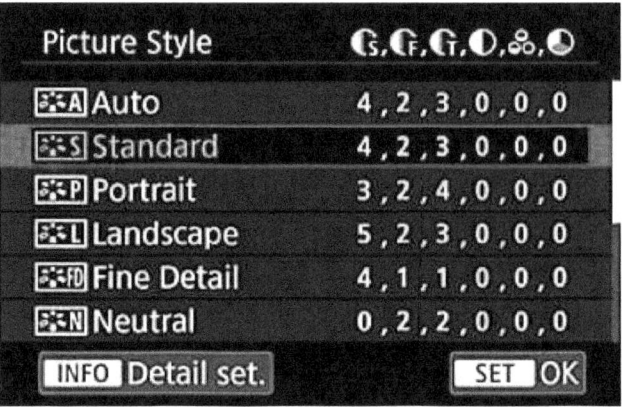

Picture Styles give you a lot of options. Canon has changed the choices for Auto, the preset color Picture Styles, and the single black-and-white Picture Style to make them better fit the needs of most photographers. You can still change the settings of any of these "canned" Picture Styles to make them look the way you want. Even better, you can use those three files to make completely new styles by using User Definition files to make new styles.

Making your color-soaked style is possible if you want your photos to have bright colors that remind you of Velvia film or the work of famous photographer Pete Turner. If you want to make the room feel more charming, choose colors that are softer, less bright, and less contrasty. It can be helpful to take shots outside on cloudy or overcast days if you are in a place with more contrast.

You can see that the graphic at the top of the page with the icons shows what the current value is for each choice. From left to right, the icons show Strength (S), Fineness (F), and Threshold (T). The Contrast icon is a half-black, half-white circle, the Saturation icon is a triangle with three circles inside it, and the Color Tone icon is a split circle. The Filter Effect is shown by overlapping circles, and the Toning Effect is shown by a painting tip. You can see them by scrolling down in the Monochrome Picture Style. Read about these settings below, and then pick them when you use Picture Styles:

Sharpness. The term for the quality of a picture is sharpness, and this measure also controls how different the edges or outlines of the picture look. Remember that changes in sharpness don't have to follow a strict rule. You can reduce or get rid of moiré effects in your picture by adding a little softness. This is done by putting an "anti-alias" filter in front of the camera, which blurs the image. When the features in your picture have a pattern that is too close to the pattern, or frequency, of the sensor itself, these effects can happen.

This could happen if the pattern made by the image's features is too much like the pattern as a whole. Canon used the factory settings for sharpening to keep the risk of losing a little picture detail to a minimum while also softening most of the moiré interference to the point where it can't be seen.

Increasing the sharpness of a picture (either in your image editor or by using a Picture Style) makes it more likely that you will get moiré patterns and those ugly "halos" around the edges of photos that are too sharp. Be careful when you make this change. In this setup, you have control over three different factors. Here are some of them:

- **Strength**. On this range of sharpness, 0 means there is almost no outline focus, and 7 means there is a lot of outline focus. Going overboard with the power can make a haze and more detail show up around the edges of the picture.
- **Fineness**. A scale from 1 (which makes the fine lines in your picture sharper) to 5 (which makes only the bigger, rougher lines sharper) tells you which edges will stand out. If you want to draw attention to a lot of small details in your picture, like a subject with a lot of texture, pick a smaller number. In this case, you should use a smaller number. In portraiture, a bigger number might be better so that eyes and hair don't stand out too much and face flaws don't get too much attention. When you are shooting a movie, you can't change the threshold or fineness.
- **Threshold**. With this choice, you can change the contrast between the areas around the sharpened edges and the edges themselves to change how sharp the outlines are. It is possible to sharpen even when there is less contrast between the edge and the rest of the picture when the scale number is low. The number goes from 1 to 5. When the cutoff is set too low, there is more noise. Higher numbers can only make things look sharper if there is already a clear difference in brightness between the edges and the pixels close by. The highest numbers might make something that looks like a poster with lots of contrast.
- **Contrast**. If you change this parameter's value, you can change the number of tones between the darkest black and the lightest white. It can be any number between -4 (lower contrast) and +4 (higher contrast). If you change the contrast

settings to low, the picture will look flatter. If you change them to high, the tones might look better, but you might lose information in the highlights and shadows.

- **Saturation**. This number specifies the color depth. Its value can range from -4 (high saturation) to +4 (low saturation). As an example, when the reds are more saturated, the red tone looks deeper and richer. When the reds are less saturated, on the other hand, the tone goes more toward lighter, pinkish colors. Too much brightness can lead to "clipping," which is when some features in one or more color channels are lost. Because of this, the RGB histograms can help you find it.
- **Color Tone**. With a value between 0 and +4, this change can make skin tones yellower or redder. With a value between 0 and –4, it can make them orange.
- **Filter effect (Monochrome only)**. It doesn't add any color to a black-and-white picture when filter effects are used on it. Instead, they change how grayscale tones are rendered to make it look like a color filter was used during the picture.
- **Toning effect (Monochrome only)**. When you tone a picture, a color overlay is added on top of it. This gives the photo a sepia, blue, purple, or green color. However, the image's tones will stay black and white.

The following are the preset Picture Styles:

- **Auto**. Changes the color settings so that scenes outside have a wider range of colors and more life.
- **Standard**. When you use the Basic Zone mode and take a picture in any mode other than Portrait or Landscape, this Picture Style will automatically apply a set of features, such as better sharpness, that are useful for most shooting situations. One of these things is a better level of sharpness.
- **Portrait**. This method increases brightness for richer colors when taking pictures, which is especially helpful for girls and kids. At the same time, it makes the skin feel softer by reducing the sharpness. This is especially good for women and kids. This Picture Style is used when you choose the Basic Mode Portrait preset. Some artists find that the Faithful method works better when painting portraits of men you want to look rougher or more manly, or when you want to draw attention to lines on the faces of older people, whether they are men or women.
- **Landscape**. This method raises the sharpness, color saturation, and saturation of blues and greens to make scenery pictures look more alive. This is the setting that is used by default when the Basic Zone Landscape mode is selected.

- **Fine detail**. For this choice to make a picture with as much detail as possible, contrast and sharpening are used, which could add some visual noise. You might guess that this level gives you the most detailed picture.
- **Neutral**. One difference between this picture style and the Standard style is that it has less saturation and contrast. It's useful when you want your photographs to look less bright or when the brightness and contrast of the photos you're taking look too high, like on a sunny beach day.
- **Faithful**. The colors in your picture should be shown as exactly as possible, with relationships between them that are close to how the human eye sees them. This is how the style is meant to be used.
- **Monochrome**. When you pick this Picture Style, your camera can only take black-and-white pictures. And if you only take JPEG pictures, the colors will be gone too. On the contrary, if you shoot in JPEG+RAW, you can add color to the RAW files once you open them in a photo editor. This is still true even if you only shot in black and white. When you play back the photos, they will only appear in black and white on the screen, but the color information is still in the RAW file and can be found later.

TIP: The Monochrome Picture Style can still be used to edit your photos even if you are only working with one RAW file and not the JPEG version. The camera knows that the RAW file is black and white, so when you open it in an image editor, it will change it to that style immediately. The camera's screen shows your pictures in black and white. There is still color information in the RAW file, though, and you can choose to import the picture with that color information chosen from the drop-down menu.

Symbols

Icons for Contrast, Strength, Fineness, and Threshold for Sharpness can be found on the screen where you choose the Picture Style. The numbers show what these Picture Style-specific choices are set to.

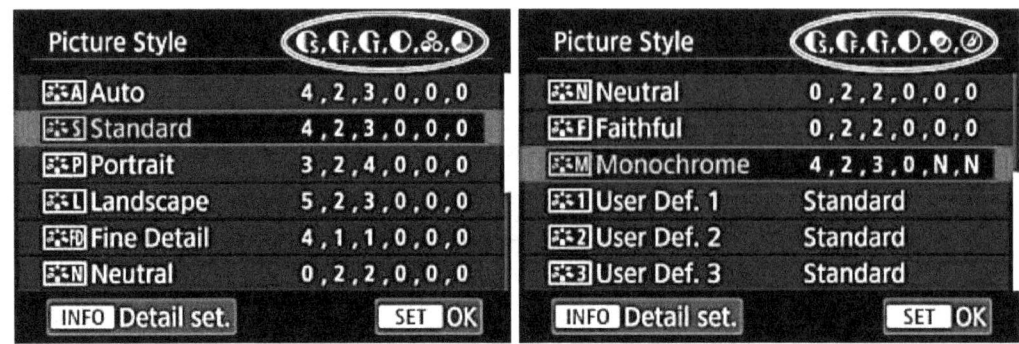

	Sharpness		
			Strength
			Fineness
			Threshold
	Contrast		
	Saturation		
	Color tone		
	Filter effect (Monochrome)		
	Toning effect (Monochrome)		

Settings and Effects

	Sharpness			
		Strength	0: Weak outline emphasis	7: Strong outline emphasis
		Fineness[1]	1: Fine	5: Grainy
		Threshold[2]	1: Low	5: High
	Contrast		−4: Low contrast	+4: High contrast
	Saturation		−4: Low saturation	+4: High saturation
	Color tone		−4: Reddish skin tone	+4: Yellowish skin tone

1. Shows the edge thinness that the improvement can be used on. The number goes down as the details that can be marked get smaller.

2. The contrast threshold sets the level of enhancement between the edges and the rest of the picture. It's more important for the shape to stand out when the contrast difference is small. Noise is usually easier to see when the number is smaller, though.

Monochrome Adjustment

Filter effect

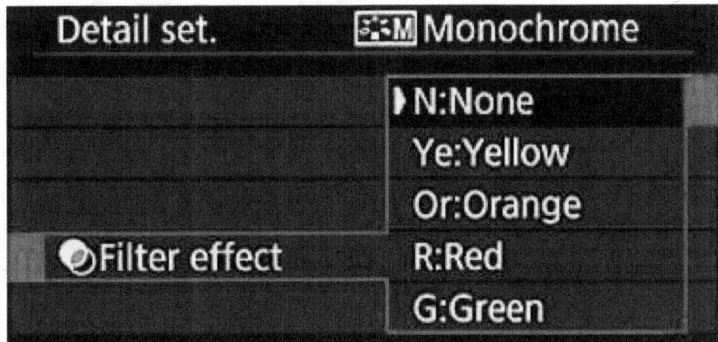

Adding a filter effect to a picture can make white clouds, green trees, or other features stand out more, even if the image is only black and white.

Selecting Picture Styles

Canon has made it very easy to choose a Picture Style. The company has separated the style selection process and the style modification process into two separate tasks so that you don't change a current style by accident. Among the Picture Styles you already have, you can choose from the following:

- **Picture Styles menu**. Hold down the QCD-1 button and use this menu item to move the cursor down the styles list until the style you want is highlighted. After that, press the SET button.
- **Quick Control screen**. To get to the Picture Styles tab, move to the right column and press and hold the Q button. Once the icon is selected, you can either turn the dial or use the directional buttons to pick the style you want to use. After that, you can press the SET button to confirm your pick.

Defining Picture Styles

It's very simple to understand the Picture Style options that are currently chosen and make changes as required. Numbers appear on the menu screen to show the values that have been set for each of the Picture Style choices. Some people who sell cameras use vague words like sharp, extra sharp, vivid, or more vivid. If the photo Styles menu is present, you can change one of the pre-set photo styles or make your own. Just do what's written below:

1. Once you've chosen the style you want to change, click the **Edit** button.
2. The **INFO** button will show you the Detail Set menu when you click it. The next screen will be for either the six color styles or the three User Def color styles. Along with the Sharpness and Contrast choices shown, you can scroll down to find two more options. Here is where you can change the saturation and color tone. Toning Effects and Filter Effects are used instead of Saturation and Color Tone in the Monochrome panel, which looks the same.
3. Pick a setting that needs to be changed. You can change the settings with the QCD-1. If you click Default Set. at the bottom of the screen, the numbers will go back to the ones that were saved before.
4. Press **SET** to change the settings of a parameter that is highlighted.
5. You can move the triangle to the number you want to use with the QCD-1. Keep in mind that the scale still shows the old number, which is shown by a gray triangle. This makes it very simple to return to the old setting if you need to.
6. After pressing the **MENU** button three times, you will be taken back to the screen that was before the menu. This will keep the setting as it is when you press the **SET** button.

When the Picture Style menu shows a Picture Style whose default settings have been changed, the changed setting will be shown in blue. This will happen with any Picture Style whose basic settings have been changed. Because of this feature, you won't have to worry about making changes to a Picture Style and then forgetting about them. The change will be saved. If you look quickly at the Picture Style menu, you can see which styles and settings have been changed.

The process for customizing the Monochrome Picture Style is a little different. There are now choices for the Filter Effect and the Toning Effect instead of the Saturation and Color

Tone settings. One important thing to keep in mind is that once you take a JPEG shot in black and white, you can't change the color to full.

You can pick **None** or any of these colors: Orange, Yellow, Red, or Green. You can also pick None, Blue, Purple, Green, or Sepia tones. You will still be able to change the Contrast and Sharpness settings after you pick a different Picture Style.

Adjusting Styles with the Picture Style Editor

The Picture Style Editor that comes with your camera can be used on both Windows and Macintosh computers, if you'd rather work with Picture Styles on your computer. It lets you change settings like Standard, Landscape, and Faithful that are already set, and it also lets you make your Picture Styles.

You can change many things about the picture, such as its contrast, sharpness, color intensity, and color tone. After making changes, you can save the file as a PF2 file. After that, you can either send this file to the camera or use Digital Photo Professional to change a RAW picture while it's being sent.

You'll be able to make and load your Picture Style by following these steps:

1. Launch the Picture Style Editor, which is sometimes written as PSE. This is not the same as Photoshop Elements, which also starts with PSE.
2. You should first open Photoshop Elements and add a RAW CR3 picture that you want to use as a guide. You can also use the Open command in the File menu or drag a file from a folder into the main window of the editor.
3. Other than Standard, choose a different default style from the ones that are given. It's important to start with a base style that looks a lot like the look you want to achieve since your new style will use all the features of the base style you choose (tweaking is easier than creating a style from scratch).
4. You can look at your old style and your new style side by side to see which one you like better. Three buttons in the lower left area of the window let you choose whether to see the old and new designs next to each other in a vertical or horizontal line.
5. If you click the **Advanced** button in the Tool Palette, the **Advanced Picture Style Settings** box will appear. This dialogue box is on the left side. Things that can be

changed on the camera itself are the same. When you're done, please remember to click the OK button.

6. Make adjustments that are thought out. There are a lot of things you can try if you know how to use the more advanced tools in photo editing software like Photoshop, Photoshop Elements, Digital Photo Pro, or something similar. Within the Tools palette, you can find more ways to change the color, tonal range, and curves. Keep in mind that these changes are much more extensive than what can be made with the camera's Picture Styles, so it's well worth the time to get used to them.
7. From the File menu, pick **Save Picture Style File** when you're done. This will save a PF2 file of the style you just made to your hard drive. In the parts that are asked for, please give your style a caption and copyright information. When you choose Disable Subsequent Editing, your style will be locked and can't be changed any further.

In the rare event that you want to make your own unique, secret design, any changes you have already made to the style will also stay hidden. You won't be able to change that style in the future, though. You should save a second copy of your unique Picture Style without checking the box that says Disable Subsequent Editing if you think you might want to change it later.

Uploading a Picture Style to the Camera

Now, use your camera to add your new look to one of your three User Defs. There are places in the Picture Style array. Follow these simple steps:

1. Once you turn on your camera, open the EOS Utility, and pick the Camera Settings/Remote Shooting choice from the splash screen. Your camera should already be connected to your computer and ready to take pictures.
2. You should choose the Shooting menu. You can tell what it is by the menu bar that shows up about halfway through the control panel on your computer screen. It looks like a white camera against a red background. This picture can be seen on your computer screen.
3. To get the Register Picture Style box to show up, you have to click on the box.

4. To change your user settings, choose one of the three User Def tabs. 1. User Def. 2. Alternatively, User Def. 3. Each tab will display the name of the Picture Style that is currently in use there.
5. Picture Styles that you have saved locally or downloaded from somewhere else will have a PF2 tag added to them when they are shown. Just click on the one you want to use, then go to the Open box and click on the Open button.
6. The box that says **Registering Picture Style File** will appear again. If you press the OK button, the camera will know what Picture Style you set in User Def. the "slot" that the tab you picked shows. Instead of "User Def," the name of the currently selected Picture Style will show up in the menu. Alternatively, User Def. 2/User Def. 3.

Color Space

If you choose this menu item, you can choose between two different color spaces, which are also called color gamuts. When you are in one of the Creative Zone modes, you can switch to this mode. The first color space is called Adobe RGB because it was made by Adobe Systems in 1998. The second color space is called sRGB, which seems to come from the fact that it is the standard RGB color space. It's possible to use a different range of colors in each of these two color gamuts when taking pictures.

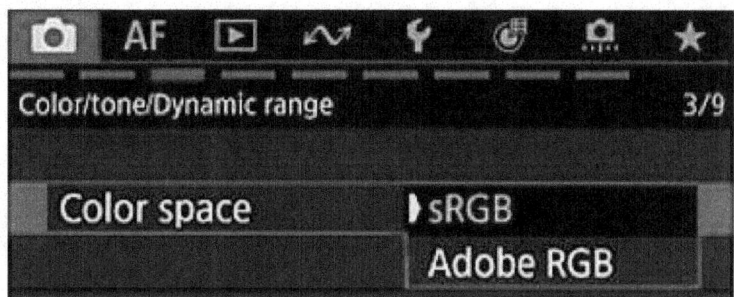

When you take a JPEG or HEIF picture with the P, Tv, Av, or M exposure modes, the Color Space menu option works right away. Every JPEG and HEIF picture you take with the camera will be shown in the sRGB color space when it is in Scene Intelligent Auto photo mode. RAW photos are the only ones that don't follow this rule.

They have information for both Adobe RGB and sRGB, but if you don't change the setting when you import the photos, your image editor will use sRGB (with Scene Intelligent Auto or Creative Auto shots) or the other color space when you load those photos. There is more information in the section called Best of Both Worlds.

You might be surprised to learn that the camera doesn't pick up every color that the human eye sees right away. Unfortunately, it's not possible because of the sensor, the filters used to record the basic red, green, and blue colors, and the parts of your computer monitor and camera that show those colors. The inks and dyes used don't exactly take in and reflect colors, so it's not possible to print every color our eyes can see.

Your printer records a different version of each color that the sensor records, the screen shows a different version of the colors that the sensor records, and the sensor itself does not record all of the colors that we can see.

There are, however, a lot of colors caught in addition to the ones we need. When you change a 14-bit RAW image to a 24-bit image (eight bits per channel), you can only make 16.8 million colors instead of 16,384 colors for each of the red, green, and blue channels. There are up to 281 trillion different colors that can be in a 14-bit RAW picture.

A color space is a picture of the set of colors that a certain piece of hardware can show or record. This hardware could be a scanner, digital camera, computer, printer, or something else. There are many more color spectrums out there.

A third color space called ProPhoto RGB, shown by the yellow triangle in the picture, is being used by professional photographers more and more because more and more color printing labs can handle it.

You can't save photos with the ProPhoto gamut in ProPhoto. But you can use Adobe Camera RAW to change RAW files to the 16-bit ProPhoto format, which gives more processing options to more experienced photographers and includes colors that humans can't see as well as the ones they can.

The picture shows that it has deeper reds, greens, and blues, even though its green and blue main colors are made up because they are outside the visible color gamut. This makes sense since they are not in the visible color range. People with specific needs can play around with ProPhoto RGB without using a professional printing service since many inkjet printers can handle cyans, magentas, and yellows that go beyond what Adobe RGB can do.

You can use 16.8 million different colors in your picture if you pick any triangle, which is also known as a color space. This is true no matter what you pick. (Think about how many colors could be in a picture if two-thirds of the pixels were each a different color!) However, as you can see from the figure, the available colors will be different. There won't be a single shot with all 16.8 million.

Expanded color spaces, such as Adobe RGB and ProPhoto RGB, are good for professional and commercial printing because they can show a bigger range of colors. It might also be helpful if a picture is going to be greatly improved, especially if it's going to be done in an advanced image editor like Adobe Photoshop, which has many color management tools that can be adjusted to work with certain color spaces.

In this case, it is very important to make sure that the picture editor is set up in the right color space. You may want to skip the automatic upgrade to Adobe RGB if you are an experienced user. This is because pictures printed from your monitor may not look as good as they do when printed from an inkjet printer. This is because Adobe RGB is used for the color space. If you want to make things look better on your screen, you can use widely available color-calibrating hardware and software to set your display's profile for the Adobe RGB color space.

Even though both sRGB and Adobe RGB can generate the same number of colors, sRGB is better at spreading 16.8 million absolute colors across a smaller part of the visible spectrum. Think of a big pencil box with 16.8 million different colors in it. New tones that weren't in the original box have been added to the standard crayons that were taken out of the original sRGB set when it was updated.

The colors in your new box are so complicated that a computer screen can't show them properly. However, they look great on a professional printing machine. As an example, Adobe RGB has more "crayons" than sRGB in the cyan-green part of the box. That being said, this probably won't help you much unless you want to print your picture using cyan, magenta, yellow, and black ink.

Photos should be saved in the sRGB color space if they are going to be printed on the user's printer. The reason for this is that the sRGB color space and the color space used by a regular inkjet printer are very close. You should pick the normal RGB color space. This is the setting that comes with most cameras and is best for the color gamut that can be seen on a computer screen or over the internet. If you want to print your picture file at a store kiosk, sRGB is the best color space to use. This is because the automatic output devices are set up to work with the sRGB color space of the end user.

Naturally, picking the right color space won't fix the issues that come up in this situation because each part of the picture chain can change or create a fairly unique set of colors. To do this, you will need to learn more about color management, which uses both hardware and software tools to make sure that all of your devices are as close to the same color as possible. As a result, the picture you see will match the picture you take, the picture on your computer screen, and the picture that you print out.

To effectively control your color, you will need at the very least a method for calibrating your computer screen. Then, you can calibrate your monitor, which will let you set it to show a uniform set of colors that you can use again and again. (What you see on the screen may change as the monitor ages or even as the lighting in the room changes.) I use Datacolor's (www.datacolor.com) SpyderX Pro monitor color adjustment software on all three of my computer screens, the two 26-inch ones and the main 32-inch one.

The gadget checks itself every week or two by temporarily attaching a small sensor to the front of the screen to read the test patches shown by the software during tuning. The device checks the amount of light in the room every five minutes and lets me know every two or three weeks when it needs to be calibrated. For the rest of its life, the sensor stays on its stand, where it measures the amount of light in the room and changes the brightness of my screens to match ambient light levels.

Clarity

You can change an image's contrast by focusing on its main tones instead of the whole picture. This is known as clarity. You can make things look clearer by increasing the contrast. You can make things look less clear by dropping it. But changes to sharpness and changes to clarity are not the same thing. This menu item can be used in the camera to change the clarity, or it can be used in a picture editor like Photoshop.

The difference between the dark and light tones in a picture will get bigger if you make it sharper. But if you make the picture clearer, the contrast between the middle tones will get greater. Some effects are similar to sharpening, but these are different because they make the image's details stand out more and lower the amount of digital noise.

As you move this menu item, you can change the amount of clarity. From -4 to +4, the slider can be moved. The default value is 0, but you can change any of the other numbers. Before getting a lot of people to use the tool, I think you should try it first. You won't be able to tell how good the pictures are until you get them on a computer. The camera doesn't show you the quality settings.

Remember that the clarity option can change the brightness or darkness of areas near the edges of your photos if they already have a high contrast level, which means they don't have many middle tones.

Highlight Tone Priority

You can get rid of highlights that are cut off or too bright.

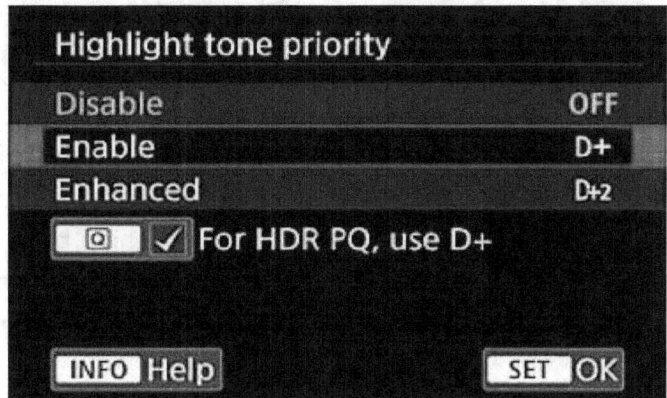

- **Enable:** When you click Enable, the shading in the outlines gets better. When you move from gray to color, it gets smoother.
- **Enhanced:** If you shoot in certain conditions, Enhanced cuts down on overexposed highlights even more than Enable.

White Balance

You can make your white balance by entering a color temperature number in the Custom menu. This can be done if you don't like the default white balance or any of the six presets (Daylight, Shade, Cloudy, Tungsten, White Fluorescent, or Flash). Yes, you can do this even if your camera has a tool that does it for you.

This screen works a lot like the one on the left end of the image below when you choose White Balance from the Quick Control screen. If you pick the K item on the Main scale, you can pick a color temperature exactly between 2,500 and 10,000 degrees Kelvin.

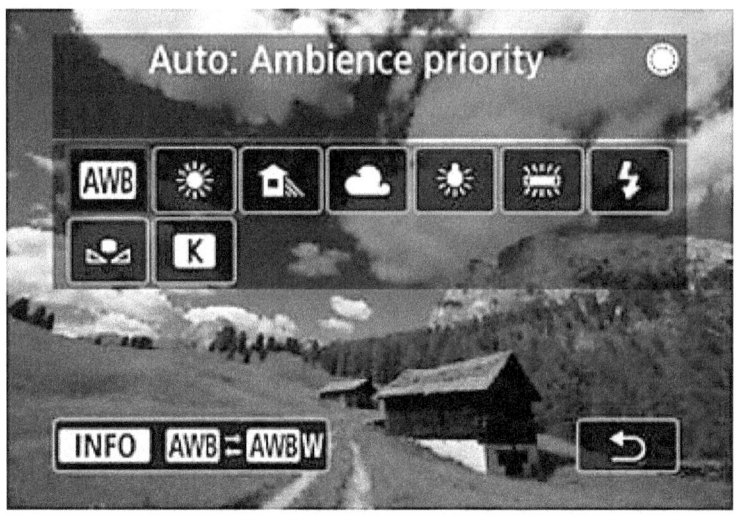

You might not be able to get a good reading on the color temperature of your scene if you don't have a color temperature meter. You might want to know the color temperatures of the pre-set options, though, in case you want to change them by selecting a different color temperature setting. If you know what the set color temperatures are, you can do this. You are given a list of the numbers that are used, and for Auto, you can choose between two options:

- **Auto (AWB).** 3,000K to 7,000K. Pressing the **INFO** button will let you choose between the Ambience-priority setting (which keeps colors bright even when lit by tungsten light) and the White-priority setting (which keeps whites neutral even when lit by tungsten light). Please make sure this choice is turned on.
- **Daylight.** 5,200K
- **Shade.** 7,000K
- **Cloudy.** 6,000K
- **Tungsten.** 3,200K
- **White Fluorescent.** 4,000K
- **Flash.** Automatically set
- **Custom.** 2,000K–10,000K
- **Color Temperature.** 2,500K–10,000K (settable in 100K increments)

Display	Mode	Color Temperature (K: Kelvin) (Approx.)
AWB	Auto: Ambience priority	3000–7000
AWBW	Auto: White priority	
☀	Daylight	5200
⛺	Shade	7000
☁	Cloudy, twilight, sunset	6000
💡	Tungsten light	3200
💡	White fluorescent light	4000
⚡	When using Flash	Automatically set*
⚙₁	Custom	2000–10000
K	Color temperature	2500–10000

It's important to choose the right white balance so that the colors in your picture look their best.

If we want to be picky, any one of the six settings (Daylight, Shade, etc.) could be wrong. But the good news is that they are probably only partly wrong in what they think. Most of the time, what you get will be good enough if you use Auto or choose a level that is close to the white balance. This is because the eye can bend in many ways.

You can always shoot in RAW and change the color balance in your photo editor after converting the.cr3 file if you need to get the color balance just right or if you don't like it when Auto or one of the presets is used. This is a choice for you if you often don't like the color balance when you use Auto or one of the other options. You can also pick a different way to white-balance.

White Balance Shift/Bracketing

With the white balance shift tool, you can change the color bias of the white balance along the magenta/green or blue/amber scale. When you change the color balance of your picture, you can make it a little more blue or yellow, a little more purple or green, or a mix of the two. You could also shoot several photo graphs one after the other, each with a slightly different color balance that is skewed in the way you choose.

Taking a look at the picture below will help you picture the process better. There is no bias at the point where lines BA and MG meet in the middle. Remember that from math class in high school? When you use the arrow keys to move the point, you can put it anywhere on the line. To find the point, you can use where the blue/amber and magenta/green lines are. The number of shifts will be shown in the box to the right of the line that says **SHIFT**.

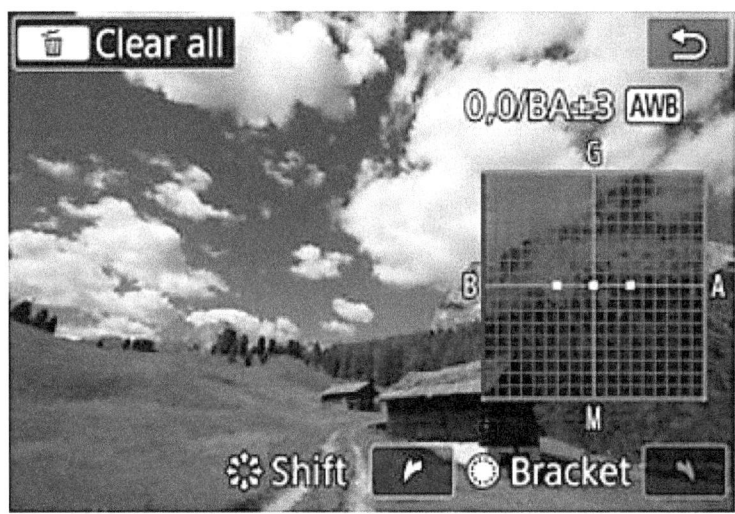

To change the white balance and to range the white balance are two different things. The changes happen along the bias line you choose when you bracket. This bracketing works a lot like exposure bracketing, but it also looks at color. You can use the bias bracketing method with any mode that only supports JPEG or HEIF. It won't work with RAW or RAW+JPEG files because the RAW files already have the information you need to finetune the white balance and the white balance bias.

The screen for making changes appears when **WB SHIFT/BKT** is pressed. If you turn the QCD-1 to the left, you can change how far apart the three dots that show the different exposures are vertically, and if you turn it to the right, you can change the range of the shift in the blue/amber dimension. When you do this, the three dots that show the images will change color. You can move the bracket set anywhere in the color space as long as you don't touch the MG or BA axes with the multi-controller joystick.

If you're not in a dark room, it can be hard to see your current shots on the LCD screen. Most of the time, it's easy to pick whether you want your picture to be greener, pink, blue, or yellow.

Lens Aberration Correction

This is the first option you'll see when you pick Shooting 5 from the menu. If the lens you're using has correction data, your camera can fix some lens flaws right away in three different settings. It used to be that some of these changes had to be made after Digital Photo Professional or a similar tool had worked on the picture. The following three things are things you can do:

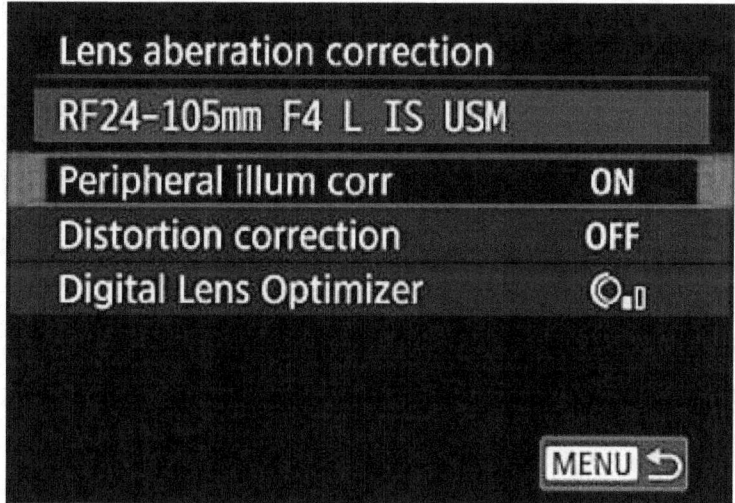

Peripheral Illumination Correction

- Dark lines on a picture, called vignetting, can be fixed.

Caution

- If the shooting conditions are right, the edges of the picture may have noise.
- As the ISO speed goes up, there will be less time to make changes.

Note

- The changes that are made will not be as big as the biggest changes that can be made with Digital Photo Professional (EOS app).

Distortion Correction

- It is possible to fix image distortion (warping).

Caution

- If you choose to fix the distortion, the angle of view might change a little. This could crop the pictures a bit and make them look a little less clear.
- The number of movies and photos that are changed could be different.

Note

- Distortion can be fixed when movies are made with RF or RF-S lenses.

Focus Breathing Correction

- If the focus points move during movie recording, it will be less likely that the angle of view will change.
- It is possible to set up this feature when Distortion correction is set to Enable.

Digital Lens Optimizer

- It is possible to fix mistakes caused by the optical properties of the lens as well as sharpness loss due to diffraction and low-pass filters.
- The Digital Lens Optimizer might show adjustment data not available or Peripheral light. You can fix this by adding the lens adjustment info to the camera with EOS Utility.

Chromatic Aberration Correction

It is possible to fix chromatic aberration, which is when colors band around things.

Note

- Chromatic aberr corr. will not show up if you set Digital Lens Optimizer to Standard or High.

Diffraction Correction

Diffraction is when the angle makes the picture less clear, but it can be fixed.

Note

- What diffraction correction does is fix the sharpness loss that comes from diffraction, the low-pass filter, and other things. This way, you can make changes even when the lens is fully open.
- This feature is hidden when the Digital Lens Optimizer setting is set to Standard or High.

Caution

- Lens distortion can't be fixed in JPEG or HEIF photos that have already been taken.
- If you're using a lens that wasn't made by Canon, you should set the changes to Disable, even if it says Correction data available.
- If you zoom in on the edges of the picture, you might see things that won't be logged.
- The correction is less for lenses that don't tell you the distance, except for diffraction correction.

Long Exposure Noise Reduction

This setting lets you choose whether to reduce noise during long exposures or not. If you don't want to use this setting, you can let the camera decide. Visual noise, which looks like a variety of different colored particles in photos, can be controlled by this setting. Some people compare the noise to the extra grain you can see in some movies shot at very high speeds. But when it comes to digital photos, grain isn't usually a good thing, even though it can be used in creative ways.

Putting on a CD while moving and then rolling down all the windows is the same thing as making noise that can be seen. It sounds like you're adding noise to the sound source. Even if you turn up the CD player's volume a bit, the signal-to-noise ratio is still pretty bad, so the tones (especially higher treble notes) that you want to hear are probably being blocked out.

When you raise an analog signal, the amount of picture information in it goes up, but the background ends up being less clear. Set the radio in your car to an AM station that is either very weak or very far away. After that, you need to make the sound better. You will not be able to hear what is being said no matter how loud you turn it up. While increasing the ISO can be helpful at times, it can also stop working at certain points for digital tools.

A lot of different kinds of noise are made by these things. If you turn up the ISO too high, noise might show up. To raise the ISO sensitivity, some random noise in the signal is added along with the photon information. The level of sensitivity goes up as you raise the ISO setting on your camera. What this means is that each pixel can be recorded with fewer and fewer photons. It's more likely, though, that one of those ghost photons will be counted with the real light particles in the world.

Most of the time, you can use ISO 800 or 1600, but there will still be some noise. That's right, ISO 3200 can also work well. The camera and its digital processing chip make it possible for noise levels to be low. This means that settings as high as ISO 800 or 1600 won't cause any issues.

Putting the picture in the light for longer is the second way to make noise. Longer exposure times let more photons reach the sensor, but some photosites may act in strange ways even though they haven't been hit by a light ray. Also, the sensor makes heat because it is left on for a longer time, which could be wrongly recorded as a flood of light. Because you can change the number on this line, you can change how much noise the digital signal processor blocks.

You can do any of these:

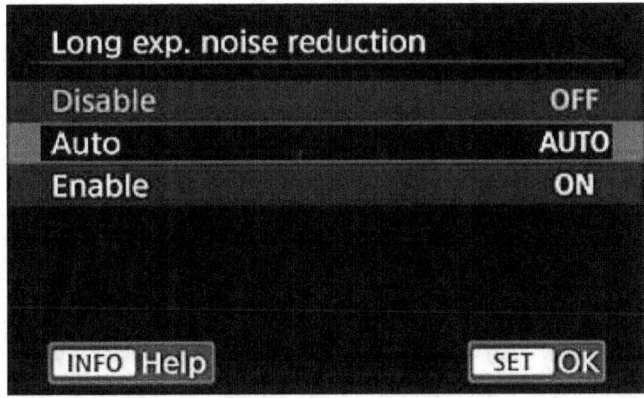

Off/Disable. Turns off noise reduction for long exposures. Even though there will be more noise, this setting is for when you want to get the most out of your picture. With this option, you don't have to wait as long to take a picture because of the noise-reduction process. If you only plan to use lower ISO settings, longer shots can make noise that isn't too bad. This will cut down on the noise that ISO boosting makes.

This is because longer exposures make the noise worse. You might be getting a photograph of a river that flows over rocks at ISO 100 while the camera is on a stand. Following that, you would use a neutral density filter and a long exposure to make the water that is hitting the rocks less rough. You can get more information from your pictures if you turn off long exposure noise reduction. This is especially true for parts that aren't moving. Pick Off if you don't want to wait. Because it might take twice as long to take a picture with Auto or On and the noise reduction process.

Auto. There is long exposure noise if you use shots that last one second or more. To find it, you take a second exposure that is clear and compare it to the first picture. Any noise in the dark-frame picture is taken out of the real picture before it's saved on the memory card. It only saves the picture that has the noise fixed.

On/Enable. The dark-frame reduction method is used on all pictures that are longer than one second if this option is chosen. This choice might be useful if you are working with a high ISO setting, which will make noise worse, and you want to get rid of any extra noise that long shots might cause. On many pictures taken in Auto mode, noise reduction will be used, even though it wouldn't have been used on those photos otherwise.

TIP: You can only take a certain number of pictures at a time while the dark frame is being exposed, and the screen will be blank when you are shooting in Live View mode. At this point, white balance bracketing won't be used.

High ISO Speed Noise Reduction

When you raise your camera's ISO setting, the second type of noise shows up. You can choose how much or how little of this noise reduction to use by setting this line. While noise reduction does lower the amount of noise, it does take away some information. This input, on the other hand, lets you do that. Standard noise control is on most of the time. If you don't want noise reduction at all, you can choose between Low and High.

Noise reduction is done to the whole picture when you raise the ISO. You can get rid of noise by lowering the ISO. This will make dark places look better. Keep in mind that the most ongoing shots you can take will be much less if you choose the High-quality setting. This is because it takes a lot longer to process each photograph when the quality setting is higher.

You can choose any of these:

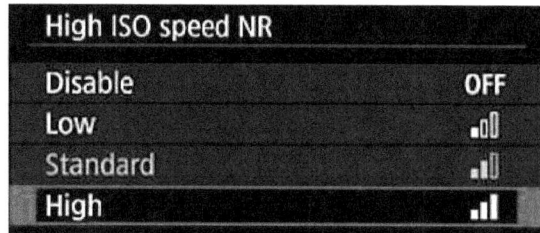

- **Disable**. The amount of noise that is used will not go down any further.
- **Low**. This cuts down on how much noise reduction is used. The picture will look grainier after this, but the small details will still be there.
- **Standard**. When the ISO number is low, noise reduction is stronger in the shadows of an image. If the ISO number is high, it's not as strong in the middle of an image.
- **High**. When more extreme noise reduction is used, the picture looks mushy and loses some visual clarity, which some viewers may find noticeable and unpleasant. The longest burst of shots that your camera can do without stopping will be a lot shorter because this choice processes pictures.

- **Multi Shot Noise Reduction**. As long as this setting is in place, the camera will keep taking four different pictures. Then, just in case the shots moved, they are lined up, and a method called dark-frame subtraction is used to join them. This method doesn't handle random images that are caused by noise. It's a better picture than the High pick.

Make sure the camera is on a stand and the subject of the photograph is not moving before you use Multi-Shot NR. Picture Quality must be set to RAW, RAW+JPEG/HEIF, or Dual Pixel RAW. You also can't get to it if you use flash, live view, take multiple or Bulb shots, or do autoexposure/white balance bracketing.

Dust Delete Data

You can take a picture of any dust or other things that are stuck to your camera if you choose this option from the menu. Digital Photo Professional comes with software that can quickly find and get rid of dust in your photos. The software will use the information about where the dust is to find it and clean it up.

You should take the Dust Delete Data picture often because it's your last line of defense against sensor dust. If you choose this menu item, the time and date of the last change you made will show up here.

Select Dust Delete Data, make sure the OK button is chosen, and then press the **SET** button. UHF waves will be used on the low-pass filter that sits on top of the sensor as the first step in the camera's self-cleaning process.

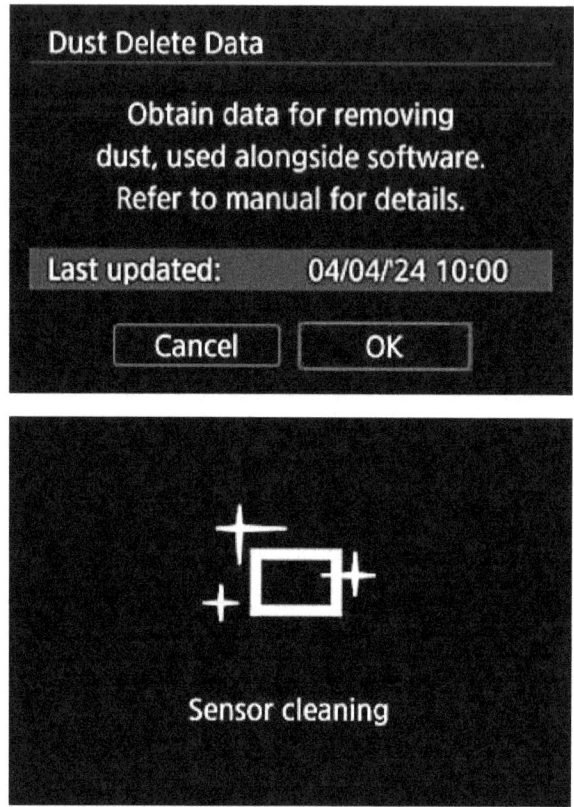

- You'll see a message after the picture sensor has cleaned itself. It will make a noise while it's being cleaned, but no picture will be taken.

After that, the screen will tell you to press the shoot button. Face the camera toward a white card that is all one color. First, put the lens into manual focus. Then, move the focus ring to the right until it reads "infinity."

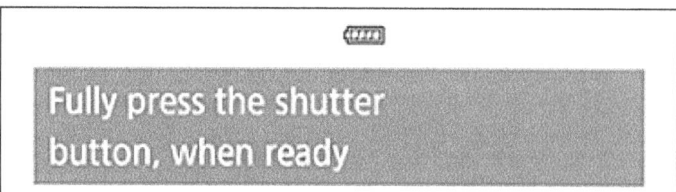

- A new piece of white paper or something else plain white should fill the screen when you shoot from 20 to 30 cm (0.7 to 1 ft) away.

- You can get the data even if the camera doesn't have a card in it because the picture won't be saved.

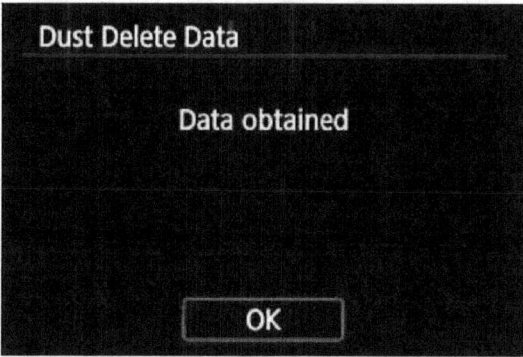

- The camera will read the Dust Delete Data as soon as the picture is taken. When the Dust Delete Data is found, a warning will appear.
- An error message will appear if the information can't be found.

Dust Delete Data Appending

Everything it takes from now on will have the Dust Delete Data added to it. The best thing to do is to get Dust Delete Data right before you shoot.

There is advice in the Digital Photo Professional Instruction Manual about how to easily get rid of dust spots with Digital Photo Professional by EOS.

It doesn't change the size of the file when you add Dust Delete Data to photos.

Caution

- If the Cropping/aspect ratio is set to 1.6x or you use RF-S or EF-S lenses, you won't be able to get Dust Delete Data.
- When [Distortion correction] is on, you can't add Dust Delete Data to photos.
- If the item has a pattern or design, the Digital Photo Professional (EOS software) might identify it as dust data. This could make it less accurate at getting rid of dust.

Multiple Exposure

With this feature, you can merge up to nine different photos into one big picture. You don't need an image editor like Photoshop to use it. Maybe that will be a fun way to remember how cool it was when you could make complicated photographs right in the camera.

Before digital cameras came along, putting together collages of several photos was a cool, groovy, far-out, hep/hip, phat, sick, and amazing thing to do. More and more people are taking the easy way out by taking two or more pictures and then putting them together in an image editor like Photoshop.

But Canon's multiple exposure function is great if you are willing to plan ahead of time or don't mind making some happy mistakes. The RAW data from the camera can be used to make one picture out of two or more shots. When you do this, photos will blend better than when you weren't good at Photoshop.

Canon has also taken away a part of the feature that was making some cameras very annoying. You no longer need to change the menu to add more shots to each set. You can set it up once and forget about it if you want to take a lot of shots at once. But don't forget to turn it off when you're done!

You can only take one picture at a time when the camera is in low light, high dynamic range, or movie mode. When setting up your camera, you need to do one of the following things before you can start taking multi-exposure pictures.

As soon as you click Disable, the multi-exposure option is off. You can quickly pick either of the two On choices instead, though. This is the master control that lets you pick between two types of multiple shots and turn them on and off while keeping the other settings you've set.

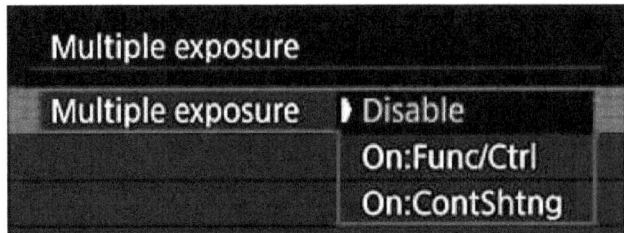

- **Disable**. Turns off multiple exposures.
- **On**: **Func/Ctrl**. In the Function and Control-priority mode, you can change how the camera works between sets of shots. Each set of shots is taken right away by the camera. This lets you see how your pictures turned out and change any settings you need to, like the brightness. When I take a lot of shots, I like to try new things. This mode works best for me when I want to carefully arrange things in the picture between shots or when the subject isn't moving around much. This camera's main flaw is that it shoots slowly all the time, so it's not ideal for recording action scenes.

You can check the exposure level, overlap alignment, and other things by pressing the Playback button at any time during the shooting process in Function or Control-priority modes. If the picture isn't what you wanted, tap the Trash button to see four other choices:

- o **Undo last image**. The picture you are looking at will be taken down, and you will be able to see one more.
- o **Save and Exit**. Each picture will be saved, but shooting will have to stop before it can begin again. The single exposure and the whole picture will be saved if you pick **All Images** from the Save Source Images menu. Only the picture that has been put together will be saved if you choose to save only the version that has been changed.
- o **Exit Without Saving**. The shooting with many exposures has stopped, and there are no more pictures saved.
- o **Return to the Previous Screen**. You can use this to go back to the last screen you saw.

- **On: ContShtng**. When the camera is set to Continuous Shooting-priority mode, it can work in continuous mode. I use this technique to take pictures with more than one exposure at live ballet and dance performances. I won't be able to plan every picture graph, but I do want to be able to record every move as it happens.

You can't look at or play back pictures, use the tools, or undo the last shot you took while you were taking pictures in this mode. Also, because photos are taken so fast, the only thing that will be on your memory card is the picture that was made by putting all the pictures together.

Multiple Exposure Control

You can choose how the shots are put together with the Multiple Exposure Control tool. You can do any of the following:

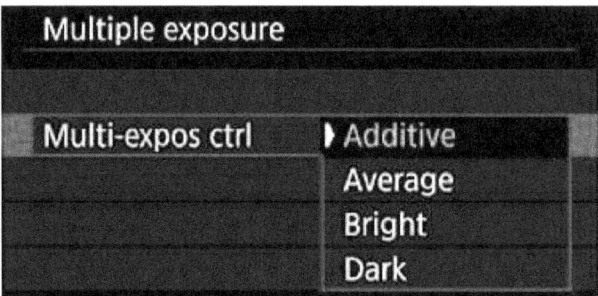

- **Additive**. From now on, all of the shots in the set will have the full exposure. Since the background was black and the subject was moving but not overlapping, the cumulative exposure effect made it look like two separate photos were put together into one.

For each shot, though, you can change the amount of exposure by setting exposure adjustment. You can also merge shots in this mode. As a general rule, you should change the exposure by one stop for two shots, 1.5 EV for three shots, and 2 EV for four shots. To get a certain level of realism in the way that overlapping pictures look, you can figure out the amount of negative exposure adjustment by hand.

- **Average**. The right amount of negative exposure adjustment will be made if you choose this option. This number will change based on how many shots you are putting together to make one picture. If you take a lot of shots of the same scene instead of different things, the background will get the same amount of light as if you only took one picture.
- **Bright**. In this case, complex methods are used to match the first picture in a set with the photo graphs that will be added to it in the future. Once that is done, this style gives more weight to the parts of the picture where pixels meet that are brighter. The basic thoughts behind this are the same as those behind Photoshop's lighten layer blending and other image tools.
- **Dark**. This choice is like the Bright choice, but the darker dots are more important. You might not fully understand how Bright and Dark modes change your pictures

until you use both of them. When to use one over the other is more of a matter of taste than anything else, so I can't say for sure.

Number of Exposures

In each multiple-exposure set, you can pick from two to nine different pictures. Choose an option, press the **SET** button, then turn the QCD-1 dial to choose how many shots to take. When you first start to play around with this tool, I suggest that you start with three different settings. With practice, though, you'll quickly learn when to take pictures that need more than one shot to be put together.

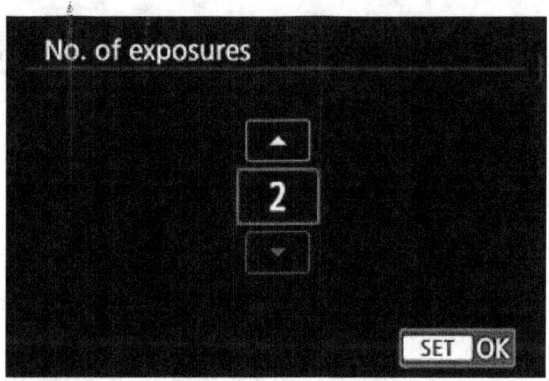

Save Source Images

Multiple exposure shots need to be taken one at a time, and then they need to be put together before the final picture can be saved. You might already know this. The sensor won't get overloaded and lose data this way, and the camera can cleverly put the pictures together by combining them and using exposure correction and other pixel tricks to make the final picture. These steps are not the same as movie multiple exposures, where all the pictures are taken on the same photosensitive frame and each new picture is added to the ones that are already there.

If you choose All Images, all of the images will be saved for later use. If you choose Result only, only the picture that was made when the images were joined will be saved. There are pros and cons to both of these tactics. There is a chance that the merge you make by hand will be better than the one the camera does for you. You can also get to the shot that turns out to be a keeper on its own without having to deal with the other photos that were mixed in. One bad thing about Every Image is that it takes more time and memory card space to save.

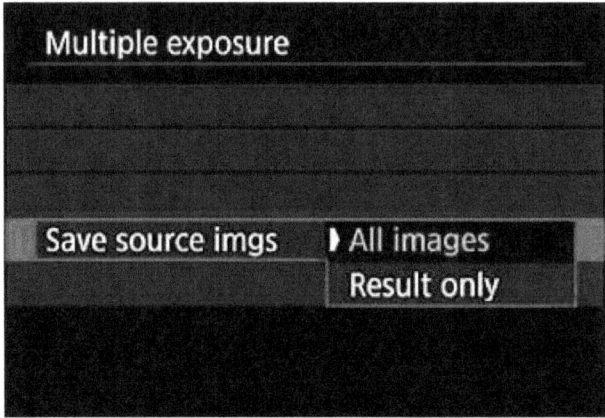

Continue Multiple Exposure

You can pick 1 Shot Only or Continuously. If you just want to take one set of multiple exposures, pick 1 Shot Only. Then, turn off Multiple Exposure and start taking it normally again. If you pick this option, you will be able to do this. Choose the Continuously option if you don't want to stop shooting to go back into the menu system after each shot to turn the feature back on after taking a bunch of different exposures.

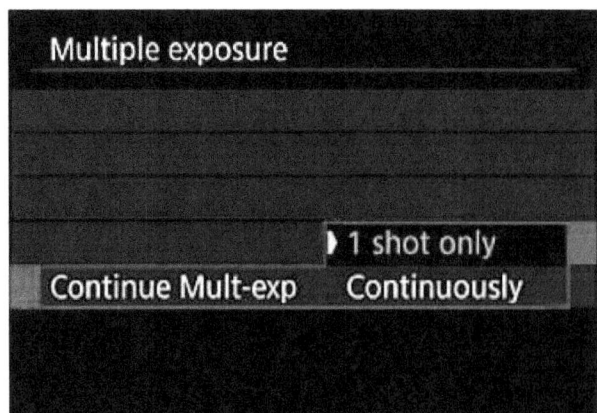

Focus Bracketing

With the camera's focus bracketing feature, a series of photos will be taken while the focus is slowly changed between each one. After that, it can move from the point that is closest to the subject to the point that needs to be the clearest. You can choose between 2 and 999 shots.

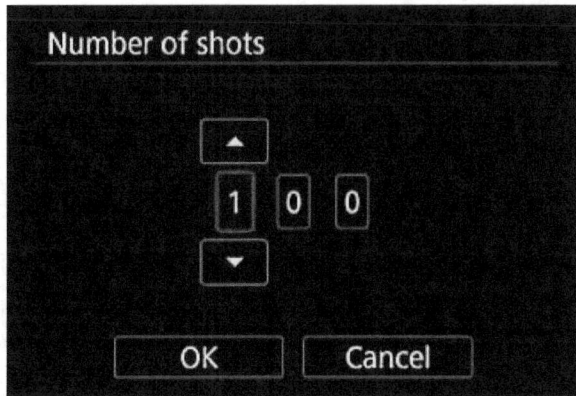

This is when you can set the Focus Increment. Tell it how much to shift the attention. This number is changed right away to match the opening number when the picture is taken.

The focus can cover a wider range with the same number of shots and focus steps when the aperture value is bigger.

Press **SET** when you're done setting up.

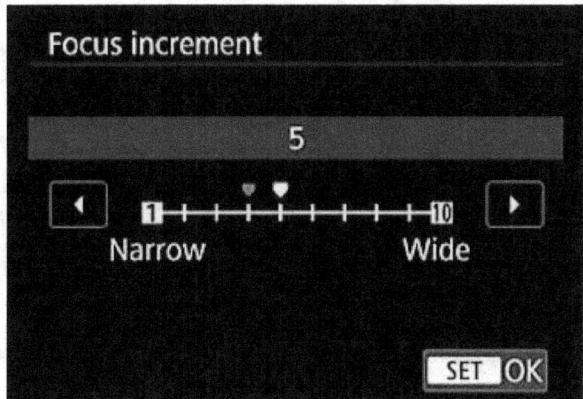

- If you select Enable, the camera will make changes based on the difference between the shown aperture value and the real aperture value (effective f/number), which changes based on the focus position. It will take into account changes in the lighting of the picture while focus bracketing.
- If you don't want to fix changes in picture brightness while focus bracketing is going on, choose Disable. Shouldn't be used to add depth to photos you've already taken in apps like DPP.

Set [Depth composite]

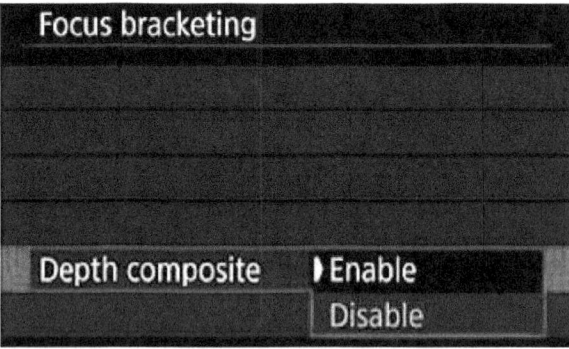

- Press **Enable** to let the camera do depth compositing. Both the source shots and the picture with the depth added are saved.
- Click **Disable** to turn off in-camera depth compositing the way you want to. It only saves shots that are taken.

Set [Crop depth comp.]

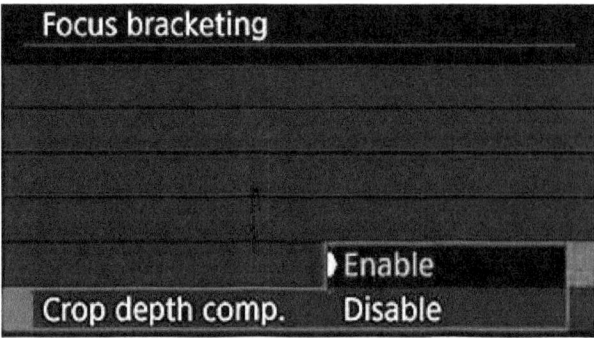

- Select **Enable** to crop images before compositing. Cutting any pictures that don't have the right angle of view for compositing alignment will fix the problem.
- If you don't want to crop these shots, click Disable. For this reason, places in the saved pictures that don't have a good enough view are marked with a black line. You can change or crop the pictures however you like.

Set [Flash interval]

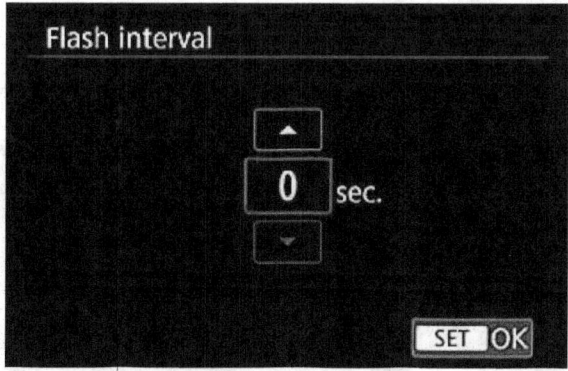

- Focus bracketing works with compatible Speedlites and non-Canon flash units that are powered by the sync port.
- If this setting is set to 0, the camera starts shooting as soon as the Speedlites are fully charged. Check the instructions of the Speedlite that comes with your camera for safety tips on how to keep shooting. If you want to use multiple Speedlites that are compatible with wireless flash photography, you may want to make the wait longer.
- For non-Canon flash units, set a good time between charges to see how long the flash lasts and how long it can be charged.

Take the picture

- To save your pictures in a new folder, press [💾] and OK.
- To focus, move the camera to the close end of the range you want, and then press the button down.
- After taking a picture, let go of the camera button.
- The camera keeps shooting, and the point of focus moves out to the horizon.

- When the focus range gets as far away as you set it, or after the number of shots you choose, no more will be taken.
- To stop shooting, press the camera button down.

Interval Timer

Up to 99 hours, 59 minutes, and 59 seconds can be set as exposure times with this setting. When you press the **INFO** button, a screen will appear where you can change the number of shots and the time between them.

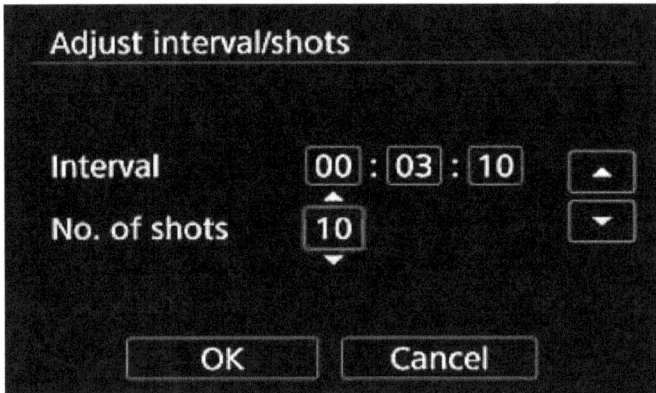

Silent Shutter Function

You can take pictures without drawing too much attention to yourself if you turn this on. There won't be as many sounds and sights that show that pictures are being taken at the same time. When the electronic shutter is used, the focusing beep sound, the sound of touching the screen, and the sound of the self-timer are all turned down. The flash stops working, the self-timer light stops blinking, and the tracking help beam stops shining.

Long-duration noise reduction is turned off. You can turn off the camera, but the shutter will still be open. You can still use headphones to listen to the sound while you record video because the headphone output will stay on. Since nothing is happening, the only sounds that are likely to be heard are your breathing and the motor that focuses the lens.

Shutter Mode

If you don't use the mechanical shutter on your camera, you can take shots without making any noise. You can also choose the third mode. An electric first-curtain shutter starts the picture and a mechanical shutter stops it. This is more like how cameras have been used for a long time.

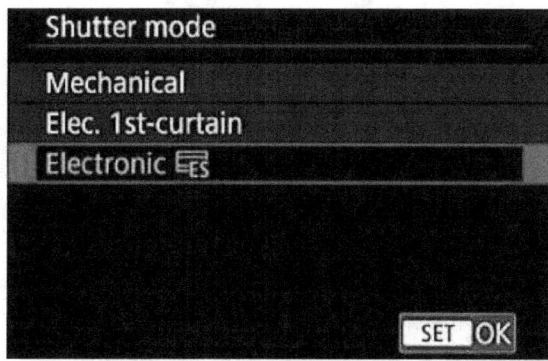

Mechanical shutter. A motorized first curtain is pulled back to show the sensor in this state, which is the normal one. The curtain stays in place until a second curtain is pulled back by a motor. People in business call this the "traditional mode." The first and second screens come together to make a hole in the middle of the sensor when the shutter speed is above 1/200th of a second and up to 1/8000th of a second.

This means that you can only see a small part of the sensor at any given time. There could be thirty seconds to one-hundredth of a second between the first and second curtains. When a mechanical shutter is used, the flash sync can only go as fast as 1/200 of a second.

To get the most dynamic range out of your shots, use a camera that moves.

Electronic 1st-curtain shutter. If the exposure time was made longer, the mechanical shutter might have bounced, which could have made the picture less sharp. That won't happen with this setting. The real first curtain needs to be taken down to do this. After the shutter is opened, the sensor will be cleared automatically to make it look like the first curtain is being opened by hand. This takes place right after the shutter opens. The exposure will last until the second curtain drops automatically, which should happen between 30 and 1/250 of a second. As you work in this mode, the speed of the electric flash will be set to 1/250 of a second.

Electronic shutter. In this setting, the exposure starts and stops itself. Up to 1/8000 of a second can be used for exposure in Tv and M mode. Up to 1/1600 of a second can be used in Fv, P, or Av mode. If you set the camera to constant shooting mode, it will always take 20 pictures per second. This is going to happen, and a white frame will show up. There are some problems with this mode's lack of noise, such as the ones below:

- To get rid of all sound from the camera, go to the Setup 3 screen and turn off the Beep option. It will beep to let you know that it has taken a picture when you use the electric shutter method.
- Neither the electric flash nor the automatic exposure bracketing can be used. It wouldn't help much to use an electric shutter because the flash burst is generally louder than the camera shutter.
- When you use a rolling shutter, it can take a long time to record a whole frame, so there is a chance that banding artifacts will show up in your pictures. This is very important when it's not possible to tell where the light source is coming from. Picture of things that are moving quickly might look off because the part of the subject being shot first will have moved by the time the camera sees the end of the subject.
- It changes from reading with 14 bits to reading with 12 bits. This lowers the dynamic range, but it also lessens the effect of the moving shutter. In parts of the picture with dark shadows, it's harder to get tones because of this. This stands out the most in scenes with ISO numbers above 400. A lower ISO setting and/or leaving the automatic camera on will give you the best results.

Release Shutter Without Card

Users can take pictures with Release Shutter Without a Card even if they don't have an SD card in the camera at the time. If you turn this setting on, the camera will keep taking pictures, but they won't be saved. Instead, the picture will be kept in the camera's memory until a memory card is put in. The picture will then be saved to the card.

You may find it helpful to be able to Release Shutter Without a Card sometimes, like when you need to take a picture quickly but don't have a memory card with you or when the memory card you are using is full. Let's say you are outside taking pictures and your memory card starts to fill up. This feature is easy to turn on so you can keep taking pictures without having to stop and switch memory cards.

When this choice is used to take a picture, the picture will not be saved forever if the camera is not connected to a memory card. This is very important to keep in mind. This memory will get full fast if you keep taking pictures without a memory card. You can't use the camera to take more pictures until you either put in a new memory card or get rid of the ones that are already there. The spare memory will fill up if you keep taking pictures without a memory card.

Touch Shutter

Touching the touchscreen on the back of the camera to take a picture is possible with this feature. Photographers who want to take a picture quickly without having to change the settings or press the shutter button by hand may find this feature very useful.

High-Speed Display

You can see a high-speed display that changes between each shot and the live picture when you are shooting in [⚡H] (high-speed continuous shooting] drive mode and a shutter mode other than the electronic shutter.

Metering Timer

You can decide how long the metering timer stays on after you do something like press the shutter button halfway. This changes how long the AE lock or exposure number display stays on.

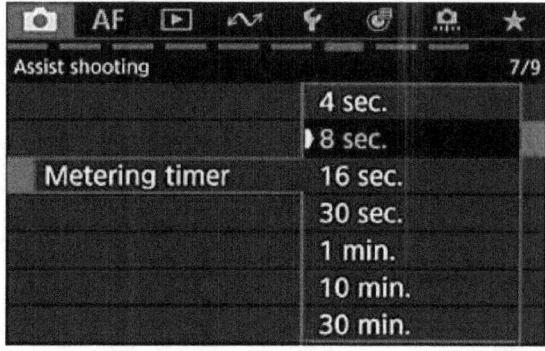

Display Simulation

When you choose Shooting 9 from the menu, this is the first choice you can make. You can choose whether the live view picture has the same brightness level as the final picture or shows a bright picture (based on the Screen Brightness setting you set in the Set-up 4 menu), which might be easier to see in bright rooms. You can pick one of the following:

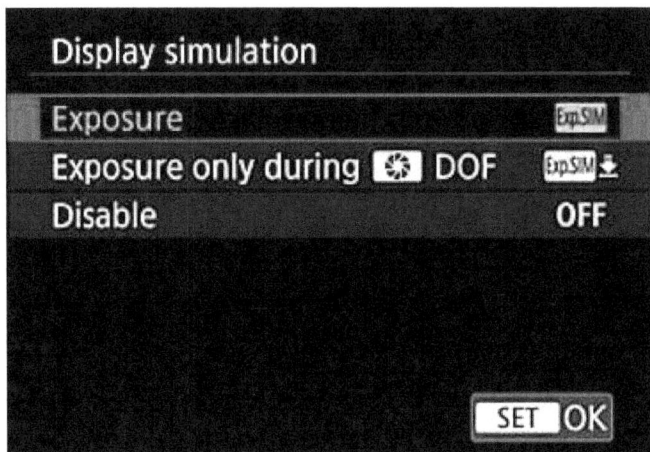

- **Exposure+Depth-of-Field**. The picture on the screen shows how bright the real picture is, depending on the current exposure settings and any exposure correction settings you have made. In real-time, you can see how your exposure settings work on a scale that is mostly right, but not quite. Use this choice. It will also show a picture of the real depth of field at the angle that was just chosen.
- **Exposure**. The brightness of the picture is changed to show the real exposure, even though the exposure was already fixed. But the depth of field won't be shown. This is the choice you should make if you want to see how the lighting changes a picture without having to see what is in focus and what is not.
- **Exposure Only During DOF Preview**. At first, the view picture is as bright as the camera came with it. But if you press any button you may have set as a depth-of-field sample button, it will change to match your exposure settings. For this to happen, you need to press that button.
- It will work best for you doing it this way whenever you need to check the exposure while you're shooting. I like this setting the most because it lets me plan my shots on a big, bright screen while still being able to see how brightness and depth of field will change the picture.

Optical Viewfinder Simulated View Assist

If you miss the optical viewfinder experience, this function will take you back to that time. Just recently, the electronic viewfinders in mirrorless cameras have started to get as clear and easy to see as the big, bright optical viewfinders found in digital (and film) SLR cameras. It wasn't long ago that this changed. This picture was taken with the Canon EOS R5 Mark II, which has an organic light-emitting diode (OLED) sight that lets it see farther in low light.

This option was first added to the EOS R3, which costs more. As long as you haven't made any big exposure compensation changes, it changes the scene's general brightness in the electronic viewfinder (EVF). This gives you a preview that's like using a regular optical viewfinder.

If this is turned on, Display Simulation will not run, and the tone curve will be changed to be softer. That way, the scene's blacks and whites will look lighter than its middle tones.

The EVF sample will turn into the JPEG format if the OVF simulation is not used. The tone curve for the JPEG format looks more like a S. More contrast will be made and the dynamic range will be shrunk. This feature is there, but I don't use it very often because I'd rather see a picture that looks more like the JPEGs I will make later.

AVF simulation is what you need to turn on if you want the picture to look like it was taken through an optical vision. Remember that modeling won't work on the EVF or LCD screen if you watch the sample on an external monitor that is connected to the HDMI port.

Blackout-Free Display

This option for the display gets rid of the blackout that happens when continuous shooting starts. This makes it easier to shoot things that are moving.

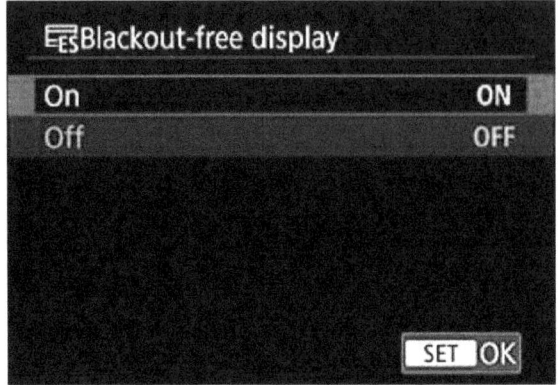

Shooting Information Display

You can change the information that appears when you take a picture on different levels of this post. Many things can be seen on the lens or the LCD screen on the back of the camera while you are taking pictures. But it can be hard to understand when you see all of that information over and over again.

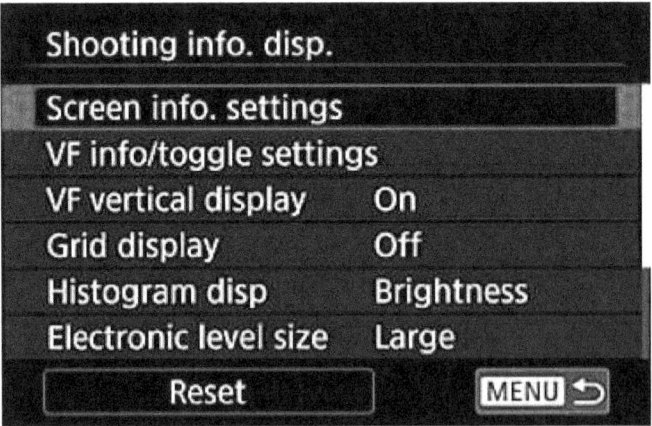

- **Screen Information Settings**. When you press the **INFO** button, five different types of information will show up on the LCD screen.
- **Viewfinder Information/Toggle Settings**. Three different camera views can be shown or hidden.
- **VF Vertical Display**. If you turn this function on, the screen will show different information when you stand the camera straight up.

- **Grid Display**. You can pick a grid that is 3x3, 6x4, or 3x3 with diagonal lines. You can also get rid of the lines on the LCD screen and camera.

Histogram Display. This property can be set to one of two options:

3. **Brightness and RGB settings**. It's possible to choose between the RGB live histogram (which shows all three main colors) and the Brightness live histogram.
4. **Display Size**. Pick between the Large and the Small.

Lens Information Display. This property can be set to one of four options:

- **Focus Distance Display**. What you set may mean that the focus distance is only shown in manual focus mode when the camera is focusing. In this case, it could be at any time or not at all.
- **Unit**. It is possible to change the settings so that the focus distance is shown in either meters or feet.
- **Focal Length Display.** You can pick whether to show the screen the present focus length or not.
- **SA Variable Amount.** The amount of spherical aberration that can be fixed with lenses that can handle this change, like the RF 100mm f/2.8 Macro of course.

Reset. This setting changes the numbers of the settings above back to how they were before.

Reverse Display

A mirror picture can be shown if you shoot with the screen facing the person (toward the front of the camera).

Viewfinder Display Format

You can still see through things that are in your way, even if you can't get rid of them all. On the view, you can pick from two different kinds of screens. The rest of the information is shown on top of the frame on Display 1. Your picture is in the viewfinder. Some of the information is shown in a black bar below the screen.

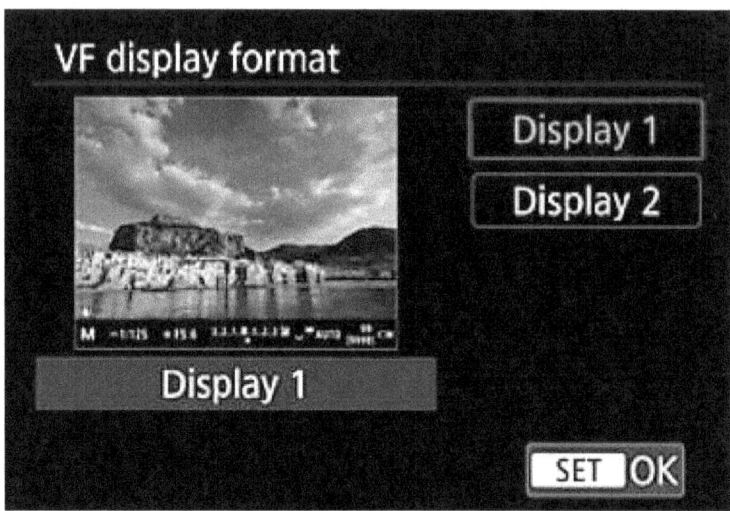

Display 2 will have black bars on the left and right and above the frame if you choose it.

There will be no picture frame on top of these black bars; the extra details will be shown inside them. When you press the **INFO** button, the sight will switch between the different information screens that you set up in the Shooting Information Display setting.

Display Performance

This setting affects whether the screen uses more power and whether things that move quickly are shown more easily. I always use the Smooth setting because I don't use less power and never run out of batteries.

Chapter 8

EOS R5 MARK II Custom Settings

If you want to change how the Canon EOS R5 works to fit the way you shoot, you can use the Custom Functions Menu. This menu lets you make changes to the camera, such as the autofocus settings, brightness settings, and more. You can change how the camera handles focusing, how it figures out how much light there is, and what each button does.

For each setting, the Custom Functions Menu lets you change how the camera works. This lets you change it to fit your needs better. People who want to take sports, portraits, or landscape photos can set the camera to work best for those kinds of photos. This menu lets you change how the camera works in more ways, so you can make each time you shoot something different.

Tab Menus: Custom Functions

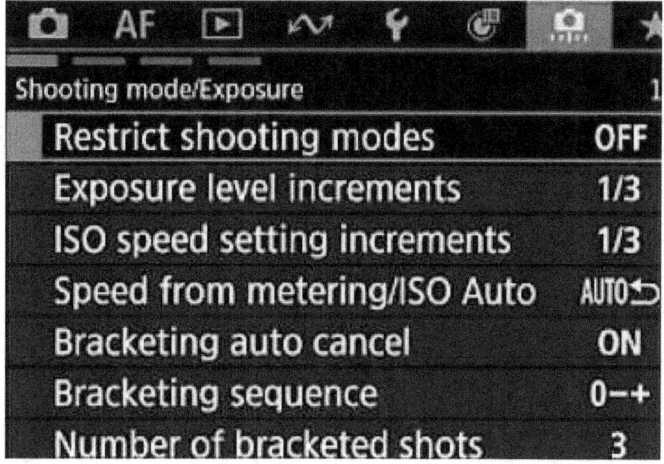

Restrict Shooting Modes

The MODE button lets you choose which shooting modes to use.

You can choose from Fv, P, Av, M, Tv, BULB, C1/C2, or C3. Then press SET to make it official. Press OK to save the change.

Exposure Level Increments

In 1/2-stop increments, you can change the camera speed, aperture value, exposure compensation, AEB, flash exposure compensation, and other settings.

- 1/3: 1/3-stop
- 1/2: 1/2-stop

ISO Speed Setting Increments

You can change the ISO speed setting increase to a full stop.

- 1/3: 1/3-stop
- 1/1: 1-stop

Speed from Metering/ISO Auto

While the metering timer is still going, you can change the ISO speed if the camera changes it during metering or the metering timer for ISO Auto operation in P/Tv/Av/M/B mode.

- AUTO⤺ : Restore Auto after metering
- AUTO⤸ : Retain speed after metering

Bracketing Auto Cancel

You can turn off AEB and white balance bracketing when the power switch is off.

- ON: Enable
- OFF: Disable

Bracketing Sequence

Setting up AEB and white balance bracketing can be changed.

- 0−+: 0, -, +
- −0+: -, 0, +
- +0−: +, 0, -

AEB	White Balance Bracketing	
	B/A Direction	M/G Direction
0: Standard exposure	0: Standard white balance	0: Standard white balance
−: Underexposure	−: Blue bias	−: Magenta bias
+: Overexposure	+: Amber bias	+: Green bias

Number of Bracketed Shots

With white balance and AEB, you can change how many shots are taken.

When Bracketing order is set to 0, -, +, this table shows the shots that will be made.

- **3: 3 shots**
- **2: 2 shots**
- **5: 5 shots**
- **7: 7 shots**

(1-stop/step increments)

	1st Shot	2nd Shot	3rd Shot	4th Shot	5th Shot	6th Shot	7th Shot
3: 3 shots	Standard (0)	−1	+1				
2: 2 shots	Standard (0)	±1					
5: 5 shots	Standard (0)	−2	−1	+1	+2		
7: 7 shots	Standard (0)	−3	−2	−1	+1	+2	+3

Safety Shift

If the light changes on the subject and the autoexposure range can't get the standard exposure, the camera will change the setting that was manually picked to get the standard exposure. What you set for aperture and shutter speed works in both TV and AV modes. You can use ISO speed in mode P, mode Tv, or mode Av.

- OFF: Disable
- Tv/Av: Shutter speed/Aperture
- ISO: ISO speed

Same Expo. for New Aperture

You can switch lenses, add an extension, or use a zoom lens whose maximum aperture value can be changed. If you do any of these things, the largest aperture value might go down and the smallest f/number might go up when taking in M mode (manual exposure) and setting the ISO speed manually instead of using ISO Auto. This function changes the ISO speed or shutter speed (Tv value) right away to keep the exposure the same as before (1), (2), or (3). This stops the matching underexposure.

As soon as you press ISO speed/Shutter speed, the ISO speed changes right away within the ISO speed range. When the ISO speed is changed and the image can't be kept, the shutter speed (Tv number) is changed right away.

- OFF: Disable
- ISO: ISO speed
- ISO/Tv: ISO speed/Shutter speed
- Tv: Shutter speed

AE Lock Meter. Mode after Focus

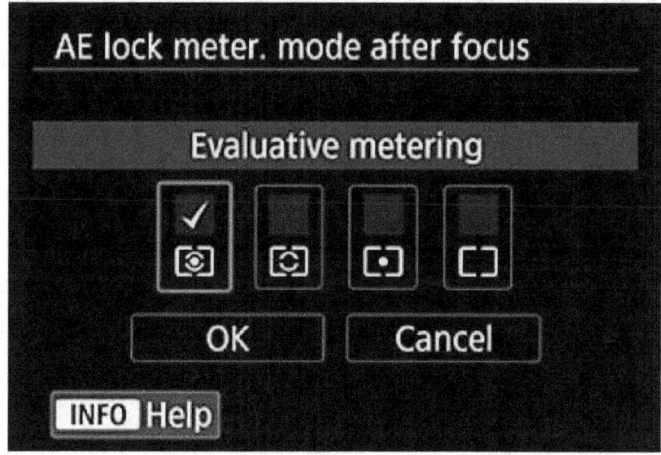

Once the subject is in focus with One-Shot AF, you can lock the exposure (AE lock) for any metering mode. The exposure will stay locked as long as you press the shutter button halfway. For AE lock, check off the sensing modes you want to use. Press OK to save the change.

Set Shutter Speed Range

You can choose from a range of shutter speeds for each Shutter setting. You can choose a range for the shutter speed when you're in Fv, Tv, or M mode. When the setting is P, Av, or Fv and the shutter speed is set to **AUTO**, the speed is based on the range you choose. When making a movie, this doesn't happen. Press OK to save the change.

Mech Shutter/Elec 1st-curtain

- **Lowest speed**: It's possible to set the lowest speed to anywhere from 30 seconds to 14,000 seconds.
- **Highest speed**: You can set the highest speed to be between 1/8000 sec. and 15 sec.

Electronic

- **Lowest speed**: The slowest speed can be set for 30 seconds to 8000 seconds.
- **Highest speed**: You can set the highest speed to be anywhere from 1/16000 sec. to 15 sec.

Set Aperture Range

You can pick the aperture value range. In Fv, Av, M, or B mode, you can set the aperture number by hand in any range you want. You can set the aperture value to **AUTO** in Fv mode, P mode, or Tv mode. This will make the aperture value stay in the range you choose. Press OK to save the change.

- **Max. aperture**

You can set it from f/1.0 to f/64.

- **Min. aperture**

You can set it from f/91 to f/1.4.

AE Microadjustment

Caution

Here's how to change the standard amount of exposure. This is helpful if taking with autoexposure and not adjusting the exposure makes your photos look too dark or too light.

- **OFF: Disable**
- **ON: Enable**

Press the button and then choose **Enable** to get to the screen where you can make changes. ±1 stop, which is 1/8 of a stop, is how much you can change the auto exposure. Photos will be less underexposed if you move it to the right, and more overexposed if you move it to the left.

FE Micro Adjustment

The flash can give off different amounts of light. Helpful if the main subjects of auto-flash photos taken without flash exposure adjustments often look too dark or too light.

- **OFF: Disable**
- **ON: Enable**

To make changes, press the Q button and then choose **Enable**. You can change a normal flash's brightness by ±1 stop, which is equal to 1/8 of a stop. If the main subjects are getting too much light, move the setting to the left. If they are getting too little light, move it to the right.

Limit Continuous Shot Count.

You can set the highest burst size to shoot continuously. It will stop taking after a certain number of shots if you hold down the shutter button and set the setting for continuous shooting.

You can set it anywhere from 99 to 2 shots. The setting goes back to **Disable** when you press the **DELETE** button.

As long as **Disable** is set, shooting can go on until the largest burst shown at right in the viewfinder is used up.

Add Cropping Information

You can arrange photos as if you were using a medium- or large-format camera (6x6 cm, 4x5 inch, etc.) because adding scaling information shows vertical lines for the aspect ratio you picked when you shot.

When you take a picture, the camera doesn't crop it before saving it to the card. Instead, it adds information about the aspect ratio so that you can crop them in Digital Photo Professional (EOS software).

When you shoot pictures on a computer with Digital Photo Professional, it's easy to crop them to the size you set.

- OFF: Disable
- 6:6: Aspect ratio 6:6
- 3:4: Aspect ratio 3:4
- 4:5: Aspect ratio 4:5
- 6:7: Aspect ratio 6:7
- 5:6: Aspect ratio 10:12
- 5:7: Aspect ratio 5:7

Av Setting Without Lens

You can pick whether the aperture number can be changed even when the lens is not attached.

- OFF: Disable
- ON: Enable

There is no need to connect a lens to change the aperture setting. So this is helpful when you're ready to shoot and already know what aperture value you want to use.

Default Erase Option

You can change which option is picked by default in the erase menu when you press the **Erase** button while playing back pictures or looking through them after taking them.

When you press the **SET** button, you can quickly delete pictures as long as you don't press **Cancel**.

- 🗑: [Cancel] selected
- 🗑: [Erase] selected
- RAW: [EraseRAW] selected
- J/H: [Erase non-RAW] selected

Release Shutter w/o Lens

You can pick whether you can take pictures or movies without a lens.

- **OFF: Disable**
- **ON: Enable**

Retract Lens On Power Off.

If you want, gear-type STM lenses like the RF35mm F1.8 Macro IS STM can be set to shrink right away when the camera is turned off.

- **ON: Enable**
- **OFF: Disable**

Add IPTC Information

There is a way to add IPTC (International Press Telecommunications Council) information to JPEG, HEIF, or RAW photos while you are taking them. You can do this with the EOS software. This helps with keeping track of files and other tasks that need IPTC help.

If you want to know how to add IPTC information to your camera and what kinds of information you can add, read the EOS Utility Instruction Manual.

- **OFF: Disable**
- **ON: Enable**

Custom Function C. Fn 5

Clear all Custom Func. (C.Fn)

Choose [📷] to clear all custom functions. All Custom Function settings are cleared when you press the C.Fn key, except for the Customize buttons and knobs settings.

Chapter 9

Image Review and Playback

This is where you can change how the Canon EOS R5 Mark II looks at and handles photos and movies after you take them. Watch movies and look at pictures on your memory card from this menu. You can also remove or lock them. You can also rate photos, make movies, and tell the app to automatically rotate photos.

You can also see information about the shooting, enlarge photos for a more in-depth look, and make artistic or simple changes like cropping in the Playback Menu. It's easier to organize and go over your work when you can do it all from the camera.

Playback Menu

You can choose how to show, look over, copy, and print the pictures you've taken from the seven blue-coded Playback options. These choices are on the camera's back. Not many of these things have settings that are already set.

Some of the only ones that do this are Image Jump with Main Slider (10 pictures), Magnification (2X), and Control over HDMI (Disable). Most of these are functions, not settings, so there aren't many fixed numbers for them. You can pick one of the following:

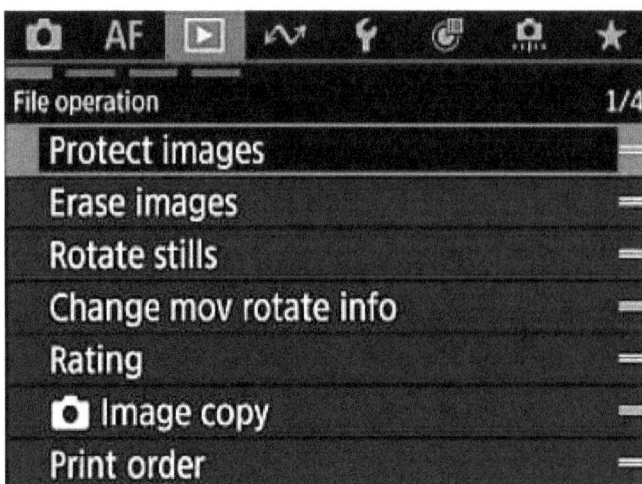

Protect Images

That's right, Protect Images lets you lock some photos on your memory card so that no one can delete them or write over them. You won't be able to delete or overwrite important photos by accident. This is a good way to keep important pictures safe, like wedding photos or family photos. If you keep these picture graphs, you won't lose them if you take them out of the memory card by accident or if the card stops working.

The Playback 1 menu has seven things. This is the first one. It's possible to mark a picture as secure so that someone doesn't delete it by chance another time. You can do this by pressing the **Erase** button or selecting **Erase Images** from the Playback menu.

In the Quick Control menu, you can find Protect under **Playback**. You can also use this item from this menu. To protect the picture, press the MENU button and pick **Protect** from the Playback 1 menu. This will help you protect one or more pictures.

One of these screens will appear:

Default screen. By default, the screen shows the following options:

- **Select Images**. From the present card, you can pick which pictures to use by scrolling through a grid of tiny icons.
- **Select Range**. By clicking **SET** on the first picture and then the last picture and clicking **SET** again, you can pick a run of pictures.
- **All Images in Folder**. Pick out each picture in the box. If there is more than one folder, you will be shown a list of them. To pick the area that is now highlighted, press the **SET** button.
- **Unprotect All Images in Folder.** Choose a folder and let anyone see all the pictures in it.
- **All Images on Card.** Keep every picture on the card safe.
- **Unprotect All Images on Card.** Take off the protection from all of the photos on this card.

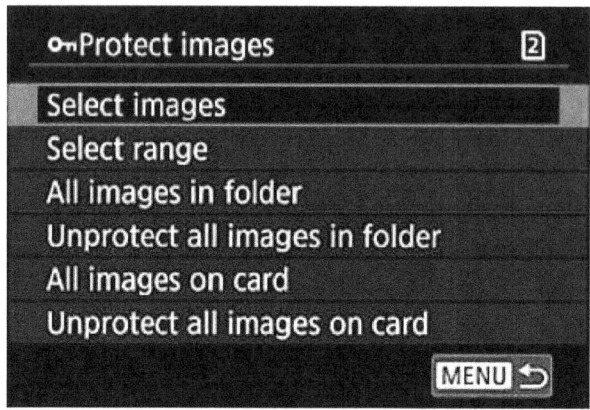

Erase Images

You can Select and Erase Images, Select Range, All Images in Folder, or All Images on Card when you choose this item from the menu. With the first three choices, you can pick which pictures to delete from a card. With the fourth choice, you can delete them all. Pictures that have already been saved will not be deleted. The Format function, on the other hand, is often faster and gives you more details.

This function does some of the same things that the Protect Images function does. This screen will appear if no Image Search Conditions are given. It lets you do the following:

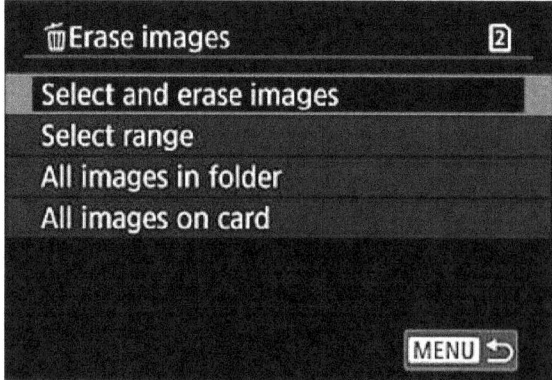

Select and Erase Images. To move from one picture on your card to the next, press the left and right arrow keys. You can get rid of a checkmark or remove a picture by pressing the **SET** button. When you press the Q button after making all of your choices, a confirmation box will show up. Click Cancel or OK and **SET** to finish.

Select Range. Does the same thing as the choice to cover the area. Choose **Select Range**, then pick out the first picture in a series, and press the **SET** button to give it a name. Once you've picked the last picture to erase, press **SET** a second time. Make sure you want to remove the pictures by pressing the **Q** key.

All Images in Folder. You can now see a list of the folders on your memory card. A message will ask you to accept after you press **SET**. It will also let you know that Protected pictures will not be deleted after you confirm your choice.

All Images on Card. You will be asked to confirm it when you're done with this step. Picking **All Images on Card** will get rid of all the pictures on the card. The only pictures that will stay are the ones that were sealed. The pictures on the memory card will be erased, but the card itself will not be lost.

You can do one of these things after setting the Image Search Conditions in the Playback 5 menu:

- **Select and Erase Images**. As you look through a short list of pictures, you can pick any picture that's already on the card.
- **Select Range**. Pick pictures that fill the whole card.
- **All Found Images**. If none of the photos you protected were saved, get rid of all the photos that were found using the search terms you chose in the Set Image Search Conditions line.

Remember that deleting pictures from your memory card with **Erase image** will not free up space on the camera's internal memory.

Once you have saved all of your pictures to a computer or another drive, you will need to format the memory card to use the extra room. When the card is cleaned, the picture on it is erased so that it can hold new information.

Rotate Stills

If you go to the Setup 1 menu and choose the **Auto Rotate** option, you can set up the camera to rotate pictures that were taken vertically. You can also spin a picture by hand while it plays by using this menu item. To rotate stills, go to the Playback 1 menu and choose it. Next, use the QCD-1 to look through the photos on your card until you find the one you want to turn. Last, press the **SET** button.

The picture on the screen will be 90 degrees to the left. The screen will be turned 270 degrees if you press the **SET** button again. Don't forget that you can move pictures in the menu that comes up when you press the Q button while watching.

Change Movie Rotate Info

People who have recorded movies on their phones know that they can be turned from side to side or even flipped over while the recording is going on. With this item, you can change the orientation of the movies you take with your camera so that they can be watched on other platforms in either portrait or landscape mode.

This choice only changes how your phone and other devices show your movies. Videos will always be shown side by side on the camera's screen. In the Set-up 1 screen, you will need to turn on the choice that says Add Movie Rotate Info.

From the Playback 1 menu, just choose this option. Then, turn the QCD-1 to choose a movie to watch.

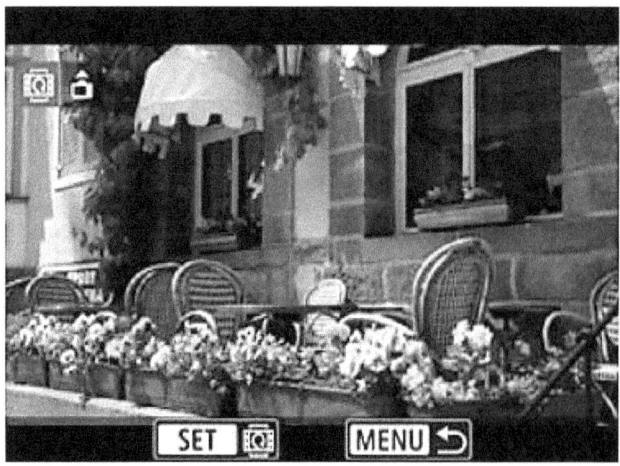

When the video is played again, there will be an icon in the upper left corner of the screen with an arrow inside it that points to the side of the movie frame that is shown at the top of the screen. The direction is always at the top. It will move to the right and then to the left when you press **SET**.

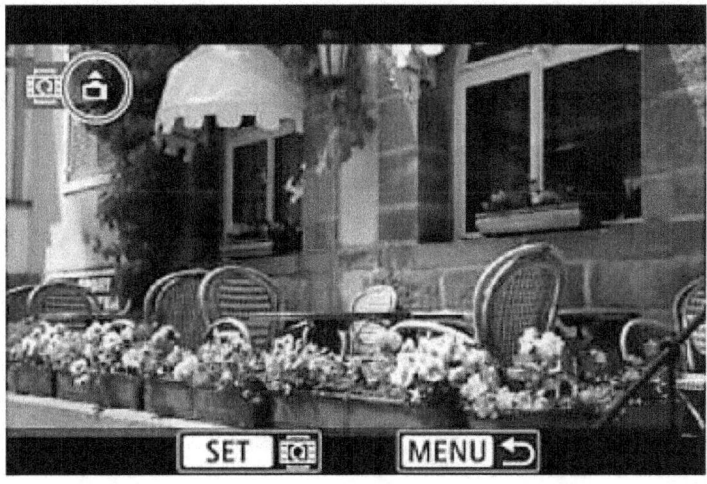

Rating

As the song plays, press the **RATE** button more than once to leave a review. Giving photos or movies you've taken a number is helpful if you want to rate their quality or use the number system to show something else. With this item, you can turn off the score tool. It lets you give shots one, two, three, four, or five stars.

Picture Jump only lets you see pictures with the grade you give them. You were told to take pictures at a track meet with a lot of different events. You could give each event with a jump one star, each event with a run two stars, each event with a throw three stars, each event with a jump four stars, and each event with a dash five stars. After that, you could use the Image Jump tool to see only shots from a certain group.

Still, the waypoints are given can be changed so that it works for many types of groups. Wedding pictures can be put into groups, such as those of the bride and groom, their parents, their guests, and the staff. Take pictures of kids for school photos. For first graders, you might give one rate, for second graders, another, and so on.

This tool can be used for a lot more than you might think at first. Digital Photo Professional also lets you use scores to choose which photos to use in a slide show or to pick photos for you. You can pick either of these two options.

There are three ways to rate a movie or picture:

RATE button. If you press the RATE button more than once, you can give it any number of stars, or no stars at all. The only way this will work is if the Rate Button Function setting is set to Rate in the Playback 6 menu. You can also not write a review at all. When you press the Rate Button Function button, you can set the maximum number of stars that can be given. As an example, you could not let scores be less than or equal to three stars.

Quick Control menu. When you press the **Q** button while the Playback mode is still on, the Quick Control menu comes up. This is where you can rate things as well. This picture is in the left column, next to the third picture from the top.

This menu entry. To use the Ratings menu item, just do these things:

1. Get on the menu and pick **Rating**.
2. Press Select Images, Select Range, All Images in Folder, or All Images on Card to pick which pictures to rate.

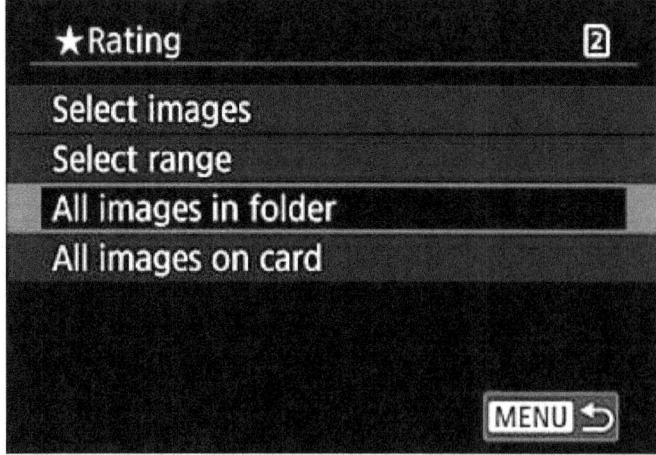

3. When you see the movie or picture you want to rate, press **SET**. You can also pick a bunch of pictures, all the pictures in a folder, or all the pictures on a card.
4. To rate the QCD-1 from one to five stars or to take away a star, turn it now. You can rate as many shots as you want.
5. When you're done, press **MENU** to leave.

Image Copy

The best thing about cameras with two memory card slots is that I can use both of them at the same time without switching cards. Making backups of your files on two cards is one of the best things about having two. You can use these when you're not near your computer, like when you're traveling. These are some of the things I do:

- **Shoot to two cards simultaneously.** You can use this right away to make a backup of your pictures in case the ones on your main card get lost or damaged. There should be about the same amount of room on both of your cards. Go to Record Functions + Card/Folder Settings in the Set-up 1 menu and choose Record to Multiple. You can now record more than one card at once.
- **Make a copy.** You can copy pictures from one memory card to another with the Image Copy tool. Do not use two cards at the same time when you take pictures. This slows down the camera. Instead, use only one card when you take pictures. Make a copy on a second card at the end of the day. This way, you won't miss any of the important times in your life. You can copy any number of pictures you've taken from this menu item, from one to all of them.
- **Make copies to distribute.** It will be easier and faster to make multiple copies of a picture if you buy memory cards.

You can copy pictures from one memory card to another by following these steps, which can only be used when the camera has two memory cards in use at the same time:

1. The screen below will appear on your device when you choose **Image Copy** from the **Playback 1** menu. Which card will be the source? The number on the line tells you this and how much space is left on the card that will be the destination.

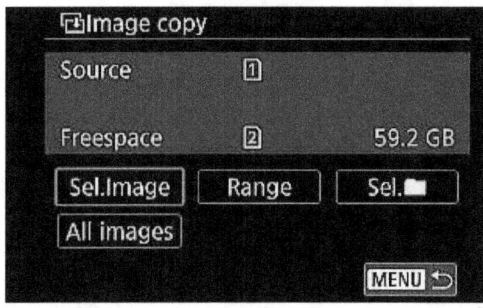

2. You can choose from All Images, Range, Select Folder, and Select Image on the first screen. Select Image lets you choose just one photo. Press the **SET** button to pick the option.
3. You can choose the Select Image, Select Range, or Select Folder method. This will bring up a screen with a list of files that can be seen on the source card. You can't see this screen. Pick the folder that was touched by pressing the **SET** button. Steps 3 and 4 will not be done if you pick All Images.

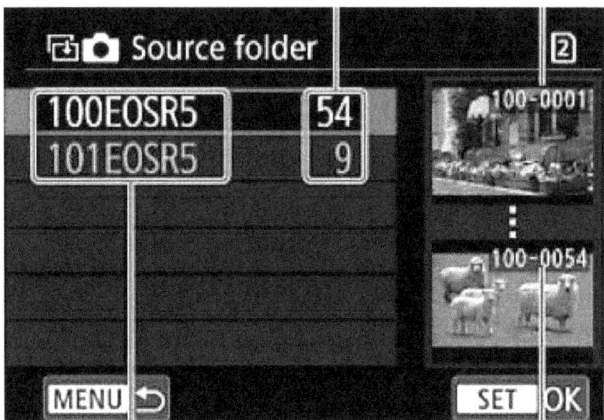

4. If you go to the File menu and choose Select Image or Range, you can choose which pictures to copy. After clicking Select Folder, you won't have to do Step 4. Remember that you can only copy pictures from one place at a time.

    o **Individual images**. As you look through the pictures, press the **SET** button to mark the ones you want to copy. If you're ready to move on, press the **Q** button after picking out each picture.
    o **Range of images**. This makes a picture list that you can look through. Press the **SET** button when you find the first picture in the range. To find the picture that is now shown, use the multi-controller joystick. Then press **SET** again. To be sure of your choice, press **Q**. To move forward, press **Q** again.

5. It displays the groups on the different memory cards. To choose one, press **SET**. If you want to make a new folder with a name of your choice, press Create Folder. You can also change the folder's name on the Canon text-entry screen.
6. After you pick which pictures to use as a source and where to save them, the screen below appears. Following the **Cancel** option, you can either press **SET** to go ahead or stop the process. In this case, you can either skip the picture and send a

new one, or you can stop the transfer if the target address already has an image with the same file number. The names of the two files will always be the same and never change.

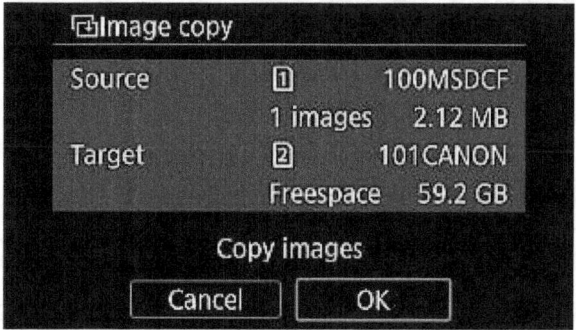

7. There are different speeds for memory cards, so the time it takes to copy will rely on how many photos you want to move. To leave the menu, press the **SET** button when you see the image below.

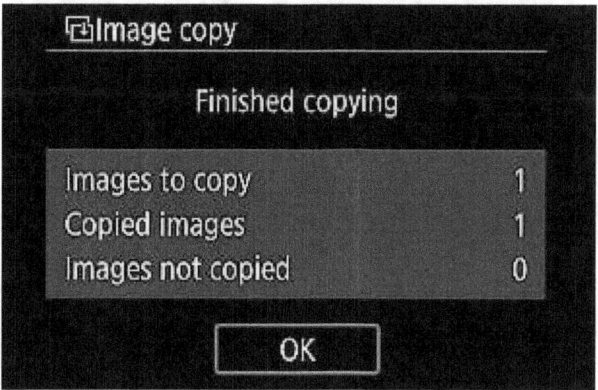

Print Order

The Playback 2 page only has two things, and this is one of them. Almost all digital cameras can now handle a file called DPOF, which stands for Digital Print Order Format.

This type of file lets you tell your camera which photos on your memory card to print and how many of each to make. People who have a printer that can read memory cards will be able to see this. The people at the picture lab will be able to read your memory card and use what they see to make prints for you.

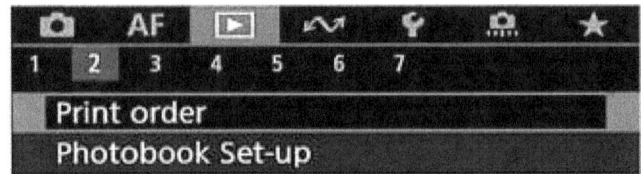

Once the pictures you've chosen are marked for DPOF printing, you can either print them yourself or take your memory card to a digital lab or machine that can read the print order and make the copies you want. You can't order pictures or RAW files. To place a DPOF print order, do the following:

1. Choose **Print Order**. Hit the **Set up** button.
2. It will show you the screen where you can place a Print Order. To make Setup the current choice, use the arrow keys. Hit the **SET** button.

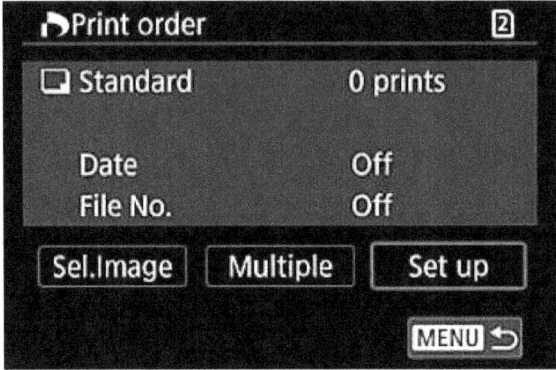

3. As for the Print Type, you can pick Standard, Index/Thumbnails, or Both. After that, you can pick whether to put the Date or File Number on the paper or not. It is not possible to show both the date and the file number at the same time. In the print order, you can't pick a different print type for each picture; the same print type will be used for all of them. To get back to the Print Order screen, press the **MENU** button.
4. Bring Sel. Image (pick out single photos) or Multiple.

    o When you use Sel. Image, the motion tools let you look at the pictures, and the SET button lets you choose which ones to print. Select pictures and press the Thumbnail/Zoom In button to see them as thumbnails. To get back to the single-image view, press the Magnify/Zoom Out button.

- o You can choose a Range, mark all the items in a folder as marked, delete all the items in a folder, mark all the items on a card as marked, or delete all the items on a card. To pick a range or group, press the SET button. To get back to the print order screen, press the MENU button.

5. If you pick single photos instead of a range, folder, or card, you can use the up and down buttons to pick from one to ninety-nine pictures of the same picture. They can be used after a picture is picked. When it comes to index pictures, you can only change whether the chosen picture is included or not. You can't change how many copies there are. Press the SET button to confirm. With the up and down buttons, you can pick from different picture plots. To get back to the Print Order screen when you're done, press the **MENU** button.
6. On the Print Order page, there will be a new option called Print if the camera is connected to a PictBridge printer. You can make that choice. There are a few things you need to do to the Paper Settings before you can start printing. One more way to leave the Print Order page is to press the picture release button on your camera. Next, make sure that both the printer and the camera are off. In a printer, store booth, or digital minilab that works with it, take out the memory card and put it in the slot.

RAW Processing

This is the first menu item on the Playback 3 page. Double Pixel RAW data can be used with this item, along with normal RAW files.

You can turn your RAW pictures into JPEG or HEIF files right in the camera, but not S RAW files. There have been no changes to the original RAW file. Only RAW and DPRAW shots that work with your device will be shown if you choose this option in the menu.

Here are the steps you need to take to begin:

1. Click on **Select images** on the first screen to pick out a single RAW shot. Click on Select Range to pick a set of pictures that will keep coming up. By turning the QCD-1, you can go from one good shot to another. Instead of the magnifying glass, press the button and turn the Main dial counterclockwise to show a set of search pictures.

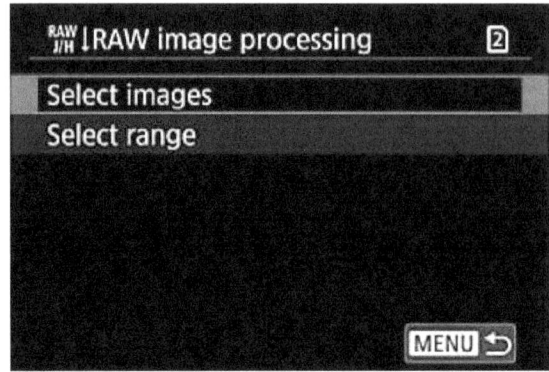

2. To pick a picture to work on, press **SET**. It will have a checkmark next to it. Press the **Q** button to move on after making your choice.

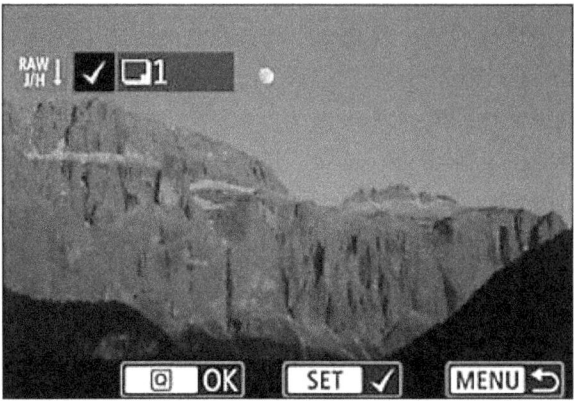

3. The camera will quickly make JPEG copies of the RAW image(s) you picked and ask you to confirm that you want to save a new file if you choose Use Shot Settings on the next screen. Go to Step 4 if you want to change the settings. If you pick Use Shot Settings, the settings that were in place when the picture was taken will be used. When the HDR PQ Settings are set to Disable, JPEGs are created. HEIFs are made if not.
4. There is a screen with many options that can be changed. Pick out the number you want to change with the joystick that has more than one control.
5. Everything will be set up the same way it was before the RAW file was shown. If you want to change a number, press SET and then use the Main dial or QCD-1 to make your pick. Click the Magnify button to make a part of the picture bigger and look over changes that are hard to see. To make sure you want to go back to the main page, press SET.

6. Now you are free to change any or all of the settings that are left. To remove everything you've done so far, just press the Trash or Erase button.
7. After making changes, you can press the **INFO** icon to see how the pictures looked before and after we made the changes. It will say **After Change** next to the picture, and the parameters that have been changed will be shown in orange in the upper right part of the screen. The **After Change** picture and the **Shot Settings** picture can both be seen if you turn the QCD-1. Once you zoom in, you can see how the Digital Lens Optimizer changes things. To get out of Compare mode, press the **MENU** button.
8. The Save button [⇧] is in the bottom right corner of the screen, just above the Return line. Click it when you're done making changes. Click Save to begin a new file. Press the Cancel button to end the process. If the picture was taken with a ratio other than 3:2, that ratio will be used to show and save the document.
9. When you pick a few shots, you'll be asked if you want to work on them more. Click **Yes** to go ahead.
10. You can select the one you want the camera to show: the Original Image or the Processed Image.
11. Process all of the pictures you want to use if you have more than one picked out.

In-Camera Upscaling

You can double the number of pixels in your JPEG or HEIF files in both the left and right directions, and the total number of pixels can be quadrupled. You can upsize pictures that were taken as JPEGs or HEIFs and have a size of L.

Caution

- Processing a picture could take a while.
- Shooting won't happen until the processing is done.
- This picture can't be made bigger.
    - Pictures taken with Cropping/aspect ratio set to something other than Full-frame
    - RAW pictures
    - Pictures taken with cameras other than an EOS R5 Mark II
    - picture sizes that have already been blown up

- Pictures that have been enlarged, cropped, or removed, either on the camera or in editing software.

- Sometimes when you shoot, the picture won't turn out the way you thought it would.

Resize

- Pick this item from the Playback menu.
- You can use the touch screen or the arrow keys to move from one picture to the next. It only shows pictures that can be changed in size. One of them is a large, medium, or small JPEG or HEIF picture. Some types of photos and movies, like Small 2 or RAW ones, can't be changed in size.
- Press SET to pick a picture and change its size. There will be a pop-up choice on the screen with three sizes of smaller images: M, S1, and S2. The QCD-1 dial can be set to Medium (3984,265, 11 megapixels), Small 1 (2976,84, 3.8 megapixels), or Small 2 (2400,1600, 3.8 megapixels). Now you can choose.

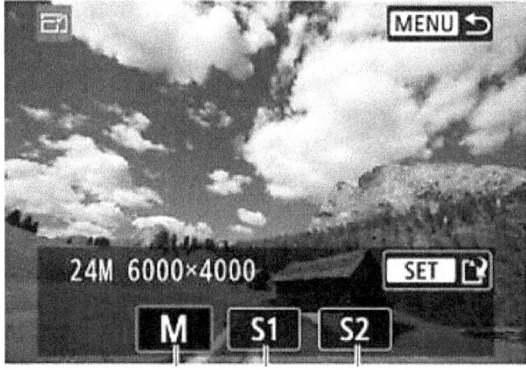

- You can't make a picture bigger than it is now. I mean, you can't save a picture that is Medium size as a Large size picture.
- To save it as a new file, click **SET**. Then, click OK on the next screen to confirm your choice. You can also click Cancel to close the app without making a new copy. The picture doesn't change from the last one.
- Just like with other Playback menus, the Quick Control menu that appears when you press the **Q** button lets you change the size of any picture.

Cropping

Just pick it and press the **SET** button to use it. There is a picture that works. Choose a picture that you want to cut out with the QCD-1. Once you've picked out a picture, press **SET** to see the screen.

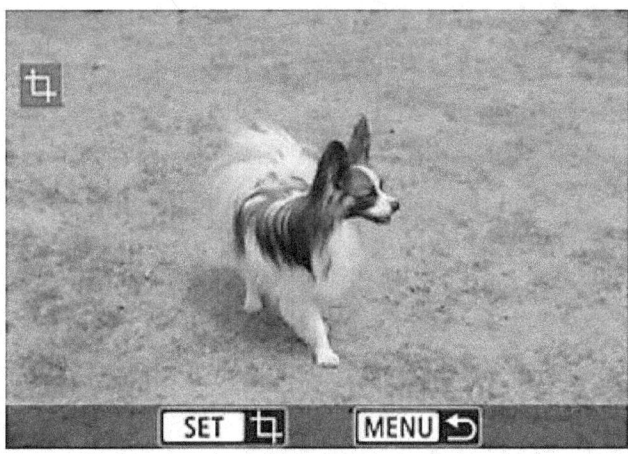

In the cropping screen, you can use any of these tools:

Select adjustment: There are function buttons in the top row of the screen that you can use to make changes. From left to right, turn the QCD-1 so that any of these are marked:

- **Change the crop view. Enlarge/reduce the crop**. Grow or shrink the crop. When this option is picked, turn the QCD-2 so that the green cutting frame gets bigger and smaller. You can use the multi-controller joystick to move the cutting frame around in the picture.
- **Straighten the image. Correct for tilt**. This choice will add a grid on top of your picture when you press SET. You can set tilts of up to 10 degrees. Little by little, the QCD-1 will change direction as you turn it. To make small changes (0.5 degrees at a time), tap the lines in the top row on the monitor. The grid helps the pictures line up. To finish and become sure of this change, press SET.
- **Change aspect ratio.** The aspect ratio of the cutting frame will change between 3:2, 16:9, 4:3, 1:1, 2:3, 9:16, and 3:4 if you keep pressing SET while this option is chosen.

To save the picture you just edited as a new file, choose this option, press **SET**, and then press **SET** again. The whole of your original picture is saved.

Slide Show

SlideShow lets you watch movies or pictures one after the other without having to manually switch between them. It's more fun and takes less time this way. Just pick Slide Show from the Playback menu to use this feature. During playback, you can stop the slide show by hitting the **SET** button. This lets you get a better look at a picture. You can also press the **INFO** button to change how much information is shown for each shot. These two buttons can be found on the top panel. Like, if you want to judge how exposed a bunch of pictures are, you might want to look at both the pictures and the histograms that go with them.

Here's how to get your slideshow ready:

1. Every picture on the card will be picked automatically when you switch to Slide Show mode. Move on to the third step if that's what you want. If you want to pick out certain pictures, go to Step 2.
2. You can filter the picture graphs that are shown in your slide show. Rate, Date, Folder, Protected, and File Type (RAW, RAW+JPEG, JPEG, or Movie) are some of the factors you can use.
3. To begin setting up the device, press the **Set up** button.

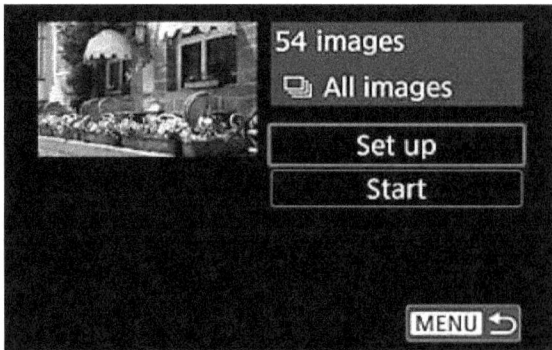

4. To make a screen with a list of play times, select Display Time and press the **SET** button. For each picture, the play time is different: 1, 2, 3, 5, 10, or 20 seconds. To be sure, press the **SET** button.

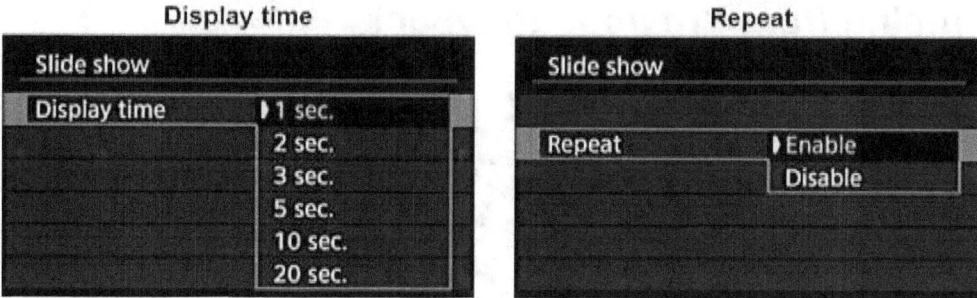

5. Press the **SET** button and the Enable button at the same time to play the show over and over.
6. Press and hold the **MENU** button to end the Setup.
7. Select Start and press the **SET** button to begin the show. Instead, press the **MENU** button to end the show you just set up. Please remember that the size of the picture file will determine how long each slide is shown.
8. When you want to play again, press the **SET** button. If you press the **INFO** button, you can see different information screens for still shots. There is no need for the camera to turn off by itself after a certain amount of time. Playback will still happen. If you change the Main dial, you can change how loud the videos are. As the movie plays or stops, you can see a new slide by turning the QCD-1. On the QCD-1, you can find these two settings.

VR Preview

You can get a feel for how VR content will look on VR displays on the camera screen if you use lenses with the EOS VR System.

Setting Image Search Conditions

You can choose which images to show based on the words you used to look at. After setting the search terms, the only things that can be done are to playback and show the pictures that were found. After a picture has been checked, you can protect it, rate it, play a slide show, delete it, and do other things.

Resuming from Previous Playback

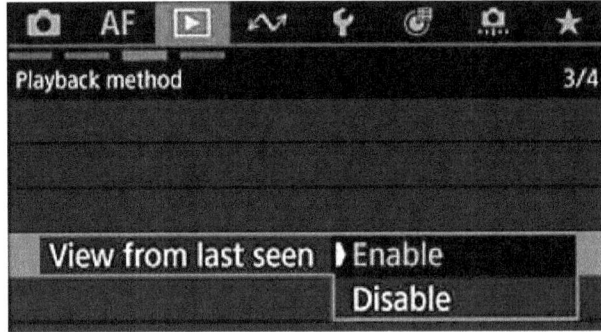

- **Enable:** If you haven't just finished shooting, playback will begin with the last picture shown if this option is turned on.
- **Disable:** The last picture you took is played back when you turn the camera back on.

View from Last Seen

The behavior of this item tells you what happens when you restart playback and look through your pictures. If you want to use it, the most recent picture shown during the review process will be shown when playback starts. The most recent picture taken by the camera is shown when playing is turned off.

Since I am always taking pictures, I usually don't turn this setting on because I want to be able to see my newest pictures as soon as I take them. You would want to go back to the picture you were most recently focusing on, though, if you were looking through a lot of photos while doing something else, like cropping or shrinking them.

Magnification (Approximate)

This parameter lets you choose both the starting point on the screen and the starting magnification for the magnified view that will be used during playback. Find out how often you look closely at your photos to help you choose the first magnification setting for your lens. You can choose from the following options:

Magnification. You can choose from three options:

- **2X, 4X, 8X, 10X (from the center of the frame).** If you pick one of those choices, the first expanded view will be either 2X, 4X, 8X, or 10X, and it will be in the middle of the frame.
- **Actual Size (from selected point).** If the picture is focused automatically, it will be in the middle of the frame. If it was focused by hand, it would be around the edge of the frame. The point of focus is in the middle of the 100% zoom.
- **Same as the last magnification (from the center point).** It will use the amount of magnification you were using before and place it roughly in the middle of the picture.

Magnified position. This sets the first place where the picture will be blown up. You can work from the Center or the Focus Point.

Maintain position. When you look into a picture, you can move around, but you can't get lost in the frame. This lets you see how the same part of an image, like a person's face, looks in a bunch of pictures that were taken one after the other.

Blur/Out-of-Focus Image Detection

Mostly by looking at the faces in JPEG/HEIF photos of people, this feature can automatically tell if an image is blurry or out of focus. You can set a level of blurriness or loss of focus, and all photos are sorted, saved, or scored based on that level.

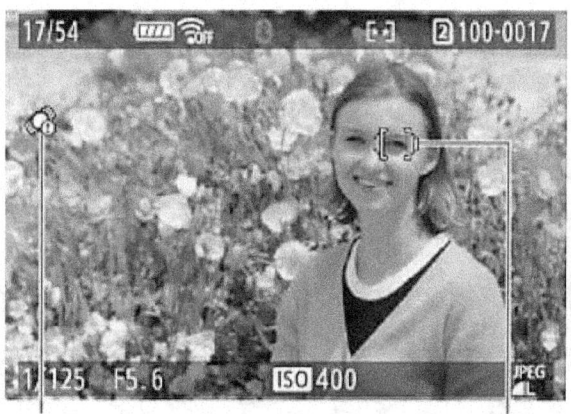

Displaying the Highlight Alert

You can set the overexposed highlights to blink on the video screen. To get a better result, set the exposure compensation to negative and try again. This will give you more detailed gradation in the flashing areas where you want it to be shown properly.

Playback Information Display

Pressing the **INFO** button during replay will switch the camera between the three screens that can be seen. There is a clean screen with no information on it, a screen with basic information, and a screen with more detailed information and the choice of multiple data panels on the shooting information screen. This item lets you pick which of the many screens will show up when you press the **INFO** button.

You can add or remove displays by following these simple steps:

1. Getting in through the menu. There's a screen. There is a tick next to each option on the screen. There are ten that can be used with the R5 Mark II.
2. Choose the panels you want to see with the INFO button and then press the **SET** button to mark them as seen. Pick the choice with a checkmark next to it, then press the **SET** button to hide a display. Please remember that you can still see panels that aren't checked off by scrolling down on the Shooting Information page with the multi-controller.

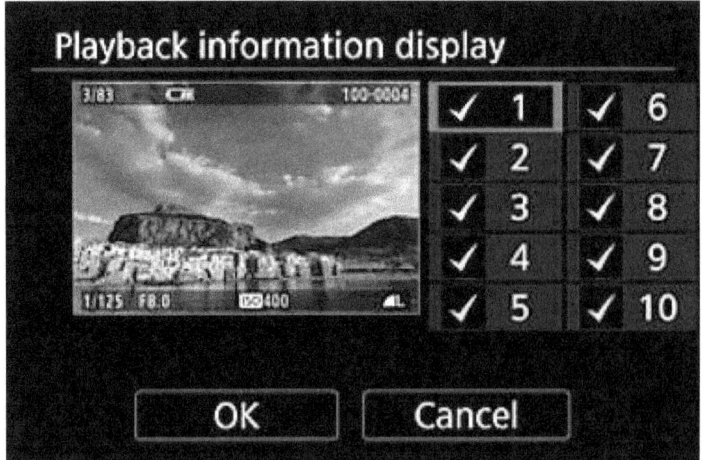

3. You can check off more than one box. During playback, the No Information screen will only show up if none of the other options are chosen.
4. In the lower-left area of the Playback Information Display screen, highlight OK and click the **SET** button. This will finish setting up the screen.
5. When the Shooting Information screen shows up during Playback, use the multi-controller joystick to switch between the options that are shown. If you need to see the Shooting Information screen, press the **INFO** button.

AF Point Disp.

If you choose the Enable choice, the AF point (or points) that were used to find focus will be shown in red. Perhaps a lot of places would be brought to your attention if automated AF point selection was used.

Playback Grid

As the video plays, you can choose to turn off the grid show completely or put a 3x3, 6x4, or 3x3 plus diagonal lines grid over it. From the Shooting 9 menu, go to the **Shooting Information Display**. This will show you the same grid of options while you're shooting.

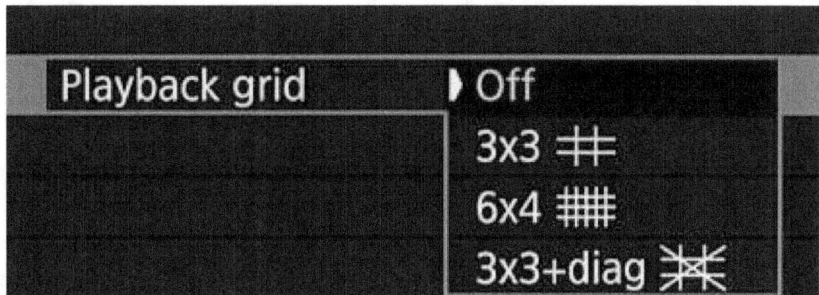

Movie Play Count

This setting lets you decide if the Time Code, an exact positioning marker or index, or the movie's recording and playback time, also called Rec Time, is shown on the screen. You can change the Movie Play Count choice in either of these menus (Movie Shooting or this one), and it will show up differently everywhere right away. Under the Movie Shooting menus, you can find more choices for Time Codes.

Conclusion

The Canon EOS R5 Mark II is a significant upgrade from its predecessor, offering new and exciting features that cater to both professional and amateur photographers. Its game-changing pre-capture shooting, advanced autofocus capabilities like Eye Control AF, and a stacked CMOS sensor greatly enhance both speed and precision. Hybrid photographers will particularly appreciate the seamless switch between stills and video modes, and the enhanced image stabilization makes it perfect for handheld shooting. With improved battery life, weatherproofing, and customizable settings, the R5 Mark II is a versatile and highly efficient tool for creative expression. Whether shooting fast-paced action or delicate portraits, this camera excels across a range of scenarios, making it an excellent choice for any photographer looking to push their boundaries.

INDEX

A

Anti-Flicker Shooting, 141, 142
Aperture, 12, 14, 15, 16, 17, 18, 19, 20, 22, 23, 24, 25, 26, 27, 28, 30, 31, 33, 34, 35, 36, 37, 38, 39, 40, 41, 43, 44, 45, 131, 144, 149, 205, 207
Aperture Range, 207
Auto Lighting, 81, 125, 136
autoexposure, 182, 205, 207
Automatic Reset, 62, 63
Av Setting, 209

B

battery life, 3, 151, 233
Bracketing Sequence, 204
burst of shots, 181

C

camera keeps shooting, 192
CANON folder, 63
Change Movie, 215
change the number of shots, 193
change your photos' color, 135
Clear Settings, 82, 154
color temperature, 125, 135, 172, 173
Continuous Shot Count, 208
Cropping, 112, 139, 184, 208, 224, 226

D

dark and light tones, 171
Date/Time/Zone, 70
Display Simulation, 197, 198
DOF Preview, 197
DPOF printing,, 221
Dual Shooting, 7, 113
Dust Delete, 81, 182, 184

E

Electronic shutter, 195
erase everything on your memory card, 68
Erase Images, 212, 213, 214
ETTL Flash mode, 151

F

Factory Preset Code, 66
File Name, 65, 67, 68
Flash Custom Function Settings, 154
Focus Breathing Correction, 177
Format Card, 68

H

High-Speed Display, 196

I

Image Detection, 230
image detection setting, 9
Image Stabilization, 10, 11, 14, 15, 16, 17, 18, 19, 20, 22, 23, 28, 33, 34, 35, 36, 38, 39, 40, 43, 44, 45
Interval Timer, 137, 193
ISO Speed, 136, 144, 181, 203
ISO Speed Setting, 203
ISO speed settings, 140

L

landscape, 10, 19, 29, 37, 38, 70, 155, 202, 215
Language, 53, 71

M

Manual Reset, 62, 63
Mechanical shutter, 148, 194
Metering, 146, 155, 156, 157, 196, 203

metering timer, 196, 203
Micro Adjustment, 208
Monochrome Adjustment, 164
Movie Shooting, 74, 109, 232
Multi Shot Noise Reduction, 182
Multiple Exposure, 137, 185, 187, 189

P

photographer, 2, 5, 6, 42, 159, 233
photographers, 1, 2, 7, 9, 10, 12, 14, 15, 16, 17, 19, 20, 21, 22, 23, 24, 25, 26, 27, 28, 29, 30, 31, 33, 34, 35, 36, 37, 38, 39, 40, 41, 42, 43, 44, 45, 46, 66, 118, 126, 138, 141, 159, 169, 233
photojournalists, 9
playback, 56, 59, 119, 130, 133, 227, 228, 229, 232
Playback, 56, 58, 109, 133, 186, 211, 212, 214, 215, 217, 218, 220, 222, 225, 227, 228, 229, 231, 232
portrait, 2, 10, 20, 24, 30, 41, 42, 43, 46, 155, 215
Protect Images, 212, 213

Q

quality settings, 54, 172
Quick Control screen, 164, 173

R

Recommended Tv Setting, 143
Resize, 225
Retract Lens On Power Off, 210

S

save your pictures in a new folder, 192

sharpness, 13, 22, 24, 29, 35, 42, 43, 158, 159, 160, 161, 166, 171, 177, 178
Shooting Information, 81, 127, 199, 201, 231, 232
Shooting menus, 232
Shooting Modes, 81, 202
Shutter Mode, 194
Shutter Speed, 131, 206
SlideShow, 227
social media, 7, 9
stop shooting,, 193
Straighten the image, 226
System Frequency, 72

T

Telephoto Lenses, 13
Time-Lapse Movie, 137
Touch Shutter, 196

U

upgrade, 170, 233
Uploading a Picture Style to the Camera, 167
Upscaling, 224

V

Viewfinder, 75, 76, 77, 81, 198, 199, 200

W

weatherproofing, 233
wedding, 9, 12, 25, 28, 34, 42, 212
White Balance, 81, 135, 172, 173, 174
Wireless functions, 151

www.ingramcontent.com/pod-product-compliance
Lightning Source LLC
Chambersburg PA
CBHW062213220526
45471CB00009B/3180